CONCEIVING THE OLD REGIME

CONCEIVING THE

OLD

Pronatalism and the Politics of Reproduction
in Early Modern France

Leslie Tuttle

UNIVERSITY PRESS

2010

OXFORD
UNIVERSITY PRESS

Oxford University Press, Inc., publishes works that further
Oxford University's objective of excellence
in research, scholarship, and education.

Oxford   New York
Auckland   Cape Town   Dar es Salaam   Hong Kong   Karachi
Kuala Lumpur   Madrid   Melbourne   Mexico City   Nairobi
New Delhi   Shanghai   Taipei   Toronto

With offices in
Argentina   Austria   Brazil   Chile   Czech Republic   France   Greece
Guatemala   Hungary   Italy   Japan   Poland   Portugal   Singapore
South Korea   Switzerland   Thailand   Turkey   Ukraine   Vietnam

Published by Oxford University Press, Inc.
198 Madison Avenue, New York, New York 10016

www.oup.com

Oxford is a registered trademark of Oxford University Press

Library of Congress Cataloging-in-Publication Data

Tuttle, Leslie, 1967–
Conceiving the old regime : pronatalism and the politics of reproduction in early modern France / Leslie Tuttle.
   p.   cm.
Includes bibliographical references and index.
ISBN 978-0-19-538160-3
1. France—Population policy—History.   2. Family policy—France—History.
3. Fertility, Human—France—History.   I. Title.
HB3593.T93 2010
304.6´3094409032—dc22   2009030071

9   8   7   6   5   4   3   2   1

Printed in the United States of America
on acid-free paper

For J. H. E.

ACKNOWLEDGMENTS

I am grateful for fellowships and grants from the Fulbright Program and from Princeton University that funded the beginnings of this book. At the University of Kansas, my research has been funded by grants from General Research Fund, the Office of International Programs, and the College of Liberal Arts and Sciences. I extend special thanks to the Western Society for French History for the Amy Millstone Fellowship that first enabled me to expand my research into *la France profonde*. My thanks, also, to KU's Hall Center for the Humanities and the office of the Vice Provost for Research for their generous support of this project in its late stages.

Over the years, I have benefited from the warmth of many scholarly communities. The staffs at the Bibliothèque Nationale and Archives Nationales in Paris provided expert help from beginning to end. My tour of departmental archives gave me a new appreciation for the richness of France's history and for the dedication of its archivists. I would like to single out the staffs of archives in Auxerre, Caen, Valence, and Laon for their kindness to a foreign scholar finding her way. Thanks, also, to Robert C. Ritchie and the marvelous people at the Huntington Library in San Marino, California, for the gift of an office in 2006–07 and the intellectual fellowship that went with it. I benefited from the comments of fellow scholars at the University of California, Los Angeles, the University of California, Santa Barbara, and fellow participants in the Folger Shakespeare Library workshop "In the Maelstrom of the Market," in particular Martha Howell, Katherine Crawford, and Julie Hardwick. At the University of Kansas, my History Department colleagues in the "Junior League" read parts of this work in various guises over several years, offering excellent advice and collegial support. My thanks to Jeff Moran, Paul Kelton, Liz MacGonagle, Megan Greene, Nathan Wood, Katherine Clark, Jennifer Weber, Karl Brooks, Sheyda Jahanbani, Jacob Dorman, Greg Cushman, Ernest Jenkins, and Kim Warren for making my workplace intellectually lively and friendly. I also benefited from suggestions from colleagues at the Gender Seminar and Early Modern Seminar at the Hall Center for the Humanities, in particular from the creative minds of my esteemed colleagues and friends Luis Corteguera and Marta Vicente. Fellow early modern francophiles at KU, including Allan Pasco, Bruce Hayes, Paul Scott, and Mechele Leon, provided camaraderie and essential advice.

Long ago, Eric Brian's sage advice helped me conceptualize my subject as an intellectual problem. David Bell, Rachel Fuchs, Hugh Hochman, Sara Melzer, Kathryn Norberg, and Kristin Stromberg Childers shared their expertise in response to my queries. Friends and colleagues including Hilary Bernstein, Lisa Bitel, Michael Breen, Greg Brown, Sara Chapman, Paul Cohen, Cynthia Cupples, Natalie Dykstra, Marie Kelleher, Cheryl Koos, Peter Mancall, Jen Popiel, Rebecca Sokolovsky, and Helen Sheumaker have seen this project evolve over the years, and have, perhaps unbeknownst to them, played an important role in what it finally became. I hope that they will accept my sincere thanks. The advice of readers including Barbara Diefendorf, Bill Jordan, Tony Grafton, Sarah Hanley, and Carolyn Lougee Chappell has helped me immeasurably. My advisor, Natalie Zemon Davis, inspired me even before I met her with the astonishing insight, energy, and empathy she brings to the study of history. After knowing her as my teacher and friend, I understand that she brings these qualities to all parts of her life, and my esteem for her and gratitude for her influence in my life only grows as time goes by. Finally, I thank Susan Ferber at Oxford for her generosity, excellent sense of humor and sound advice at each step of the publishing process, Gwen Colvin for her keen eye and patience, and Mary Brooks for expert last-minute editing.

My friends and family have been mostly patient as they waited for this book to be done, and I want to acknowledge how much their support means to me. For long-term summer fellowship I thank Jonathan Field, Jayme Filippini, David Kaiser, Jen Keller, Amy Monaghan, Rich Schoenstein, Jim Sherman, and all the "youngs" and "olds" who have congregated at the red farmhouse. Thanks to my cherished Lawrence friends Jackie Stafford, Gregg Ventello, Maryanne Leone, and Phyllis and Louis Copt. My parents Jerry and Carol Tuttle, my sister Laura, and my mother-in-law Janice Earle, believed, sometimes against all the evidence, that someday this book would be finished. In a work that treats the subject that this one does, I cannot refrain from observing that my mother is the eighth of twelve children that my grandmother, Marie Kunze Wilson, a schoolteacher, and her husband Belva Wilson raised and launched into the world. My grandmother Wilson has been much on my mind as I wrote, as has my other grandmother, Margaret Bruce Tuttle. I inherited the joy that learning and reading bring me from them. Last and most, I thank my husband, Jonathan Earle, for the gift that sustains me, namely his company and conversation every day of our life together.

CONTENTS

CONCEIVING THE
OLD REGIME

Introduction

During the early morning hours of August 8, 1735, in the French provincial city of Auxerre, about a hundred miles southeast of Paris, Marie-Anne Pichery, the thirty-seven-year-old wife of a tanner, gave birth to a daughter. The newborn was swaddled and carried to the parish church of St. Pierre-en-Vallée, where her paternal uncle and eldest sister, acting as godparents, gave her the baptismal name Gasparde Bienvenue. Later that same day, her father, François Bourdillat, summoned officials from the town hall to his home; now that this new baby had arrived, Bourdillat needed these officials to produce a document verifying that "God had blessed his marriage with the number of twelve children born of him and of Marie-Anne Pichery, his wife."[1]

In response to Bourdillat's summons, two city officials made their way to the outlying parish where the bourgeoning Bourdillat family lived. When the officials crossed the threshold from the street into the Bourdillat home, they may have found neighbors and relatives celebrating. Customarily, the community gathered in the hours after a baptism to welcome its newest member and offer thanksgiving for the safety of mother and newborn.[2] The newly delivered mother was probably resting in her bed, attended by a midwife or lying-in maid. Perhaps she was receiving visitors who brought gifts for her and for her newest daughter, and offered their compliments on her fecundity. Marie-Anne Pichery was extraordinary in this respect; this was her sixteenth confinement in twenty-two years of marriage. Although it was a day for celebration, the couple's fertility had not protected their household from the ravages of infant mortality. They had already buried four of their children, probably lost during infancy, and at least three more would die in young adulthood.

If the city officials raised a glass of the local wine with the happy father they failed to note it. Sticking to the essential facts for their administrative record, they reported examining the baptismal certificates of and then laying their eyes upon all of Bourdillat's twelve living children: Marie Françoise (aged 18), Louise (17), François Pellerin (16), Claude (14), Anne (13), Pierre Estienne (11), Marie Anne (10), Florent (9), Marie Louise (7), Pierre Louis (4), and Claire Radegonde, who was just a few days shy of her first birthday. Finally, François Bourdillat presented the newest member of the family, just back from the baptismal font: Gasparde Bienvenue, that is, Gasparde "Welcome."

Gasparde's middle name was unusual, but apt, for her birth was a particularly welcome event for the household. When duly registered in local records, the fact that François Bourdillat had fathered twelve living children would earn him full exemption from royal taxation. Abundant procreation marked him as an exemplary subject of the king, and justified conferring on him one of the most coveted privileges that French law could offer. Bourdillat was not alone. During the last century and a half of the Old Regime, thousands of French households took advantage of the incentives for reproduction set out in a 1666 royal edict "offering concessions and privileges to those who marry before or during their twentieth year . . . or to fathers with ten to twelve children."[3]

The birth of a tanner's daughter in a provincial town may seem like a mundane domestic event, far removed from the functions of keeping order, collecting taxes, making war, and building empires that historians have traditionally identified as central concerns of the developing states of early modern Europe. Yet the events surrounding Gasparde Bienvenue Bourdillat's birth are testimony to the growing political significance the Old Regime government in France accorded to human fertility. By the time Louis XIV began his personal reign in 1661, many of the educated, elite men who served the king had come to regard procreation as a fundamental political concern. They considered the human capacity to procreate a political resource far too valuable to be left outside the sphere of royal influence. Building on these convictions, the royal government mobilized the governing tools at its disposal—in particular the offer of fiscal privilege—in an attempt to shape the marital and reproductive behavior of the king's subjects. This book traces the history of this experiment in procreative engineering, examining what it tells us about the changing relationship between family and state during a pivotal era in French history.

The pages that follow pursue these themes by tracing the creation and implementation of Louis XIV's November 1666 pronatalist edict, called by a variety of names throughout the following decades, most often the "Edict on Marriage." The 1666 legislation was France's first national pronatalist program. While it offered a variety of incentives to encourage marriage and procreation, it reserved its most lucrative prizes for men, like François Bourdillat, who fathered twelve or more living, legitimate children. [The tapestry of various award categories and requirements to qualify are set out in table form in the appendix.]

I use a modern word—*pronatalist*—to describe the early modern laws and policies intended to encourage the birth of more French people. The laws promoted reproduction both by giving French couples incentives to have larger families and by encouraging marriage—a union from which pregnancy and childbirth was the expected outcome. While the word "pronatalist" is modern, political interest in securing a large and vibrant population was already intense in the seventeenth and eighteenth centuries.

Today, leaders in many nations consider it a political priority to ensure their country will have an increasing, or at least stable, number of workers and taxpayers, generally because this stable population is necessary to sustain the tax base that pays for social welfare programs.[4] Faced with flagging birthrates and an aging population, many nations—France among them—have enacted policies to create incentives for reproduction. In recent decades, the pronatalist policies of democratic states have usually sought to reduce the costs of child rearing, provide subsidized child care, or compensate parents for wages lost when they leave a job to care for an infant. Such policies often join fiscal incentives and support for parents to nationalistic pleas to have another baby as an act of good citizenship. Incentives, of course, have not been the only weapons in modern states' pronatalist toolbox. Many states have pursued (and some still pursue) pronatalist aims by limiting reproductive freedom; that is, by restricting access to contraception and abortion. Both these techniques—providing fiscal support for parents, and forbidding contraception and abortion—were also factors in Old Regime French pronatalism. But they of course look different against the backdrop of a preindustrial society in which neither child care nor education was provided by the state, "contraception" meant behaviors forbidden by a politically powerful, institutionalized church, and each child born was the subject of a monarchy, not a citizen of a republic.

When scholars seek to explain modern pronatalist policies, they usually start by identifying the quantifiable population "problem"—such as declining rates of growth, or the death toll of war—to which such policies supposedly constitute a rational response. But pronatalist policies always implicate ideologies and values that go deeper than a merely rational, instrumental increase in the number of human beings. As the anthropologist Marilyn Strathern mordantly observes, "When human beings reproduce themselves, they inevitably do so with already existing and thus specific forms of themselves in mind."[5] Procreation reproduces social and political relations, not just human bodies. And because all babies (at least until very recently) were the products of sexual relationships between men and women, a government's action to promote births is inevitably formed within prevailing models of gender relations and ideas about sexuality. In their quest to encourage procreation, pronatalist policies imagine and normalize specific domestic arrangements and modes of caregiving. They seek to amplify qualities traditionally associated with conjugal households and family life, and to promote the transformation of individual men into fathers, and women into mothers. If these roles arise in biology, they are nevertheless richly elaborated social identities that imply specific, gendered behaviors and legal responsibilities. Like other scholars before me, I believe that these "qualitative" factors are not accidental or incidental parts of the logic of pronatalism, whether modern or historical. Pronatalist policies, in other words, are rarely if ever indifferent to the social contexts from which human beings emerge; reproducing households and the gendered identities that function within them is an integral part of what pronatalist policies set out to achieve.[6]

Old Regime pronatalism is also different from modern pronatalism in important ways. For one, it was sustained by a different understanding about "population." Throughout the early modern period, and until Thomas Malthus's radical suggestion in 1798 that unchecked population growth posed a grave threat to social stability, political theorists generally agreed that population growth was an unqualified political benefit. Human fertility signified the blessings of God upon His people, and offered tangible, worldly benefits to a monarch. A flourishing population meant more soldiers, laborers, and taxpayers to extend the king's territory, work the land, and fill his treasury; every new subject born to a king contributed to increase the kingdom's power. As French political theorist Jean Bodin counseled in his 1576 *Six Books of the Republic,* "One must never fear that there could be too many people, [or] too many subjects, seeing as there is neither wealth nor power but that which comes from men."[7]

Within the terms of the premodern theory of population, no crisis was necessary to make a pronatalist policy make sense; encouraging more births was always an act of princely wisdom consistent with promoting national power. This was the situation in the mid-seventeenth century, when the government of Louis XIV took the step of making a royal law to promote reproduction. At that time, the French government had no empirical knowledge of the number of the king's subjects; there was neither a census nor other means to inform the king accurately of his population—indeed, the word "population" had not yet entered common usage. At the same time, Europeans who cared to think about such matters had formed an impressionistic assessment that Louis XIV's France was already the most populous state in Europe. Historical demographers have shown that they were correct; Louis XIV's twenty million subjects made him "richer in men" than his rivals.

If we look ahead fifty years to the late phase of the Sun King's reign, assessments were more pessimistic. After a dismal period of wars, harvest failuress, famine and rural misery—but still without empirical data on which to base their arguments—eighteenth-century writers claimed that the population of Europe was declining, and that France's population, in particular, was going through a precipitous decline. They turned out to be wrong. France's population rose to about twenty-eight million by 1800, representing a growth of more than 30 percent over the course of the century. Over the last century and a half of the Old Regime, then, ideas about the underlying strength and growth trends of the French population shifted, largely without relation to empirical demographic information. The conviction that population growth was beneficial remained. Populationism—the notion that population growth was a good thing—remained the orthodox conviction of educated men even as they disagreed about whether or not France's current population signalled strength or weakness. The anxiety about population decline of the eighteenth century added urgency to a preexisting pronatalist agenda, but it does not explain its reason for being.

No population crisis caused Louis XIV's government to initiate the pronatalist policy of 1666, a fact that should focus our attention again on the qualitative aspects of the Old Regime's pronatalist project. In the 1660s, as Louis XIV's advisors looked back at decades of political upheaval, they were candid about the importance of marriage and child rearing for stabilizing the political order. An unmarried man, they said, was "like a foreigner in his own country," whereas a man who married and became a father was "thoroughly tied to his fatherland and obedient to his prince."[8] Potentially unruly and self-indulgent individuals, they believed, thought twice about their actions when they had progeny whose honor and fortune were at stake. Encouraging marriage and reproduction not only promised to multiply the king's fiscal and military power, it would bind subjects to the monarchy and to enhance social discipline. Royal officials would continue to voice such beliefs throughout the eighteenth century, a fact that helps explain why the royal government continued to reward men with large families even after most officials had come to doubt that pronatalist awards ever had or could generate population growth.

This qualitative logic of pronatalism drew its strength from the political ideology of Old Regime government, which made explicit connections between the domestic and political realms. Political theorists, for example, explained the origins and nature of monarchical power by comparing it to the natural authority that parents exercised over their children. In contrast to modern democratic states, in which political authority is legitimated by the idea of a contract between individuals naturally endowed with rights, early modern kings and their subjects were taught to think of their respective political duties through metaphors of family, with the understanding that monarchical government had arisen organically out of the "natural" hierarchical relationships of the conjugal household. The political theorist Jacques-Bénigne Bossuet stressed it was a "very important truth," that "the first idea of power that arose among men, is that of paternal power," from which "kings were fashioned on the model of fathers."[9] Early modern political theory was rife with family metaphors: the king was father of his people, and must love and discipline them as would a good father; subjects owed the king obedience as children did their fathers; the household was a commonwealth in miniature, where fathers' words were law; the kingdom was an expansive, fertile household that the king should manage according to the rules of good husbandry (good husbandry was management, as the phrase went "*en bon père de famille*"). These metaphors explained the claim that political, social, and economic order in the kingdom depended on the reproduction and solidification of the natural lines of authority within the conjugal family. Theorist of royal sovereignty Jean Bodin explained the necessity for policing family life when he noted that "it is impossible that a commonwealth have any value if families, which are its pillars, are poorly founded."[10] Old Regime pronatalist policy sought to plant these pillars of a powerful, well-policed commonwealth by promoting the formation of conjugal families and the birth of royal subjects within them. In the course of doing so, it claimed the realm of licit, reproductive sexuality as proper terrain for government intervention.

Pronatalism, Fertility, and "Numeracy about Children"

This book is a study in political culture rather than historical demography. Nevertheless, it is vital to understand the demographic context of the Old Regime's experiment in governing reproductive sexuality. The advent of pronatalism came at a significant moment in the history of French, and indeed of *human* procreative behavior: seventeenth- and eighteenth-century France have offered demographers some of the earliest statistical evidence of deliberate family limitation in Europe. It is not a coincidence, I argue, that at the same time that certain French couples, mostly urban, and of middling status or higher, began purposely to have smaller families, France's royal government initiated policies intended to encourage marriage and reward men for having large families.[11]

Demographers and historians of the family attach enormous significance to the adoption of deliberate family limitation, seeing birth control as a sign that people have crossed a "profound divide ... [in] moral economies."[12] The adoption of birth control signals the waning of traditional ideas about the cosmos and humans' role in it, and the rise of contemporary Western ideas about the individual and society.[13]

Historical demographers and historians of the family have identified family limitation as both symbol and catalyst of a revolutionary shift in values away from providential acceptance of divine will and toward conscious human intervention to shape and improve the quality of human life. Following Philippe Ariès, they argue that birth control facilitated parental investment in the welfare and education of each child who was born; the prevention of births implied not less love for children but greater concern for each individual who came into the world.

Family limitation has also been connected with an evolution in gender relations. Contraception undermined religious doctrines that identified procreation as the sole legitimate reason for sexual activity. It signaled a rejection of attitudes that held women responsible for sin, and that had claimed that the pain and toil of procreation and childbearing were their means of redemption (e.g., 1 Timothy 2:15: "She shall be saved in childbearing"). Family limitation opened up new possibilities for women liberated from repeated pregnancies and endless child rearing. In addition, some historians argue that the method of contraception they

believe was most often used by married couples—withdrawal—required cooperation and communication between husbands and wives, and thus may have
promoted a revolution in sexual intimacy. For all these reasons, family limitation
is often connected to the developing ideal of affection as the basis for marriage
and family life; and by extension, interpreted as a sign of the waning of the
authoritarian, patriarchal family.[14]

In an effort to pin down the mentalities that separate cultures that practice
family limitation from those that do not, Etienne Van de Walle has employed the
term "numeracy about children." Numeracy here designates the "clear notion
about what family size ought to be" that is ubiquitous in the modern West but
often absent in environments where family limitation is not standard practice.
Americans, for example, are socialized in multiple ways to think of family size in
comparison to a numerical norm; most could probably hazard a fairly accurate
guess about how many children are found in an "average" household. This mode
of thinking is not characteristic of all cultures. As recently as the 1980s, for
example, when health workers asked women in rural Mali questions about an
ideal family size, around 25 percent gave answers that were non-numeric.
Consider the twenty-eight-year-old Malian woman, who responded to the
question "How many children would you like to have in your life?" by saying,
"Ah, what God gives me, that is it . . . I cannot tell the number I will have in my
life."[15] Another woman, aged forty and a veteran of ten pregnancies, responded
that she had wanted four children, but going on to have ten was "God's work."
When the interviewer began to discuss contraception, she added, "If God does
not want it, it is impossible to stop pregnancies. It cannot succeed. . . ."[16] The difficulty interviewers and respondents had understanding one another's attitudes
was not simply a matter of language barriers, nor was it the result of any ignorance
on the Malians' side about the biology of reproduction or the technology of contraception. Rather, researchers conclude, interviewers and respondents were
communicating across a conceptual divide regarding the legitimacy of human
agency in reproduction.

Van de Walle proposes that in the era before family limitation, French women
and men might have answered in similar ways. In his research in early modern
sources, he found little evidence of specific thinking about ideal family size in
France before the seventeenth century.[17] In order for contraception to become
the norm, he argues, individuals must develop numeracy about their reproductive lives, thinking about the size of their families both in terms of a goal to
achieve or not exceed, and as a matter that legitimately falls within their control.
"A fertility decline is not very far behind when people start conceptualizing their
family size," he argues, "and it cannot take place without it."[18]

It may seem paradoxical to link the ideational structure of family limitation
with a pronatalist policy that rewarded very large families. First, some words of

caution. More than fifty years of sophisticated demographic research has under-scored that it is wrong to assume that, in the era before measurable, deliberate family limitation, human reproduction was some sort of mystery over which Europeans exercised no control.[19] While early modern couples may rarely have discussed how many children they wished to have, fertility was nonetheless shaped and limited by social norms about who could marry and when, and by variable sexual and child rearing behaviors such as periodic abstinence and extended breast-feeding. In 1965, John Hajnal identified two characteristics of early modern Northwestern European societies—a late average age at first marriage and a high proportion of the population who remained celibate for life—as the defining elements of a "European marriage pattern" that constituted a powerful check on the growth of the European population until the eighteenth century. A late average age at marriage meant that, although we might imagine large families were typical before the era of birth control, a French woman who married in 1700 at the age of twenty-five (average age for first marriage at that time) gave birth to on average five or six infants during her reproductive life span, assuming her marriage was not ended by the death of either partner before she reached menopause.[20]

Both before and after the advent of deliberate family limitation, then, the sixteen births François Bourdillat and Marie-Anne Pichery experienced put them far outside the reproductive norm for their age. But if large families of ten or more children were uncommon in 1666, when the royal government's policy set ten children as the level for obtaining pronatalist rewards, they were far from unknown, especially among elites and in urban settings. Among these social groups, parents were wealthy enough to provide dowries to their daughters, who therefore tended to marry at a younger age. Plus, parents in these families often sent their infants to wet nurses, and as a result, women tended to become pregnant again more rapidly. These marital and child rearing practices meant that couples in those social groups had, on average, more children. For example, in the French town of Meulan, historical demographer Marcel Lachiver discov-ered that although the average number of children per marriage was 5.6, nearly 25 percent of couples married between 1660 and 1739 whose marriages lasted through the woman's reproductive lifetime sent ten or more babies to baptism. One couple in nine (11.3 percent) experienced twelve or more births.[21]

The attempts at intervention that this book investigates coincide with dramatic changes in these patterns. Over the course of the centuries it studies, reproduc-tive feats like those of Bourdillat and Pichery became increasingly uncommon; by the mid-eighteenth century, the *parlementaire* and philosophe Montesquieu would label the large families of ten or more children envisioned by the 1666 pronatalist edict "prodigies," a word connoting something that defied natural limits. Perhaps unsurprisingly, demographic data suggests that the urban and elite social groups among whom such large families had been most common were among the first to adopt deliberate birth control. Lachiver's study of couples in Meulan found that marriages between 1740 and 1789 were approximately half as likely to produce such large families as in the earlier period; only 13.9 percent of couples married in the later part of the century experienced ten or more births.[22]

I do not make these observations to argue that royal pronatalist policies had any causal relationship to the demographic transition occurring in France; my research does not suggest that pronatalist policy changed demographic behavior in any measurable way. It seems clear that royal encouragement to have larger families did not have the power to hold back the tide of deliberate family limitation in France. But Van de Walle's observations regarding "numeracy about children" do illuminate the cultural context of the royal government's pronatalist experiment, and shed additional light on the circumstances in which French couples, in increasing numbers, crossed the "profound divide . . . in moral economies," to act in ways that proved they believed procreation was a matter of conscious choice. It was within the social context of French elites—the social group most likely to produce large families—that the practices of family limitation and a political program to promote fertility were born. Indeed, the mere existence of a royal pronatalist policy provides compelling evidence that a major component of the fertility transition was already in place by 1666: the law indicated a belief, at least among the educated, elite men who formulated it, that reproduction was subject to human control.

Fertility control was without question "thinkable" for Louis XIV's influential minister Jean-Baptiste Colbert and the royal advisors who helped him formulate the Edict on Marriage of 1666. In fact, these officials demonstrated surprising sophistication in identifying how the fertility regime of their society actually worked. The king's advisors designed their policy to encourage marriage, preferably at an earlier age; they also tried (albeit with some ambivalence and little success) to raise legal barriers against monasticism, and thus to limit the numbers of men and women who remained celibate. Much of the focus of the royal government's pronatalist policy, in other words, rested on counteracting the mechanisms of late marriage and celibacy, the very controls that Hajnal named as the major checks on population growth in early modern Europe. The precision with which French lawmakers identified these mechanisms bears consideration in relation to the question of whether the European pattern of delayed marriage was an unconscious cultural mechanism or a more deliberate strategy adopted by families in order to limit the number of children they had.[23] By the mid-seventeenth century, in any case, royal advisors surmised that French men and women were making conscious decisions about the timing of marriages, balancing the likelihood of having a large number of children for whom to provide against other factors like the wealth and social status of a prospective spouse.

They assumed that fertility strategies, in other words, were an extension of the conscious planning and strategizing about marriage and inheritance that families practiced to promote their own social and economic interests.[24] The fact that royal officials sought to use their insights about fertility to promote more births rather than (as couples increasingly chose) to limit them does not change the fact that they shared with the growing number of couples practitioning family limitation a belief in the possibility, and even the utility, of shaping human fertility for earthly goals.

Pronatalist policy took shape in an atmosphere of considerable tension about the potential consequences of fertility control. Was it licit to think in such terms, inserting human decision making into the providential question of whether an immortal soul would be born? Didn't God punish men and women who pursued sexual pleasure without pregnancy? Would human beings, once they assumed control over their procreative lives, earn divine wrath, or make mistakes that might result in the extinction of lineages or nations? These anxieties lurked in the background as reproductive behavior shifted, and thinking about population grew bolder. The early political intervention studied here were, in many ways, conservative. Seventeenth-century royal officials no doubt took comfort in the fact that the behaviors encouraged by royal pronatalist policy—marrying and welcoming a large family—were consistent with the licit, procreative behavior recommended by clerics during the Catholic Reformation. The king, like the parish priest, was counseling men and women to seek the birth of children as a divine blessing. Yet despite this apparent harmony, it is worth considering whether, by enunciating reproduction as a politically useful, instrumental behavior, the royal government may actually have helped to legitimate the notion of fertility control for some of its subjects. That is, the 1666 pronatalist edict can only have promoted Van de Walle's "numeracy" about children by defining a numerical standard necessary to qualify for rewards—not just *many,* but a precise number that royal officials set out to count and monitor. In this sense, pronatalist policy promoted the conceptualization of human responsibility for fertility important for licensing family limitation. Royal policymakers and French couples may have been seeking different ends—to increase versus to limit births—but both operated on the same side of the divide of conscious choice. By moving procreation within the calculus of human action, both groups helped to generate political contests over which earthly power—the state or the individual—had the more compelling claim to control it.

Pronatalism, Families, and the French State

The story of the creation and implementation of pronatalist policy also offers an opportunity to reflect on the evolution of royal government in France, that is, on the growth of a central power structure capable of implementing its will over civil society, and reliably responsive to direction by the king and his closest advisors. Textbook accounts of European history still point to the 1660s, the first decade of Louis XIV's so-called personal reign, as a watershed moment in the development of an "absolutist" state, when the young king seized the reins of a still feudal state and steered it toward modernity. During Louis XIV's exceptionally long reign, as the story goes, the French state definitively turned the page on traditional, decentralized modes of governing and gradually built the means to project royal power throughout French society. Like his father, the Sun King never called the Estates General, a convocation of representatives from the clergy, nobility, and commoners. Not only did the king not solicit his subjects' advice, Louis XIV and his close advisors actively sought to bypass it, curtailing the right of the sovereign courts to suggest changes to royal legislation, and undermining the power of venal officers by creating rival networks of officials whom he and his minister-servants could dismiss at will. Louis installed himself at the center of the French political universe, forcing the nobility to adhere to the strict ceremonial order of life at Versailles, and using his agents in the provinces as a network to transmit his sovereign power to the kingdom's far reaches.[25]

This traditional narrative about the development of Old Regime government and the term "absolutism," which historians have often used to describe it, has been the subject of a devastating revisionist critique in recent decades. The greater success with which Louis XIV collected his taxes, organized his army, and kept the peace was not due to the implementation of "modern," rationalized bureaucratic modes of governing, the critics argue. They stress that Louis XIV's adherence to traditional social values was at least as important as any centralizing innovations in explaining how the Sun King managed to solidify and extend royal power. And, they point out, with only a few hundred nonvenal officials to govern a realm of some twenty million, the king and his government were inevitably dependent upon the cooperation of his subjects, in particular his elite subjects.[26]

The monarchy's interest in regulating marriage and reproduction have not as yet figured prominently in accounts of the changes wrought in the 1660s.[27] Yet there are compelling reasons to juxtapose pronatalism with the more familiar legal, fiscal, social, and military reforms through which (in the terms of the traditional view) Louis XIV and his government sought to build French power and to increase the authority of royal government. Royal advisors, for their part, evinced no doubt that the domestic realm was vital to their plans. They called marriage the "first foundation of republics, states, and kingdoms."[28] Far from a mere rhetorical flourish, their assessment of marriage's fundamental political importance was based on sound logic. As a legal institution, marriages established households, the productive, taxpaying entities that were the irreducible unit of premodern economy and government. Furthermore, marriages were "the seminaries of the king's subjects," sites for the reproduction of the human labor force on which royal wealth and the achievement of the king's ambitious imperial goals ultimately depended. Marriage and the family also played a vital disciplinary role in the state. Within the realm's conjugal households, men, women, and minor children had distinct roles defined by law that determined their rights and responsibilities in the broader political and legal realm. Conjugal households socialized Louis XIV's subjects, preparing each one to fulfill his or her obligations in the hierarchical social order. The preamble to the pronatalist edict of 1666 called marriage "the fecund source from which springs the strength and grandeur of states," acknowledging the conjugal household's fundamental role in creating manpower, wealth, and social stability. The king's advisors, in other words, considered marriage and reproduction essential to rebuilding monarchical authority and creating a glorious and powerful France.

When it claimed that marriage was a fundamental concern of secular authorities, Louis XIV's pronatalist edict called upon ideas that already had a venerable pedigree in early modern Europe. From the fifteenth century, and especially in the wake of the Reformation and the political realignments it engendered, European rulers, both Protestant and Catholic, had increasingly sought to exercise legislative authority and legal jurisdiction over the domestic realm. In doing so, these rulers were intervening in matters that had previously been regulated by local customary law or by canon law and ecclesiastical courts. The most typical focus of states' interest in regulating family life came through laws defining the circumstances necessary to contract a legal marriage (and thereby, it is worth noting, to engage licitly in reproductive sexuality). From the late middle ages forward, territorial rulers in France, Holland, Spain, England, and Germany made civil laws intended to limit the ability medieval canon law had granted to young people to marry clandestinely, that is secretly and without parental consent, à la Romeo and Juliet. Civil governments' efforts to ensure that marriages be publicly contracted, and that young men and women obtain parental consent to their unions were reflections of the centrality of the conjugal household in maintaining economic and social order; secret marriages spelled confusion over legitimacy, inheritance, and authority. So important was clarity on these issues that secular governments' claim to some form of jurisdiction over marriage and family formation was a common step in the evolution of modern nation-states in Europe.[29] The salience of marriage and family formation as political issues across Europe during the early modern period argues for placing state intervention in the family alongside the more familiar milestones in the development of modern states, such as the reorganization of armies, regulation of the economy, and development of legal and bureaucratic institutions.

Recent work on France has taken this step, arguing that increasing intervention in matters of marriage and family played a crucial role in the evolution of

France's royal government. In an influential series of articles, Sarah Hanley has traced this dynamic throughout the sixteenth, seventeenth, and eighteenth centuries.[30] Between 1556 and 1639, royal laws established what she called a "family-state compact," repeatedly intervening to regulate marriage and childbearing. For example, royal laws stretched the period of legal minority, forcing French young people to obtain parental approval for marriage until a woman reached age twenty-five, and a man age thirty. Young adults who dared make marital vows without parental permission risked being denied their natal family's money and prestige. If a man or woman married an underage spouse without the consent of the spouse's parents, he or she risked prosecution for *rapt,* or criminal seduction, a capital offense. Additional royal laws sought to monitor procreation. Unmarried women or widows who found themselves pregnant were enjoined to declare their pregnancies before royal judges, lest their infants' deaths be considered *prima facie* evidence they had committed infanticide. The offspring of clandestine marriages—couples who gamed loopholes in the law to marry secretly—were, by 1639, denied a share in inheritances. With these legal measures, French royal law and royal courts claimed greater jurisdiction over marriage and reproduction than had been the case beforehand.

In some ways, the king's new power to regulate marriage seems to confirm the traditional narrative of a "centralizing" state, as royal laws superceded customary laws and royal courts edged out ecclesiastical courts. But matters of family and sexuality also lend themselves to the revisionist narrative of state formation. For example, Hanley argues that the impetus for the French state's regulation of marriage and reproduction originally came not from a power-hungry monarchy, but rather from jurists. The jurists, representatives of an upwardly mobile social elite of royal officeholders, constructed a symbiotic relationship with a still fragile monarchical government. By propounding laws regulating marriage, reproduction, and inheritance, the jurists sought to protect their own family interests. When they limited the ability of young men and women to contract legal marriage without parental consent, and strictly defined the conditions for legitimate reproduction, they reinforced the authority of elite parents, enabling them to direct how property and prestige would flow to the next generation. The control afforded to parents—meaning, especially, fathers—guarded the fiscal and social capital these elites had carefully amassed. They, in turn, rewarded the royal government's protection of their family interests by investing their money in royal offices, and by providing the educated, elite labor force necessary to staff a growing royal government.[31] Rather than interpreting the regulation of family life as evidence of the centralization of power in the monarch's hands, in other words, Hanley sees the regulation of family life as evidence of a collaborative relationship between the king and France's social elites, particularly its *male* social elites. Royal legislative power helped to protect the interests of these elite men, with whom French kings shared a deeply rooted set of hierarchical and patriarchal social values, what we might call early modern "family values." These values included the determinative quality of family, breeding, and blood and the crucial role that deference to paternal power played in defining and maintaining France's social and political order.

Where does the royal government's pronatalist agenda fit in historians' effort to determine whether Louis XIV's reign is best understood as an expression of centralizing innovation or as the pinnacle of traditional collaboration with social elites? As the following chapters will show, the royal advisors who framed pronatalist policy reflected on the effort to promote reproduction both as an innovative use of royal power and a measure that embodied cherished values of French legal and political tradition. The project affirmed fatherhood as the natural origin of legitimate authority and celebrated the bonds between male heads of household and the monarch. By providing incentives for marriage and procreation, the royal government endeavored to buttress and reproduce this deeply gendered vision of social order. Yet although it celebrated fatherhood, the Edict on Marriage did not, after all, provide fathers with enhanced legal authority. It targeted male heads-of-household with normative definitions of masculinity against which their service to crown and kingdom could be measured. It sought to bend fathers' sense of familial self-interest to better serve the king's interest in securing the manpower necessary for his ambitious program of personal and national aggrandizement. In this fashion, pronatalism built on tradition to legitimize innovative experiments in governing. Royal government intervention in fertility represented a concerted effort to subject marriage and sexuality to the priorities of "reason of state."

Louis XIV's pronatalist edict of 1666 inaugurated a long and ongoing history of pronatalist intervention in family life on the part of the French state. Early modern pronatalism is evidence that sexual and reproductive behavior have been targets of secular government intervention for longer, perhaps, than many would guess. Early modern Europeans came to see that the universal human need to procreate is shaped into particular patterns reflecting different cultures' core values, and that these patterns have powerful implications for both individuals and governments. France's identity as a nation-state took shape amidst vibrant discussion of the possibilities and dangers inherent in governing this universal human experience. The halting efforts of the developing early modern state apparatus to encourage men and women to "be fruitful, and multiply" offers a window into this oddly persistent theme in French political life. Through the hopes and disappointments of royal officials and the couples with whom they interacted, we see how the intimate lives of men and women and the public world were connected both at the level of ideas and in the day-to-day governing practices of the Old Regime.

ONE

The Politics of Fertility in Seventeenth-Century France

W hen Louis XIV declared his intention to rule France without the aid of a chief minister in March of 1661, the young monarch assumed control over a kingdom in which human fertility had long been recognized as a matter of political concern. As his personal rule began, the most important dramas linking human reproduction with politics revolved around the monarch himself.

In June of 1660, Louis had married his twenty-one-year-old first cousin, the Spanish *infanta* Maria-Teresa, in a ceremony on the border between Spain and France. The marriage had been negotiated as part of the 1659 Treaty of the Pyrenees; it was the human representation of a diplomatic agreement intended to end a generation of war between the two kingdoms. On the French side of the border, the royal marriage generated intense hope for quick proof of the royal couple's fertility. France had suffered through a great deal of political instability in the prior century, in large measure because no French king had managed to pass on his crown to a son of age to rule since the death of François I in 1547. As a result, Louis XIV's subjects ardently, anxiously awaited the good news of a royal pregnancy.

But as the king, his new bride, and the royal entourage made their way back toward Paris, a scandal arose from within the court itself. We can trace the scandal in the letters of Gui Patin, a Parisian physician and man of letters. In June, he reported to his provincial correspondents that Mademoiselle de Guerchi, a young woman who served as a lady-in-waiting to the Queen mother, Anne of Austria, had died suddenly under mysterious circumstances. Suspicions were aroused when the priest at the Parisian parish of Saint-Eustache refused to bury Guerchi's body. Rumor held that the corpse had been taken to the Hôtel de Condé and packed in quicklime; by hastening decomposition, someone was hoping to conceal forensic evidence. Nevertheless, the circumstances surrounding Guerchi's death soon became clear. Guerchi, an unmarried woman, had discovered that she was pregnant at the very moment when the royal marriage meant that the court would be under significant scrutiny. Seeking a solution to a problem that would soon become evident and cause shame to herself and perhaps to the royal family, Guerchi had consumed a toxic abortifacient potion.

With the king's subjects focused on the royal marriage and the hope for royal progeny, it is hardly surprising that French legal authorities reacted with alarm to

the realization that a woman within the royal court had secured a potion intended
to end her pregnancy. Guerchi, evidently, was far from unique. Patin reported
that after her death a delegation of clerics from the diocese of Paris went to
inform the officials of France's highest court that six hundred women had revealed
either an abortion or infanticide to their confessors in the past year alone.[1]
Abortion was a capital crime in early modern France, treated with rigor by royal
law since the sixteenth century. For the judges, the prevalence of the crime was
evidence both of the persistent vice and disorder troubling French society, and of
their own failure to police sexual morality in the kingdom.

The legal machinery swung into action. As he traced the progress of the
newly wed royal couple toward Paris for his provincial correspondents, Patin
also followed developments in the abortion case. In mid-June, he reported that
authorities had arrested and interrogated Madame Constantin, a well-connected
midwife. Constantin admitted that Mademoiselle de Guerchi had died in her
house, but denied giving her any medicine whatsoever. She claimed that the
young woman had arrived at her home gravely ill, and died shortly afterward,
screaming in agony. While the midwife avowed hearing something about a potion
Guerchi had taken, she denied any knowledge of what the potion was or who had
made it. The midwife's admissions were legally savvy, if unconvincing to contemporary observers. By mid-July, Patin used unusually crude language as he
reported to his correspondents "they say [Constantin's] house was a bordello,
and that lots of sluts were going there to give birth or get abortions."[2]

Patin provided some clues that opinion was divided about the case. He noted,
first, that many considered the legal evidence against the midwife too weak to
warrant the death penalty. He also speculated that *les plus grands,* powerful members of the royal court, were lobbying on her behalf. Given Constantin's profession we might suspect her protectors to have included a clientele of elite women.[3]
For their part, the judges pressed on, intent on exposing Paris's abortion underground. They scoured the city and its environs for witnesses to confirm their
suspicions. They ordered parish clergy to read a *monitoire,* a message from the
pulpit enjoining any person having information about the midwife or her collab-
orators to make a declaration to authorities.

Constantin was tortured and then condemned to death by the Châtelet
criminal court in July of 1660. She appealed her sentence to a higher court, but
the judges' rigor was unyielding. And, while the king pardoned some offenders
in the Châtelet prison to celebrate his marriage, the midwife's crimes did not
merit the same clemency; she was hanged just days before Louis XIV and his
bride triumphantly entered Paris.[4]

The events of the summer of 1660 provide one particularly vivid example of the
political stakes surrounding fertility and reproduction in early modern France. In
one way or another, of course, procreation is basic to human survival, and therefore

destined to become a matter of concern within all political systems. Even if nature leads humans to seek sexual gratification, few societies allow the crucial business of producing and raising the next generation to proceed unregulated. The reaction to Mademoiselle de Guerchi's illicit union and the fate of the child she conceived attest to the salience of these issues for Louis XIV's government and for his subjects. As this chapter will show, seventeenth-century political writers recognized that reproduction was politically significant, that how it occurred contributed, for good or ill, to the replication of specific kinds of social and political relations. Procreation was therefore a vital subject of political contemplation, argument, and action.

In modern political discourse, the measurement of "population" is the most common locus of discussions about the consequences of human reproduction for political order. In seventeenth-century France, the means to measure population did not yet exist, and the intellectual orientation that goes with such measurement was in its infancy. As a result, other ways of thinking about the political consequences of fertility and human reproduction dominated. This chapter surveys three of the most common ways that procreation was credited with political significance. The first section examines the problem of reproducing the monarch, important for the continuity and stability of political power. The second section explores the traditional, Biblical notion that a flourishing and abundant population was the sign of divine blessing, and the related notion that it was a monarch's duty to police the reproductive morality of his subjects to ensure such blessing. Finally, the last section briefly examines the development of an early "social science" of reproduction that noted historical and cultural variations in the way humans procreate, and speculated on which of these was most politically beneficial. Taken together, an important theme united these different politics of fertility: the conjugal household defined by indissoluble, monogamous marriage was the foundation of French political order. This idea would also provide the logic of early modern pronatalist intervention in the reproductive process.

Fertility and the Politics of Dynasticism

In the late sixteenth century, the influential French political theorist Jean Bodin claimed that hereditary monarchy by succession in the male line was the most natural, desirable, and durable form of government that the world had ever known. While hereditary monarchy avoided the bloody rivalries that arose from elections, however, Bodin recognized that it could leave kingdoms vulnerable to the uncertainties of human reproduction.[5] France was even more vulnerable on this score than some of its neighbors. The so-called "Salic Law" held that the French crown could not legitimately be inherited by a woman or pass through the female line. As a result, orderly royal succession in France was dependent on the timely production and maturation of a male heir to the throne.[6]

As Louis XIV's subjects looked back on the kingdom's recent history, they surely recognized that France's kings had been unlucky in their attempts to meet this high standard of monarchical fertility. Accidents, assassinations, and reproductive delays had given rise to a series of regency governments, leaving France vulnerable to political instability and civil unrest. The circumstances of the young Louis XIV's life were a case in point. In 1638, Louis XIII and his queen, Anne of Austria, had been married without issue for almost twenty-three years. When the queen gave birth to a son, the child was baptized as "Louis Dieudonné" [God-given] and his arrival greeted as a miracle. But Louis XIII died in 1643, and his widow, Anne of Austria, and her trusted minister, the Italian Cardinal Mazarin, encountered significant resistance in their attempts to exercise regency power on behalf of the young Louis XIV. Resistance spiraled into outright rebellion during the Fronde of 1648–52.[7]

Political stability was more likely when the king was an adult. Patin, the physician, alluded to this truism when he wrote, echoing the warning of Isaiah 3:12: "Holy Scripture threatens us with three things, if we anger God: they are to fall into the hands of a child, a woman, and a foreigner."[8] So it was that French men and women hoped for the birth of a royal heir (called a *dauphin* in France) as soon as possible following the king's marriage, a birth that would repair the kingdom's "disorders" by decreasing the chances that another regency government would be necessary. As Patin wrote, "May it please God that [the queen] give us a prince who will restore France and love people of good will!"[9]

The marriage of the twenty-one-year-old Louis XIV signaled to his subjects that he was crossing the threshold to responsible male adulthood, ready to rule in his own right. France's recent history of troubled successions arguably intensified the parallels between the exercise of monarchical authority and the act of successfully fathering a legitimate heir. For this reason, the king's marriage was a particularly significant rite of passage in his political life.[10] Although French kings achieved majority and thus could go through the ritual coronation ceremony at Reims at the age of thirteen, the reaction of Louis XIV's subjects suggests they were reassured when their young king married and began to exercise patriarchal control over a family. In French legal tradition, marriage emancipated a young man from the authority of his parents, an event usually marked by the founding of a new household. After their marriages, young men took up the role of a male householder in the community, paying taxes and representing their household in local political matters. In the political memoir he wrote for his son, the king himself would point to his marriage to help explain his decision, in March of 1661, to exercise his royal power without the aid of a first minister.[11]

It is even possible that Louis XIV's impending fatherhood was a factor in his decision to inaugurate his personal rule. Throughout the fall and winter of 1660–61, as Cardinal Mazarin's final illness grew more serious, court watchers like Patin kept track of the appetite and behavior of Maria-Teresa (now Queen Marie-Thérèse) looking for signs of a pregnancy. The announcement of the queen's pregnancy coincided with the death of Cardinal Mazarin; the man who had acted, in many ways as a political "father" to the young monarch died that same week that the king learned he would himself become a father. Patin noted on March 7, 1661, that the queen had taken to her bed, arousing courtiers' suspicions. One of the king's first acts in the days following Cardinal Mazarin's death on March 9 was to proclaim a feast day in honor of Saint Joseph. Patin reported that the queen sought the saint's intercession so that she might bring safely to term the child that she expected in about seven months.[12] To the great relief of the king's subjects, the queen's pregnancy resulted in the birth of a male infant and dauphin of France, Louis, on November 1, 1661.

The birth of an heir relatively soon after the king's marriage worked to quell much of the lingering anxiety about Bourbon succession. Although several of the five offspring of the king and Queen Marie-Thérèse were sickly and did not live long, the dauphin survived to produce sons of his own. As an illustration of the importance of fertility to the king's exercise of power, however, it is worth noting that the representational apparatus of the royal government did not hesitate to proclaim the king's fertility even before it was proven. The young king had adopted the imagery of the sun, the greatest of all fertility symbols, even before his marriage. The meaning of the symbol was made explicit in a medal that was struck to celebrate the marriage, bearing the Latin phrase *Faecundis ignibus ardet,* or "he burns with fertile fires."[13] It did not hurt matters, either, that the king repeatedly proved his potency by fathering illegitimate offspring. His mistresses gave birth to at least sixteen royal children throughout the 1660s and 1670s. Although fertility was not the only or even the most important of the kingly qualities proclaimed in royal propaganda (the adult Louis XIV was more often depicted as Mars than as Apollo), the king's masculine fertility was understood as an important adjunct to and guarantee of his political authority.[14]

We can see these fertility themes at work in almanac images produced in the first decade of the king's personal rule. As Abby Zanger has shown, ephemeral works like broadsides and almanacs were important in the construction of Louis XIV's public image in the early phases of his reign. In these years of significant political transition, the young monarch needed to remake himself in the guise of a mature king at the head of a stable state, and his accession to masculine authority over a household served this purpose.[15] Consider, in this respect, the 1669 almanac engraving titled "Peace presented to the king, united with Abundance, supported by Force and Victory, who promise France a golden century" (figure 1.1). On the left, the image features the seated king, next to his queen. The king holds his arm around the dauphin, who would have been about seven when this image was created. The royal couple and the heir to the throne are surrounded by

FIGURE 1.1 "La Paix presentée au roy unie à l'abondance soustenue de la force et de la victoire qui promet à la France un siècle d'or," Collection Hennin 4491. Bibliothèque Nationale de France.

allegorical figures. Ceres, representing abundance, presents her daughter Peace, holding an olive branch and beehive, symbols (the image instructs us) of a coming golden century. The peace to which it referred was France's success in the War of Devolution, concluded by treaty in 1668. A banner describes the scene, promising that the recently concluded peace will usher in a "gentle" reign characterized by "beautiful laws." As was often the case with almanac images, the image made reference to events of the recent past as it projected their significance into the future represented by the calendar of the coming year; the "beautiful laws" referred to the king's ongoing project of legal reform. From this legal reform effort would be born the pronatalist law encouraging the king's subjects to marry and become fathers just as he had.

The engraving emphasized the relationship of these political achievements to fertility and dynastic continuity through the king's doubling with a miniature version of himself. The monarch protectively embraces his son and heir, in every respect a copy of the father. Even the king's well-turned leg—a common element in depictions of Louis XIV often interpreted as a phallic reference, or sign of his virility—is mimicked in the dauphin's exposed leg and large shoe buckle mimicking his father's.[16] If these suggestions of Bourbon potency were not emphatic enough, the monarch's scepter (another phallic symbol connected to the exercise of royal authority) with its fleur-de-lys (yet another phallic symbol) flies outward and upward from the boy's midsection as the child points back toward his father's leg.

This was not a mere royal family portrait; the image emphasized the continuity of Bourbon rule. At the same time it subtly instructed viewers in the complicated politics of royal succession. The king's relationship with his eldest son and heir was at the center. Pendant images in the lower center and lower left celebrate the ceremonial baptism of the dauphin. Yet beyond this central message stressing Louis XIV's success in ensuring the likelihood of an orderly father-son transmission of the crown, the viewer is reminded of other possibilities—in essence, the image reveals a dynastic back-up plan. The small-framed depiction at the bottom right refers to the birth in 1668 of the dauphin's younger brother, Philippe-Charles, duc d'Anjou (a child who was to die in 1671). Behind the king, Louis XIV's brother Philippe, duc d'Orléans, hovers as yet another copy of the king, ready if need arises. Note, though, that the duc d'Orléans' legs, like those of every other adult man in the main image, remain hidden to the viewer; Philippe's existence was crucial, but his potency constituted a potential challenge to political stability, or at least a distraction from the hope for untroubled succession that the image sought to convey. It is also important to recognize that Louis and Marie-Thérèse's living daughter, Marie-Thérèse de France, born in 1667, is totally absent from the image; as a female, she was irrelevant to the questions of succession and of the exercise of monarchical power which are its subject. In these ways, the almanac image emphasized the potency of Louis XIV and his ability to assure direct transmission of the crown. Placing the French king's procreative role at the symbolic center, the image made monarchical fertility the bedrock upon which France's golden century of military success, civic order, and national prosperity would be built.

Fertility did not lose significance even as Louis XIV aged, fathered children legitimately and illegitimately, and became a grandfather. Another almanac image, from 1687, reiterated the significance of royal fertility, going so far as to display the bed from which Bourbon kings emerged (figure 1.2). Titled "The hopes of France in the blessed fecundity of Madame la Dauphine," it features Maria-Anna of Bavaria, wife of the then twenty-six-year-old dauphin, resting in her bed after the birth of her third son, Charles, duc de Berry, on August 31, 1686.

The dauphine's reproductive role is emphasized in the image's title, but in every other way the foreign princess is literally upstaged by and rendered a passive observer to the Bourbon dynastic pageant her fecundity has made possible.[17] At the focal center, a still virile Louis XIV, then in his late forties, stands in as proxy father offering a gesture of paternal benediction as his third grandson is presented by the allegorical figure Happiness (la Félicité). Other men of the royal family stand beside him as if to reassure viewers of the depth of the Bourbon dynasty, despite the fact that the dauphin was by that time the king's sole living, legitimate son. Again, the artist draws attention to the king's legs. One of the dauphin's legs is visible too, while other men's legs are hidden. On the right, court ladies display the duc de Bourgogne and duc d'Anjou, the new baby's older brothers. These "heir and a spare" grandsons of the king stood before the newborn in the line of succession. Again, the image highlights the fertility of the royal family as a guarantee against the miseries that had afflicted the kingdom in previous generations.[18]

The irony in examining the 1687 almanac image is that the reproductive good fortune it trumpeted was not to last. By the time of Louis XIV's death in 1715, every one of the king's direct male descendants pictured in the engraving was dead. In 1714, when disease had claimed all males in direct line to the throne except the very young Duc d'Anjou, the aged king was reduced to maneuvering to place his legitimated sons Louis-Auguste de Bourbon, duc du Maine, and Louis-Alexandre de Bourbon, comte de Toulouse, children of his liaison with Athenaïs de Rochechouart de Mortemart, Madame de Montespan, in line for the throne. And then, having failed to do so, upon Louis XIV's death his throne passed to his five-year-old great grandson.[19] Despite the king's astonishing fertility—he had fathered more than twenty children—his longevity meant the kingdom was subjected to another regency government.

In the 1660s, of course, French subjects watched their young king with no inkling of this future; their anxieties came from their vivid memories of the political upheavals of Louis XIV's childhood. From his marriage until the birth of

FIGURE 1.2 "Les Esperances de la France en l'heureuse fécondité de Madame la Dauphine," Collection Hennin 5556. Bibliothèque Nationale de France.

a presumptive heir they watched for the proof that their young monarch would conquer this obstacle to political stability, setting himself apart from his father in a fundamental way. For that reason, the marriage and the arrival of the dauphin Louis in 1661 may have been a more important moment in the reestablishment of French monarchical authority in the aftermath of the Fronde than the recent historiography of the era has acknowledged. The images analyzed here serve as reminders of the fact that the virility and mortality of the king were related, politically salient issues. Hereditary monarchy made fertility and human reproduction ineluctably political matters, central to the security of the state and to the exercise of power. Louis XIV's government understood this fundamental connection, and crafted the king's public image to emphasize the monarch's symbolic role as sun and carnal role as father. The king must count as fortunate that for most of his personal reign, he appeared to enjoy the blessing of fertility within his own household.[20]

Fertility: Divine Gift and Political Advantage

The political significance of fertility did not end with the youthful, virile monarch; fertility was a characteristic of his kingdom, too. Historical demographers estimate that in 1661, Louis XIV became sovereign over between 18.9 and 21.8 million subjects. This made France by far the most populous nation in Western Europe. None of its imperial competitors—not England, not Holland, not Spain—had human reserves rivaling those of the Sun King.[21]

A common axiom of early modern political theory held that "men are the true riches of a kingdom," and by that measure, as seventeenth-century writers saw it, Louis XIV's France was rich indeed. Despite their lack of statistics, the writers and statesmen of the mid-seventeenth century were firmly convinced that France was Europe's most populous state. They attributed growing political significance to the factor they called "peopling" (peuplement). Much as the monarch's success in producing heirs signaled divine favor and the promise of a glorious future, they saw France's densely peopled landscape as a demonstration of God's blessing and an implicit legitimization of their monarch and his goals. France's natural abundance and fertile, multiplying population were harbingers of imperial greatness.

The conviction that France was particularly densely populated had grown over the course of the seventeenth century. In the 1615 Traité de l'oeconomie politique, Antoine de Montchrestien proclaimed that the French king had "an advantage . . . that no other prince in the world can match: your France alone can flood and cover the world with men."[22] Montchrestien, a poet, playwright, and early economic theorist, littered his work with paeans to France's fertility. He likened the kingdom to a swarming anthill, boasting of France's "inexhaustible abundance" of "so many millions" of men.[23] In Montchrestien's view, the kingdom's human bounty was a sign of its latent potential, but it also presented something of a challenge for its ruler. Like a good householder must manage his domestic labor force, the French king needed to enlist the teeming masses of his kingdom in some orderly, productive enterprise.[24]

Population claims like Montchrestien's may seem suspiciously like flattery of the French monarch, but outsiders tended to agree with his assessment. Seventeenth-century British travelers, for example, penned jealous descriptions of France's wealth in human beings. John Evelyn, who visited France several times during the 1640s, noted the French proclivity for "Prolifique multiplying," and his countryman Ellis Veryard, visiting later in the century, observed that France was "fertile and abounding" in every kind of natural product, including the humans that made it "the most populous Country of its extent in Europe."[25] Despite reversals caused by war, by the Fronde, and by famines afflicting some French provinces in the early 1660s, political observers continued to believe that France enjoyed bountiful fertility and a large population, qualities that set it apart from its European neighbors. As the royalist political writer Paul Hay, Marquis du Chastelet, wrote in 1669, France had many natural advantages: the beauty of its landscape, its climate and soil conducive to agriculture, its pure air, and—most of all—the "incredible number" of its people, a truth "of which even the most ignorant have entire and certain knowledge."[26]

One sign of the growing political significance that seventeenth-century statesmen attributed to France's fertility was their increasing interest in the methods that might be used to quantify and manage the monarch's human resources. Jean-Baptiste Colbert, the powerful minister of Louis XIV who would become the architect of royal pronatalist policy, was also an early patron of the development of quantitative demographic methods. In the 1670s, Colbert supported the publication of weekly bulletins listing the number of births and deaths in Paris. He also demanded colonial officials perform yearly, nominative censuses in France's colonies—the first the royal government would attempt. The royal government never applied such measures to the densely populated metropole during the reign of Louis XIV.[27] But throughout his tenure as controller-general, Colbert did seek to collect information about what we would today call population trends. He occasionally asked provincial intendants and other informants for their assessments about whether the number of taxable households in a given region seemed to be increasing, and whether peasants celebrated their weddings with more or less pomp.[28] These kinds of proto-demographic inquiries supplied impressionistic information about the general state of the populace.

At one level, collecting information about the French population served practical administrative needs. It might aid in the repartition of the tax burden or, as we will see, be used by the king's officers as a gauge of whether his policies to enhance his population had been effective. At the same time, the growing trend toward collection of statistical information had important symbolic consequences. As theorists and historians have stressed, the creation of channels for information about the "peopling" of France played a role in extending royal power; by making the realm's vital statistics more visible to the king and his government, and by illustrating to French subjects that the king cared about such matters, fertility and human reproduction were more explicitly marked out as a terrain for royal political action.[29]

Louis XIV's administrators worked to increase the information available to the king, and were beginning to explore quantification as a tool of government. Yet it is crucial to stress that the modern discourse of population simply did not exist in the seventeenth century. Indeed, the language of numbers did not become the dominant way to represent the relationship between human fertility and the state until late in the eighteenth century. While modern demographers can quantify the French king's demographic advantage over his rivals, the government of Louis XIV had no statistical information about the French population. In the 1660s, even the word "population" had not yet entered the French lexicon.

In the era of Louis XIV, discussions of peopling were carried out in qualitative rather than quantitative terms. Writers drew inspiration from historical and religious sources, figuring population not as a numerical value but as a gauge of divine blessing. The Old Testament tradition proved a particularly rich source of such ideas and an inspiration for many seventeenth-century writers. God's plan for humanity, they noted, included the charge to "be fruitful and multiply" (Genesis 1:28), and his blessings were shown in the Psalmist's promise that "your wife will be like a fruitful vine within your house; your children will be like olive shoots around your table" (Psalm 128:3). In the Bible, abundant human reproduction also had explicit political resonance. This was clear, first, in the story of God's covenant with Abraham; the promise to make Abraham's offspring as numerous as the stars in the heavens (Genesis 15:4–5), they claimed, was a guarantee that his descendants would eventually dominate the promised land.

Jacques-Bénigne Bossuet, Bishop of Meaux and preceptor to Louis XIV's son, developed Old Testament motifs in his *Politics Drawn from the Very Words of Holy Scripture,* a book of political advice he started for his royal charge.[30] Bossuet observed via scripture that a flourishing population stood for a kind of perfect harmony in the state: "In the enumeration of the immense riches of Solomon, there is nothing finer than these words: 'Judah and Israel were innumerable, as the sand of the sea in multitude.'"[31] And, this whole "innumerable people 'ate and drank . . . every one under his vine and his fig-tree, and rejoicing.'" The populous land of plenty was a vision of true, Biblical "felicity" to which a good monarch should aspire.[32]

Works like Bossuet's reflected a traditional aesthetics that envisioned abundance itself as beautiful. But Bossuet's choice to make an abundant, well-fed people the gauge of the "true" riches to which monarchs should aspire was also timely political commentary. The part of his *Politics* treating population was drafted in the early eighteenth century, at a moment when the promise of Louis XIV's early reign had been shaken by long and costly wars, and by famine and illness in the French countryside; the death toll of these crises was high. Bossuet's fulsome praise for the beauty of an abundant population rejoicing over a bounteous harvest, in other words, was a reminder of the king's primary responsibility to watch over the well-being of his people. When the king forgot this first duty, his previously 'innumerable' people would become immiserated and depleted.[33]

How should a monarch seek to repair his losses and ensure a growing, flourishing population? Bossuet offered the prince policy suggestions drawn from the Bible and inspired by the sexual morality of the Catholic Reformation era. Rather than arguing for economic aid or tax relief, he suggested that the blessing of fertility depended upon the moral health of the French people. The king cultivated his population by repressing vagrancy, favoring marriage, and opposing illicit unions. Illicit unions were defined by their inability or intention not to result in procreation: "Let those unions which are meant to bear no fruit, and which have avowed sterility, be cursed by God and man," Bossuet fulminated.[34] Protecting the blessing of fertility thus demanded royal policing of sexual and marital order within the kingdom.

Bossuet's fertility politics remained thoroughly traditional and religious. But his contemporaries were increasingly likely to base their thinking about population in secular rationales. Seventeenth-century political theory held that population was not only a blessing, but a source of worldly political advantage in the contest among nations. By an ineluctable natural law, many argued, populous states expanded at the expense of their neighbors.[35] France's dense population thus promised to facilitate and even to justify French expansion in Europe and in the Americas. A writer named d'Orgeval argued the point in the treatise he addressed to Louis XIV: "The more men there are, the more conquerors in order to possess a greater share of the land that belongs to them by right, because God blessing their generation, He must increase the land that nourishes them." A wise prince always paid close heed to the reproduction of his subjects, because, as d'Orgeval succinctly stated, a flourishing population "renders us masters of all things."[36]

It was clearly a widespread notion that the fertility of France and its people gave it the potential to become Europe's dominant imperial power. A number of writers expressed this idea through a corporal idiom that likened the kingdom to a body composed of limbs, organs, and humors. In this idiom, French populousness indicated that the kingdom was a healthy, virile body pulsing with fecund energy. These youthful, masculine qualities gave it great potential to act, although they also might incline it to disorder and aggression. For Montchrestien, populous France was a restless body charged with superfluous humors. He recommended, in essence, that it release these humors as "seed" by sowing French colonies on distant shores.[37] The metaphor of the realm as an energetic masculine body was evoked, also, as a cause for anxiety by France's neighbors. John Evelyn, seeing France's ample population and rich agriculture, understood that they made it by nature a redoubtable enemy, with a "belly fortified for that cruel Beast called War."[38] In an age before the now familiar numerical language of population, such corporal metaphors provided a figurative language to describe how the fertility of individuals was linked with the fate of the commonwealth as a whole.

The twin beliefs that fertility was a blessing and that political strength arose from a large population had an important logical corollary: France could not have too many people. The concept of "overpopulation" did not make sense in the terms of seventeenth-century population thinking. Considering that the French king's subjects frequently observed grinding poverty, begging, and vagrancy, it is not surprising that some observers expressed occasional doubts. Nevertheless, political theorists urged their contemporaries to resist the conclusion that France was overpopulated; if human beings were the source of all wealth and national strength, whatever "disorder" their abundance seemed to engender was best understood as a problem of order and morality. Human nature led people to go astray, and lapse into idleness and crime. Like a shepherd, the king was blessed if he had a large flock, but it was his solemn responsibility to discipline the wayward. As the king explained in the memoirs he wrote for the dauphin, the business of a prince was to "know the art of making both [the people's] numbers and their opulence serve the glory and well-being of his kingdom."[39]

In fulfillment of this princely art, the era of Louis XIV witnessed widespread efforts to suppress vagrancy and to force the poor and underemployed to work. The royal government cooperated with a range of provincial projects spearheaded, for the most part, by pious urban elites. Broadly speaking, the crown and seventeenth-century French social elites agreed that forced work both had economic benefits and served to redeem the poor from the sinful bad habits that bred social disorder, notably theft, drunkenness, sedition, and illicit sex.[40] After the Fronde, royal legislation enabled experiments with poor relief by offering privileges to help fund local initiatives. These included the creation of hospitals and homes for abandoned children or for prostitutes. Most notoriously, the period saw the founding of penal workhouses that sought through incarceration to instill discipline and moral order among what contemporaries considered the criminal poor—adults physically capable of gainful employment repeatedly caught begging in the streets.[41]

As Bossuet suggested, shepherding people toward the moral order of marriage and reproductive sexuality was part of a prince's duty. In this sense, illicit sexuality was, for contemporaries, a particularly troubling sign of the disorder and moral squalor of the poor. Marriage offered a remedy; when men and women married and founded stable households, the destabilizing sexual passion that had bedeviled humanity since the fall of man was usefully channeled into productive fertility. Legitimately married parents, united by the sacrament of matrimony, produced workers, soldiers, and merchants who understood their duty to God and to king. By contrast, illicit sex was disordered and could literally reproduce disorder. The pious men and women who joined charitable confraternities and visited poor households complained that poor men and women neither married in the church nor bothered to have their infants baptized. Without benefit of the sacrament, their unions offended morality, resulted in the birth of illegitimate children, and then left those unfortunate youngsters contaminated with original sin.[42] The situation tended to reproduce itself; elite men and women thought that young, poor women ignorant of religion would "fall" or be lured into vice. When this happened, the disorder was often embodied in an illegitimate child. In the content of post-Tridentine sexual values organized around sacramental marriage and the generation of saints for heaven, illicit sexuality constituted an unacceptable threat.[43]

The quest to eradicate prostitution constitutes the best-known example of how these values coalesced into action during the sixteenth and seventeenth centuries. Although prostitution had been tolerated, and even organized as a trade in many medieval cities, it came increasingly to be seen as an intolerable offense against social order. A royal ordinance of Charles IX had outlawed brothels in France in 1561, but this was more a statement of principles than effective legislation. In actuality, it was local governments who bore the responsibility to police prostitution. Over the next century, responding to the Catholic Reformation piety and domestic values of a broad section of the French public, city fathers closed brothels and prosecuted, in particular, the procurers and procuresses who recruited young women into the sex trade. Confraternities and charitable institutions turned their attention to saving fallen women—often, it seems, by locking them up and subjecting them to austere penitential regimes. These efforts met with limited success because women's vulnerability to poverty and men's willingness to pay for sex did not disappear.[44]

The quest to repress prostitution and extramarital sexuality more broadly was tied to fertility and reproduction in France. Contemporaries believed that "debauchery" had a number of consequences for "peopling." Generally, they reasoned, it resulted in fewer births. A long tradition of medical argument suggested that promiscuous sex was mostly sterile. Some medical theories held, for example, that prostitutes overused their sex organs and thus were unable to conceive; nature supposedly preferred moderate sexual activity for successful generation.[45] By a similar logic, confessors advised childless couples to atone; sexual sin was often punished by infertility. As time wore on, experience would prove

the limitations of this logic. Charitable establishments cared for increasing numbers of abandoned children widely assumed to be the fruit of illicit unions. It was
clear to everyone that these infants had been conceived outside marriage; they
were the fruit of illicit unions rather than the supposedly ideal reproductive scenario—pregnancy occurring to married couples calmly and piously seeking
progeny. As they observed these trends, concerned men and women were led to
analyze the accidents and "disorders"—for example, the exploitation of domestic
servants and the garrisoning of troops—that helped to explain how these children had been conceived.[46] By the eighteenth century, the phenomenon of illegitimacy would prompt reconsideration of traditional ideas about conception and
generate reflection on the social and economic circumstances that shaped fertility.[47] Throughout the seventeenth century, however, religious and political
writers expressed continued faith in sacramental marriage as the key to ensuring
the blessing of God and thereby maximizing the fertility of the populace.

The abandonment of infants aroused suspicions of a related, hidden crime.
Many feared that unmarried women, because of shame, concealed their pregnancies and resorted to abortion and infanticide. Discouraging this "false honor"
had been the official rationale for the royal edict of 1556 against clandestine pregnancy, which required unmarried women and widows to register a declaration of
their pregnancy before local officials or risk prosecution for infanticide should
their infant die.[48] This regime of legal surveillance had a number of consequences.
Many women took advantage of the law to name the father of their child, seeking
damages for failure to fulfill a promise of marriage and financial support to defray
the costs of birth and infant care. Despite its illegality, abortion was nearly impossible to police; it only rarely came to authorities' attention, often, as in the case
of Mademoiselle de Guerchi, when the pregnant woman herself suffered grave
illness or death as a result. Discovery of infanticide was more common, and royal
judges faithfully penalized this crime to the limits of the law.[49] The draconian
punishment meted out to the unfortunate women prosecuted for the crime
reflected judicial authorities' suspicions—no doubt true—that the cases that
came before them accounted for only a minority of actual occurrences, and that
the "anti-fertility" crimes of abortion and infanticide were common.

Indeed, despite new laws and harsh penalties, Louis XIV's advisors suspected
that thousands upon thousands of potential royal subjects perished at the hands of
their parents. One Bineteau, describing himself as "a provincial doctor and faithful subject of his majesty," wrote to Colbert in 1666 to propose the royal
government make a concerted effort to arrest and incarcerate the thirty thousand
beggars and their wives or concubines whom he estimated were currently roam-
ing France. Doing so would reveal that many of the poor who claimed to be
crippled or blind were frauds, he contended, more than capable of earning their
living by labor. It would also contribute to "the glory of God and the good of the

kingdom," because it would "avert every year the strangulation of ten thousand infants that these unfortunates cause to die without baptism."[50] The numbers Bineteau attached to this social problem—which suggested that one in three of the vagrant poor committed infanticide every year—rested on no discernible empirical evidence. They were, rather, a sign of elite anxiety about the murderous social disorder and wastefulness represented by illicit sexuality. Likewise, Bineteau's suggestion for royal action illustrates that the spirituality and politics of fertility were, for most French people, closely allied. He believed that incarcerating the poor would not only ensure the survival and efficient use of French manpower to build prosperity, it would literally save souls by ensuring baptism of infants born within the kingdom's charitable institutions.

In the France of the young Louis XIV, then, common political wisdom held that France was uniquely blessed in its fertility, and that it was incumbent upon the monarch to protect and build on this blessing through surveillance of marriage and sexual morality among the broader population. The coalescence of this pro-fertility political regime was not inevitable. In Germany, as Ulrike Strasser and Lyndal Roper have shown, both Protestant and Catholic governments constructed legal rules that, in essence, criminalized reproduction among the poor. Local officials enforced laws that forbade men and women from marrying, and thus from legally having sex or conceiving children, unless they proved they had sufficient resources to maintain a household.[51] In France, by contrast, marriage and the prospect of procreation that went with it was not legally restricted based on property. To be sure, the resources to form an independent conjugal household were out of the reach of many, and young women from modest backgrounds often toiled for more than a decade in order to earn the dowry that enabled them to form an independent household.[52] Yet there is little sign that French elites or the crown ever enacted legislation to prevent the poor from marrying and reproducing. Indeed, providing modest dowries to facilitate the marriage of poor women and repentant prostitutes constituted a popular form of charity during the era of Catholic Reform.[53] In Bourbon France, continuing faith in the spiritual and political benefits of the fertile conjugal household won out over concerns about an expanding underclass.

Fertility as Historical and Cultural Variable

Thus far, this chapter has examined two highly traditional ways that human reproduction crossed into the terrain of early modern French politics: dynasticism and the belief that human fertility was a divine blessing. By the seventeenth century, the politics of fertility had come to embrace a third, less traditional set of considerations. Informed by history and by stories of travel and discovery, writers were increasingly inclined to take note of the historical contingency and cultural specificity of reproductive arrangements. At one level, seventeenth-century thinkers regarded procreation as the fulfillment of a natural human imperative, a process that linked all of humanity, past and present. Yet political theorists, philosophers, and statesmen were also aware that beyond this basic universal fact, the way the world's people set out to reproduce themselves showed fascinating diversity. Practices of marrying, begetting children, defining family, and marking what was sexually permissible varied enormously across time and space. Moreover, the differences appeared to have significant consequences for human fertility. The observation of this diversity called the "naturalness" of European procreative values into question; and, arguably, increased the scope for political action. After all, if the world's peoples were distinguished in important ways by the fashion in which they reproduced—that is, if fertility varied in relation to human law as well as natural law—this implied that human reproduction was a suitable terrain for government.

Both the study of history and encounters with other cultures during the Renaissance could lead toward relativism regarding human sexuality and reproduction. The intellectual trajectory of the sixteenth-century French skeptic Michel de Montaigne is illustrative. In order to buttress his conclusion that no law of behavior garnered truly universal approbation—"Let them show me just one law of that sort—I'd like to see it,"—Montaigne took apparent delight in cataloging some of the most exotic and shocking practices governing marriage, reproduction, and family relations in other cultures.[54] In some nations, he noted, mothers married their sons; others embraced infanticide, a good number favored wife-sharing, and some even praised father-eating. "Nothing in short is so extreme that it is not accepted by the usage of some nation," he concluded in the "Apology for Raymond Sebond."[55]

Montaigne's thought on these matters softened somewhat in later writing. For example, he expressed a less extreme view ten years later, concluding that perhaps there was one truly natural law, by which he meant "an instinct that is seen universally, and permanently imprinted in both the animals and ourselves": it was the affection of parents for their offspring. At the same time, he admitted that he found his own "taste strangely blunted" in this respect. Montaigne wrote that he had not found his own infants in the least bit lovable, at least not until they had passed through their formless, and then monkey-like stages.[56] Montaigne's own indifference to fathering, of course, undermined his statement that paternal love was natural. And if the affection of fathers was a social custom rather than a natural fact, what might this imply about the patriarchal conjugal household that his countrymen proclaimed to be the divinely ordained basis of social order? Was it also a fragile human construct? A natural impulse clearly led both humans and animals to reproduce, but Montaigne did not appear convinced that it led infallibly to any specific conjugal or political arrangement.

What lessons could be drawn from the observed variability of marital customs? Montaigne wrote that his reading of ancient philosophers led him to believe that the sages he and other educated Europeans revered would have found Christianity's strict sexual and marital ethics ludicrous, preferring a system of "wives held in common and without obligation."[57] Montaigne was not arguing that the French should practice the sexual openness he read about in his books; he was, however, comparing his own culture's practices to alternatives attested in history. By the seventeenth century, it was common for Christians, and in particular Catholics, to see their own marital requirements as particularly rigorous, "constrained" as Montaigne had put it, or "very severe" according to the late seventeenth-century ethnographer of marriage customs Louis de Gaya. Perhaps, they thought, reformed Catholicism, with its emphasis on monogamous, indissoluble marriage, restrained rather than encouraged fertility. To introduce his survey of the marriage ceremonies of the worlds' peoples, for example, Gaya remarked that "most other religions, in order to render marriage easier, freer, and more fecund, receive and practice polygamy and divorce."[58]

In weighing the pros and cons of other traditions, seventeenth-century writers began to see links between reproductive systems and political regimes. This was nowhere clearer than in the utopian literature that flourished during the seventeenth century. In his *City of the Sun,* published in 1623, the Dominican friar Tommaso Campanella was inspired by Plato's *Republic* to imagine a reproductive system that set all Christian taboos aside, and placed sexuality and reproduction completely in the service of secular government. Campanella envisioned magistrates selecting breeding couples from the participants in mandatory sessions of nude calisthenics. The magistrates would urge the couples to procreate at the precise, astrologically propitious moment, and offer them a special bed surrounded by statues of political and military heroes. Early modern lore held that a woman's imagination had the power to shape the developing fetus, so surrounding the couple with images of virtuous men was meant to transmit civic virtue to the child as it was conceived. Campanella's fantasy about breeding a race of civic-minded supermen constitutes a particularly radical example of where the political contemplation of reproduction could lead. Still, most utopian writers took the time to address marital practices and family organization, a recognition that the way societies organized procreation was revealing and politically significant.[59]

By the middle of the seventeenth century, the notion that marital and reproductive regimes had important political implications had spread well beyond the libertine intellectual elite. In the 1630s, the Parisian physician, philanthropist, and publisher Théophraste Renaudot held Monday afternoon conferences where an audience of one hundred curious Parisians participated in open discussions on matters of science and philosophy.[60] The assembly turned its attention to the relation of politics and fertility several times, such as when it debated the "means to render a place more populous" and "whether it is better [for the purposes of generation] that a man have several wives, or a woman several husbands."[61]

The anonymous participants in Renaudot's debates displayed familiarity with the marital and reproductive customs depicted in classical history, literature, and law. The basics of their population science went something like this: since antiquity, wise lawgivers and powerful empires had conscientiously legislated to build their human reserves. The most important example was Rome. A pantheon of ancient authors wrote about the ways that the wise Romans had carefully shaped their laws with an eye to the multiplication of their forces. First of all, Romans tolerated divorce and allowed the legitimization of children born outside marriage, accommodating their laws with human weaknesses in ways that ultimately increased the number of taxpayers and soldiers within their empire. Beyond their less stringent marital and reproductive laws, the Romans had developed legislation designed specifically to increase their numbers. The emperor Augustus passed laws penalizing celibacy, encouraging marriage, and rewarding fathers of large families. These Roman precedents, familiar to most educated Frenchmen, suggested a range of techniques that governments might use to promote population growth. This limited range of pronatalist ideas would endure into the eighteenth century and even beyond. When the government of Louis XIV would consider means to increase fertility, it was to this well-known set of Roman precedents that the king's councillors would turn.

Renaudot's meetings attest to the growth of a popular science of statecraft that addressed questions of marriage, reproduction, and population, and touched a broad public. The tendency toward instrumental thinking about sex and reproduction—posing the question, *if there were no other considerations,* what would be the best way to maximize population?—was characteristic of the libertine tenor of Renaudot's gatherings. Speakers clearly felt safe—even rewarded—for expressing ideas that challenged orthodoxy as defined in the post-Tridentine church.

Yet if learned elites made it an intellectual pastime to weigh the empirical evidence of marital variations, it would be wrong to assume that they were on the verge of abandoning their devotion to Catholic marital norms. They remained embedded within a Catholic religious culture that recognized marriage's supernatural goal of sacramental grace as equally important to nature's goal of procreation.

In the end, recognizing the political wisdom of Roman pronatalist precedents did not necessitate a rejection of the basic religious doctrines regarding marriage propounded at the Catholic Council of Trent (1545–63). How, then, did seventeenth-century French writers and their readers balance the spiritual and political possibilities of marriage in their minds? No theme in the early modern debate about marital regulation serves to illustrate their struggle better than their writing about polygamy.

The Canons of Trent had declared anathema those who denied that marriage was a sacrament, those who denied that religious celibacy was a still holier path than matrimony, or that legitimate marriage was monogamous and indissoluble. Formally, then, polygamy was forbidden to Christians. Yet the rule posed some historical problems; first, anyone familiar with *Genesis* could see that the patriarchs had been polygamists. To explain this aberration, Catholic theologians invoked a historical explanation. Fertility had been the primordial rule; as a result God had originally approved the practice of polygamy specifically because at creation it was necessary to people the earth. In the "plenitude of time," however, when the world had been sufficiently peopled, God had sent the Messiah to release his people from the requirement to "increase and multiply." Jesus had, instead, "raised the flag of virginity," instituting the higher ideal of celibacy.[62]

For seventeenth-century Europeans, however, polygamy's history was not as historically remote as the age of the patriarchs. Just a century before, when the Protestant Reformation had intensified challenges to the traditional Catholic marital regulation, the anabaptists of Münster had revived the custom, offering as justification the notion that in the past God had chosen this marital order for multiplying His chosen people.[63] The Münster experiment with polygamy was soon rejected by all confessions; both Protestant and Catholic powers closed ranks to reaffirm the identification of Christianity with monogamy. The twenty-fourth session of the Council of Trent in 1563 condemned the "false notions" and "pernicious contagion" introduced by "impious men of this age" who had dared to suggest that Old Testament marriage customs were favored by God. Jesus Christ, it reminded them, had instituted the rule of monogamy. After condemning those who claimed that marriage was not a sacrament that conferred grace (and thereby rejecting the Protestant position), the Council proclaimed its second anathema against anyone who "saith . . . that it is lawful for Christians to have several wives at one time, and that this is not prohibited by any divine law."[64] In 1563, the outrage of polygamy merited it a higher position on the list of anathematic errors than divorce, rules governing consanguinity, and even the mandate of clerical celibacy.

The intensity of its condemnation did not erase the history of polygamy in the Judeo-Christian tradition or the abundant evidence of its practice in other cultures. In the seventeenth century, most writers tended to associate the custom of having multiple wives with Islam, especially with the Turks whose lands sat threateningly near to Christian Europe. Seventeenth-century French texts often credited polygamy for the enormous armies with which the Ottoman Empire terrified Christian Europeans. Interestingly, Christians projected their own secularizing tendencies onto their Islamic neighbors, judging that polygamy in the

Ottoman Empire was a custom based on instrumental politics rather than religious commitment. The Turks, some said, had adopted this custom as a means to gain advantage in their perpetual conflict with Christians.[65]

At Renaudot's conferences, the anonymous speakers largely agreed that fertility offered political benefits and that polygyny favored fertility. Christians rejected having multiple wives, but this practice could not be considered contrary to the law of nature, they argued, given that so many of the worlds' peoples practiced it. Polyandry, or the custom of having multiple husbands, was a different matter; since a woman with multiple husbands could not produce offspring more quickly, this marital variation supposedly practiced by the Amazons and Ancient Britons was judged a "monstrous" offense against natural law by the assembly.[66] The grounds for judging polygyny acceptable, in other words, were that it seemed to promise more efficient human reproduction. It thus reflected the view espoused by many writers that "the multiplication of men is the true goal of nature."[67]

As Carol Blum has astutely observed, the "pseudopragmatism" of early modern discussions of polygamy concealed a number of "erotic subtexts and agendas of domination."[68] The distinction between polygyny, which was natural, and polyandry, which was not, served to naturalize the principle of male dominance over women. As they imaginatively explored the natural laws governing sex, European male intellectuals reconciled frustrations about the sexual limitations imposed more consistently on Catholic men after Trent. Thinking about the natural and political logic of taking many wives offered them a mental escape into a fantasy world where men exercised uncomplicated dominance over women and enjoyed unfettered access to sex. The natural, fertile, polygynous utopia they imagined recuperated marriage as a gateway to erotic pleasures. This ostensibly natural plan for human sexuality stood in sharp contrast to the consistent message enunciated from the pulpit and through secular governments' marital laws: namely, the idea that marriage was a serious civic responsibility that enjoined men to preside responsibly over a household and sustain a reproductive partnership with one woman until death. It is no coincidence, in other words, that interest in polygamy grew even amidst a crescendo of texts and laws protecting monogamous, indissoluble marriage, and extolling it as the natural model of good order in society and government.[69]

Many writers were content to observe that the most efficient means to ensure human reproduction was not the monogamous, indissoluble marriage demanded by their religion. But some reconciled their Christian sexual values with the importance of fertility by refuting the claim that polygamy produced population increase. According to Philippe de Béthune, it was in fact monogamy that best served the multiplication of mankind. Redeploying the notion that sexual moderation was necessary for reproduction, Béthune argued that the sexual demands upon a polygamous man caused him to father weaker children less likely to live. In addition, his paternal care was too limited to allow him to raise his numerous progeny to adulthood. If the Turks had large armies, he judged it was because they controlled a vast territory and not because they practiced polygyny.[70] Jacques Chaussée, an ardent apologist for Catholic marriage, agreed. If having multiple wives increased fertility, then Turkey, Persia, Japan, and other lands ought to be "infinitely populated." And yet these regions were less populous than Europe, or so he claimed. The conclusion Chaussée drew was that "although the marriage bed (*le couche*) of Europeans contains only two people, it remains much more fertile than that of these Infidels, however many they sleep with."[71] Rather than questioning the Catholic tradition of monogamy, these authors fully reconciled Christian monogamy with the profertility imperatives of nature and statecraft.

Seventeenth-century discussions about human sexual nature and its political repercussions were often carried on in the abstract, where alternatives to the principle of monogamous indissoluble marriage could be safely confined to historical time, other nations, utopias, or an imagined state of nature. In these places, human reproduction might test different rules and result in more fertile outcomes. Such discussions did not actually intend to argue that French law or Catholic tradition should change to embrace the logic of maximal fertility. They served, instead, to point out the tensions between what nature intended, reason of state endorsed, and divine law enjoined. Ultimately, this thinking worked to expand the terrain of monarchical political action. Observations about the links between marriage, fertility, and national strength and prosperity legitimized the monarchy's regulation of marriage and sexuality.

As this chapter has shown, questions about the best ways to organize reproduction were posed at the same time that French Catholics reinforced their commitment to the religious and political order represented by the monogamous conjugal household. In this sense, abstract discussions of the "best way" to organize reproduction were not entirely divorced from the real exercise of politics. Polygamy, for example, was not as remote as it seems if we take unformalized plural marriages into account. Before the Reformation, French elite men often fathered children with mistresses and concubines. After Trent, and in conjunction with the stigmatization of illicit sexuality and extramarital reproduction, social acceptance of this pattern of elite reproduction effectively ended. By the seventeenth century, royal law more resolutely excluded illegitimate offspring from sharing in the estate of their fathers, or from inheriting noble status.[72] Louis XIV himself, of course, would become a major offender against these developing mores by fathering more than a dozen children out of wedlock. While the king's reproductive success may have eased his subjects' dynastic concerns, his advisors recognized his extramarital procreation posed a delicate political problem. Perhaps the most unusual of Jean-Baptiste Colbert's services to his royal employer was concealing the infants' illegitimacy by having them baptized under the names of fictive parents. Colbert and his wife fostered the royal bastards for a time in their own household.[73] When the king later used his royal authority to legitimate his surviving bastards, and then tried to insert them in the line of succession to the throne, the move inspired moral as well as political indignation. By the end of his long reign, then, the king himself would experience the success of his own government's effort to enforce the principle that monogamous marriage was the best way to ensure the reproduction of social and political order.

A century of contemplation about the relationship of politics and reproduction had indeed proven that no one system of reproduction governed all nations, but it had also established monogamy and indissolubility as the hallmarks of specifically Catholic marital and reproductive practices. Fertility was politically important, but the quest to enhance it had to respect the specifically "French" way of marrying and procreating. How that was to be achieved is the subject of the next chapter.

Making Pronatalist Law

uring the fall of 1667, the diarist Olivier Lefèvre d'Ormesson recorded a story of courtship gone wrong. An up-and-coming royal official, Jean-Jacques Charon de Ménars, sought marriage with Mademoiselle de Janvry, a rich heiress. The prospective groom had impressive connections, as he was the brother-in-law of the royal minister Jean-Baptiste Colbert. But the young woman's family demurred, offering as an explanation that she was too young. They would not consent to her marriage until she was at least eighteen years old.[1]

Charon de Ménars did not accept this rebuff. He claimed that he and Mademoiselle de Janvry had exchanged love letters, and that she had promised to marry him; he even claimed to have proof of the fact. So assiduously did he press his suit, d'Ormesson reports, that the young woman's mother, "fear[ed] violence," and moved her daughter to a Paris convent.

The convent of the Hospitalières de St. Gervais offered shelter, but even its cloister did not protect the young woman from the prospective groom's powerful connections. On the basis of Charon de Ménars' claims to be holding evidence of a promise of marriage, it seemed possible to some that the young woman was being imprisoned in the convent against her will. At that point, King Louis XIV himself became involved in the marital intrigue. He sent an envoy to the convent to interview the young woman to "know her will." The woman denied that she was in love with M. de Ménars, or that she had exchanged letters with him. But this envoy did not know what Mademoiselle de Janvry looked like, and Charon de Ménars raised the suspicion that an imposter had taken her place. So another envoy was sent in the company of a young woman who could identify Mademoiselle de Janvry. This time, the king's representative was none other than Archbishop of Paris Hardouin de Péréfixe. The archbishop was no mere visitor to the convent but an official of the church with legal jurisdiction over it. In the midst of this second interview, Mademoiselle de Janvry's mother arrived (she had probably been summoned by a friendly insider). She was livid about the pressure brought to bear on her daughter, and poured out to the archbishop "everything that anger suggested to her." Ignorant of who had sent him, Madame de Janvry then went to "throw herself at the king's feet" and beg for royal protection against the forces arrayed, as it seemed, to force her to accept the match for her young daughter. "Madame," Louis XIV replied, "You have no cause to complain about the Archbishop. It is I who sent him. Your daughter clearly does not want de Ménars, and I will involve myself no further."[2] And there the matter ended.

D'Ormesson's story illustrates the multiple ways that marriage could be a political issue in early modern France. Forming marital alliances was a matter of the utmost importance as elite families sought to build family fortunes, protect their social position, and also to ensure the health and happiness of their children. By the time this episode unfolded, the principle that parents had the right to deny consent to the marriage of a young woman like Mademoiselle de Janvry was enshrined as a central principle of royal legislation regulating marriage. Yet the personal involvement of King Louis XIV as matchmaker and sovereign patron of de Ménars' courtship (no doubt because of the prospective groom's connections to Colbert) suggested that parental prerogative might have limits against a young monarch whose policies promoted marriage as a benefit to society and the state. What would have happened if Mademoiselle de Janvry had indicated a desire to marry? Would the king have undermined the principles of royal law?

The story also offers a glimpse of the important relationships that developed between seventeenth-century elite families and religious institutions. These cloistered, celibate spaces were essential both to family strategies and to contemporary spirituality. Convents, in particular, educated and sheltered young women in the years before they married. For many elite women, of course, the convent represented not a temporary life stage but a permanent vocation separate from— and holier than—the obligations of marriage and motherhood. D'Ormesson noted that the symbolic penetration of the inviolable space of celibacy by the prelate Hardouin de Péréfixe, especially on a mission promoting marriage, caused "murmuring against him."[3]

If d'Ormesson found the marital intrigue surrounding Charon de Ménars "extraordinary" it was likely because it unfolded in the midst of significant discussions about royal power to regulate marriage. By the fall of 1667, Louis XIV had already demonstrated his ambition to intervene in his subjects' marital lives. This chapter explores the social, religious, and political ramifications of the royal government's decision to use royal legislative power to promote marriage and childbearing.

The context for royal legislative action was legal reform. From 1665 until around 1672, a royal Council of Justice met for high-level and, initially, secret discussions to plan a sweeping codification of French law. The council was charged with an ambitious goal: bringing order, coherence and clarity to France's disparate and disunited legal tradition. In the end, the major results of its work were the civil (1667) and criminal (1670) procedural reforms collectively known as the "Code Louis," and ordinances guiding procedure in forestry (1669), commerce (1673) and, finally, navigation (1681).[4]

Marriage does not usually figure in historical accounts of Louis XIV's legal reform efforts, nor do Louis XIV's laws promoting marriage figure in most histories of French marriage law. In his useful survey of the history of marital jurisprudence in France, the legal historian Charles Lefebvre painted Louis XIV's reign as a period of consolidation rather than innovation.[5] The legislative precedents that would eventually define marriage as a contract regulated by secular authorities rather than by canon law had been laid down in the royal ordinances of the late sixteenth and early seventeenth centuries. What the age of Louis XIV offered to this developing tradition were legal arguments, especially those that forthrightly asserted the primacy of a valid contract regulated by the secular authority to the marital sacrament presided over by the church. Lefebvre highlighted the bold claims of writers like the jurist Jean de Launoy, whose polemical *Regia in matrimonium potestas* (1674) defended the royal right to declare impediments to valid marriage. Launoy's work ignited fierce controversy among French jurists and clerics, and eventually found its way to the Papal Index.[6] In Lefebvre's account, the bold doctrines enunciated by Launoy contrasted with the "timid and discreet" legislative actions of the monarchy. It was Launoy's bold claims rather than royal legislation that promoted the long historical evolution toward the notion that marriage is a secular contract, a notion that did not truly bear fruit until the secularizing moment of the French Revolution.

Yet alongside the more familiar legal reforms with which Louis XIV is associated, the Council of Justice formulated two legislative initiatives that powerfully asserted royal interest in marriage. The first was what contemporaries called the "Edict on Marriage," a pronatalist measure that altered tax laws to encourage young men to marry and provided fiscal rewards for men who fathered large families. Because it seems so different from other royal legislation regarding marriage, legal historians have largely ignored the Edict on Marriage. When historians have paid attention to it, they have mostly associated the law with the mercantilist economic views and policies of Jean-Baptiste Colbert, noting that early economic theories favored population growth.[7]

But the 1666 Edict on Marriage was not merely an economic policy; indeed, "economy" was not a recognized domain of knowledge in the mid-seventeenth century. To understand the Edict on Marriage, it is important to recognize that it was created by royal jurists in the context of legal reform, and that its logic built upon the growing tradition of royal law regulating marriage and family formation. By forthrightly asserting the crucial interest of secular government in the marital and reproductive lives of French men and women, the Edict on Marriage pushed at the boundaries between sacred and secular jurisdiction over marital union in ways much like the controversial work of Launoy.

Just how controversial such measures could be is demonstrated by the second, related legislation that the Council on Justice proposed: a law designed to stem what contemporaries perceived as a troubling flight of the king's subjects into monastic celibacy. Had the measure become law, it would have raised the age of majority for making monastic professions and more strictly regulated the alliances that elite families like Mademoiselle de Janvry's formed with monastic institutions. But in the weeks after the registration of the pronatalist Edict on Marriage, hints of the Council of Justice's secret proposal to regulate religious professions leaked. It elicited such serious political opposition that the royal government was forced to abandon its plans and to redraft a more modest proposal regulating the foundation of monasteries and convents. If royal action regarding marriage remained "timid and discreet," during the early years of Louis XIV's reign, this outcome was the result of powerful political actors who successfully opposed the monarchical government's more ambitious goals.

Family Politics: Practice and Theory

No person was more responsible for the royal effort to legislate in favor of marriage and procreation than Jean-Baptiste Colbert, the former assistant to Mazarin who by 1665 had risen to become Louis XIV's most powerful advisor. Colbert was well positioned to understand the motivations of elite families to formulate advantageous marriages because he was himself a product and practitioner of such strategies. The minister could not have risen to the powerful position he achieved had his forebears not been extraordinarily proficient at precisely the kinds of family strategies that fed the tandem growth of powerful family networks and France's royal government in the early modern period.

In a world where noble birth legitimated governing power, Jean-Baptiste Colbert tried to conceal the truth that his fifteenth-century ancestors had been cloth merchants in Rouen. Through judicious management of assets, investment in venal offices, and careful cultivation of marital alliances, the Colbert family rose by the mid-seventeenth century to possess noble titles and impressive personal wealth. These family practices, as much as the minister's own talents and drive, enabled the Colbert family to become one of the most powerful ministerial clans in French history.[8]

The marital and reproductive patterns of the Colbert family were fairly typical of those within France's upwardly mobile judicial and ministerial elite, and played an important role in building the family's power. Jean-Baptiste Colbert was the second of eighteen children born to Nicolas Colbert, Sire de Vandières, and Marie Pussort. The couple's fertility was enabled, no doubt, by Pussort's youth at the time of her marriage and by the elite custom of hiring wet nurses. Pussort gave birth to these eighteen children (of whom nine survived to adulthood) in rapid rhythm, over twenty-two years between 1618 and 1640.[9] While eighteen births put the couple far above the reproductive norm for seventeenth-century France, the Colberts were not alone. Other elite French families also displayed the extremely high fertility likely enabled by early marriage and wet-nursing; the famous example of the Jansenist network anchored by the twenty children of Antoine Arnauld comes to mind. Nicolas Colbert's brothers, Jehan and Charles, were each the father of at least sixteen children, creating a large group of cousins that Jean-Baptiste Colbert would draw upon to fill positions in an extensive clientage network that extended the minister's influence throughout France.

The reproductive life of the minister Colbert mirrored in many respects the pattern of his parents. He married Marie Charon, an heiress, in 1648 when he was twenty-nine years old. The bride was ten years his junior. Over the next twenty years, from 1650 until 1670, Colbert and Charon sent at least ten children to baptism at their parish church of Saint Eustache in Paris.[10] Raising, educating, and placing so many children no doubt created challenges for any family, but among wealthy elites, expansive families could facilitate the building and consolidation of political power and social influence.

The marital and reproductive practices of families like the Colberts were also an expression of Catholic Reformation piety. One important result of Reformation-era theological controversies over marriage was a forceful reaffirmation of marriage's sacramental status within Catholicism. If this fueled legal struggles over marital jurisdiction in France, it also had the consequence of endowing marriage and family life with heightened spiritual meaning for lay Catholics. The seventeenth century witnessed the development of an intense, family-oriented piety that appears to have had real appeal for Jean-Baptiste Colbert. At night, the minister slept in a room adorned by a Titian devotional painting of the Holy Family. And, at precisely the same time he was formulating royal policies to encourage marriage and birth, he acted as *marguillier* (church-warden) in his home parish of Saint-Eustache and personally funded the adornment of two chapels that were central to the practice of family-centered spirituality: one was decorated specifically to accommodate marriages, and the other for baptisms. In his will, the minister became a charitable patron of marriage, establishing a foundation providing dowries to poor women from the vicinity of his estate in Seignelay. Like other members of the governing elite of his age, Colbert's life shows the full range of meanings attributed to marriage and reproduction: the familial, sacred, and political converged to focus on conjugal relationships and the children they produced.

Colbert and his uncle, the renowned jurist Henri Pussort, began planning the legal reform early in the young king's reign. As Colbert explained in 1665, legal reform was "the most grand and most glorious design that can enter into the mind of a king." Working to codify and order the law exercised the most fundamental attribute of royal sovereignty, the king's lawmaking power, and demonstrated the king's devotion to providing justice for his subjects. Louis XIV could do little more important to mark his greatness than become a new Justinian, leaving an ordered body of French law to posterity.[11]

Marriage, sexuality, and reproduction were already implicated in Colbert's May 1665 memorandum laying out the procedure and goals that the king might pursue in the legal reform. In it, the minister gave indication of his faith in the contemporary economic principle that the kingdom's wealth and power grew in direct proportion to the size of its productive population. Accordingly, as he thought of goals for reform of the *police générale,* the essential laws governing daily social interaction within the kingdom, he commented that "it will be very important that [the councillors] endeavor to make difficult all the conditions of men that withdraw them from work that benefits the general welfare of the state."[12] Both production and reproduction were defined as work that contributed to the general welfare. The conditions Colbert identified as harmful to the common good included what he saw as an excessive number of judicial officers, and of celibate religious.

As Colbert saw it, judicial officers produced nothing of value, living parasitically off the conflicts and misfortunes of the king's productive subjects. Colbert was not alone in worrying about a plague of judges; several of the jurists the royal government consulted for the legal reform, despite being men of the law themselves, also complained about the proliferation of judges, barristers, and legal personnel. The oversupply created incentives for more litigation, which tended to drag on endlessly, they said, causing the ruin of families.[13] Plus, the business of justice, Colbert's uncle Pussort remarked in his reform memorandum to the king, "grasps an infinity of people who might very advantageously fill your armies, cultivate the earth, and make the arts, manufactures, and commerce bloom in all the parts of your state."[14] The royal effort to promote reproduction and the king's effort to control the judiciary were connected, the journal writer d'Ormesson noted. In its drive to "multiply men for war and commerce" the royal government embarked on a program of "closing the doors as much as is possible" to judicial careers.[15]

Colbert's memorandum also worried over the size of France's monastic population. Here, too, he found general agreement among the jurists that the king consulted in the preparatory work for the legal reform.[16] Monks and nuns withdrew from the productive exchanges of civil life, often taking a significant portion of their family's assets with them, wealth that did not pass on to heirs and was often merged into the tax-exempt property of the church. In addition, celibate religious did not reproduce (at least, not legitimately), thereby "depriv[ing] the public of all the children they might produce to serve in necessary and useful functions."[17] Colbert treated celibacy as a problem that the government might address with incentives. The minister never denied that celibacy was a spiritually meaningful practice for those who were called to it, although he perhaps doubted the calling of many of those currently living as monastics. The problem, then, was to prevent those without calling from taking vows. Colbert proposed that the king seek regulations that would discourage but not prohibit religious professions, that would regulate nun's dowries and pensions, and, finally, that would "facilitate and make more honorable and advantageous, as much as is possible, the conditions of men that benefit the common good, that is to say, soldiers, merchants, farmers, and workers."[18]

Colbert was legally savvy, but not himself a trained jurist. He enlisted the service of a range of legal specialists in the course of creating pronatalist law. The most important of his advisors was Jean de Gomont, with whom Colbert had worked during his years of service to Mazarin. Gomont provided learned advice on many issues during the legal reform process, and remained closely connected to Colbert as a client. His services to the minister included the creation of a legal treatise on marriage that was designed to prepare Colbert's son, the Marquis de Seignelay, for the role as royal servant he would inherit from his father.[19] The memorandum Gomont prepared for Colbert late in 1665, pragmatically titled "Ways to Encourage Marriage and Make Religious Vows More Difficult," appears to have very closely paralleled the minister's thinking about the issues of marriage, celibacy, and state regulation.[20]

Colbert also engaged the service of a noted authority on family and customary law, Barthelemy Auzanet. Auzanet was one of the most respected consulting barristers attached to the Parlement, and author of a commentary on the Custom of Paris.[21] Auzanet collaborated with Gomont on one of the reports that Colbert requested, a brief detailing the various legal measures to encourage reproduction that had been pursued in the Roman Empire and by other "well-policed" states. The brief was intended to add luster and legitimacy to Colbert's plan by connecting Louis XIV's pronatalist legislation to precedents pursued in antiquity.

A third source of legal counsel came from Nicolas Le Camus. Le Camus was a relative of Colbert, and, at the time, *procureur général* in the Paris *Cour des aides,* the royal court with jurisdiction over most tax matters. Le Camus offered Colbert specialized expertise in the jurisprudence of taxation and privilege. Le Camus's involvement followed a pattern common in royal conversations about regulation and legislation. He drew up a proposed legal text for an "Edict on Marriages" and then wrote a report explaining the rationale for each of its articles.[22]

Collectively, the work of Colbert's legal advisors gives us a snapshot of the conversation taking place as royal officials studied and planned for the 1666 Edict on Marriage. The conversation was a legal conversation; all of Colbert's advisors on pronatalism had some form of legal training, and their ways of conceptualizing marriage and procreation as political issues bear the imprint of their legal education. Destined for careers in the law, all of these men would have, as schoolboys, feasted on a steady diet of Latin literature and the work of humanists. Their legal training focused around Roman Law, in particular Justinian's *Institutes* and the *Corpus Juris Civilis*. Their reading made them familiar with the pronatalist plans of antiquity, in particular the Roman emperor Augustus's measures to promote marriage and reward parents of many children.[23] Even more significantly, the legal curriculum clearly nurtured a profound respect for the example set by classical states, and a sense of the vital role of law in society. Law did not merely reflect cultural values or punish infractions; it had the power to shape behavior, and to *create* social order within the society it regulated.[24]

Marital union constituted the prime example of the law's power to create social order; indeed Colbert's advisors considered marriage the elemental legal institution of civilization. The marital bond was the foundation of the state, "the most important action of civil life," as Gomont explained in the treatise on marriage he prepared for Colbert's son, Seignelay.[25] While reproduction was grounded in humans' animal, sexual nature, marriage had been decreed by God to elevate the reproductive function common to all animals into an institution of civilized life. By creating the public, legal institution of marriage, humans illustrated their unique capacity to reason and to live in an ordered society. Reproduction within the context of marriage was distinct from merely "natural and fortuitous unions" and from those that were "impure and undignified."[26] Gomont's basic definition of marriage highlighted its role in producing both orderly households and the labor necessary to the common good: marriage was "the union of husband and wife [legally and physically] capable of this tie, who contract it publicly, according to the laws of church and state, in order to live together and give children to the public."[27]

Colbert's advisors respected marriage's position as a sacrament of the church, but, their briefs did not linger on spiritual questions about original sin or marriage's role in tempering the fires of the flesh. Instead, they focused on the this-worldly, procreative implications of marital union. The higher value accorded to celibacy in Catholic doctrine was indubitable but did not change the fact that "a wife and children are a form of blessing from God, as is marked in many places" in Holy Scripture.[28] Gomont, at least, espoused in his work the royalist position that was soon to be articulated publicly by Jean de Launoy, namely that civil regulation of marriage defined the legitimate marital contract necessary prior to the making of a valid sacramental bond. In the early days of Christianity, Gomont argued, it had been Roman civil law that had defined the conditions for making valid marriage, rather than canon law. The French were nowadays following this example set by the Roman empire, Gomont explained, as "in the recent past, our kings have applied themselves particularly [to marital regulation] in order to punish the disorders that had crept into this matter through moral license, the complacency of ecclesiastics and the negligence of magistrates."[29] Rather than envisioning royal regulation of marriage as the colonization of terrain traditionally under the jurisdiction of church courts, Colbert's advisor reversed the history lesson, arguing that it had been the medieval church that had seized territory previously under civil jurisdiction.

As Colbert's advisors defended the civil regulation of marriage, the reproductive function of conjugal union loomed large. Marriage was vital to civilization and government because it "[gave] new subjects to the state, and new heirs to the family."[30] But marriage was also important because the marital bond was a potent antidote to social disorder. "Engagement in marriage is an engagement with the state," wrote Auzanet and Gomont, because "those who marry are far more tied to their fatherland (*patrie*) and obedient to their prince than those who live in celibacy."[31] Marrying, establishing a household, and becoming a *père de famille* had transformative consequences, they argued; it turned potentially unruly individual men into patriarchs concerned about the well-being of their families, and therefore engaged in and responsible to the *res publica*. A father, they argued, was naturally concerned about the welfare of his family, and as a result "the public" could be assured of "his care, his work, his conduct, and even his fidelity" (meaning, in this case, his fidelity to the king rather than to his wife).[32] The obligations of fatherhood, Auzanet and Gomont argued, made men far less likely to fall victim to the laziness and crime that might tempt a man who was motivated only by individual self-interest. Marriage and the conjugal households it founded were thus the source of the king's most important reservoir of wealth—its people—and also the foundation of the whole edifice of social order. Needless to say, all these factors lent legitimacy to royal claims of jurisdiction over marriage and family life.

In making these arguments, Colbert's advisors were drawing upon an explicitly patriarchalist vision of political and social order; they identified fatherhood as the source of legitimate political authority and the essential tie that bound men together in a hierarchical political order.[33] Gomont and Auzanet opened their otherwise technical and historical brief for Colbert with a meditation on patriarchalism, describing what we might call a "great chain of fathering" that stretched from the married householder to the paternal prince to God the father. The advisors described ideal social order as an "order of subordination" of all these fathers, bound together with what they called "mystic paternity," a force that became stronger as men fathered more children.[34] Auzanet and Gomont would go on to identify more instrumental reasons why the king might promote marriage and reproduction, but it was with this ideal of patriarchal social order that they began.

For Colbert's advisors as far other early modern French jurists, defining social order as a relationship of fathers and kings rendered any independent legal identity of children and married women problematic. For example, Gomont explained that the will of a child enacted contrary to that of his or her father (particularly in that "most important" civil action of marriage) was presumptively corrupt; good law could not recognize marital unions formed without parental consent.[35] Likewise, Gomont and Auzanet argued that a patriarch's sense of his own interests encompassed those of his wife and children so completely that they were akin to his "other selves."[36] Gomont and Auzanet intended their statement to stress the positive consequences of marrying and fathering to political and social order—men's devotion to their family helped ensure their loyalty to the state—but the corollary to the notion that wives and children were fathers' "other selves" was that political order depended upon wives and children not acting as their own selves. Royal pronatalist policy thus revealed its ideological similarity to contemporary legal theories that reduced married women and children to subordinate members of the corporate body of the conjugal household. In this sense, promoting marriage and fatherhood was a project that, in spirit, reaffirmed conjugal and paternal authority, a characteristic it shared with the French marital jurisprudence that had been elaborated over the previous century.[37]

A Colbertian "Science" of Fertility

Since they understood the procreative function of the conjugal household as a vital source of the state's manpower and of social order—and also since they were tied to Colbert through webs of clientage and family—it is hardly surprising that Colbert's legal advisors endorsed the minister's idea to make laws encouraging marriage and reproduction among the king's subjects. It was a plan "befitting the King, and one that all of France must hope will produce results as great for him as it did for the Romans," as Nicolas Le Camus opined.[38] By addressing his legislative authority to procreation, the French king was following the example set by "the most politically savvy of peoples, who made laws that survived longer than their empire itself."[39] The remaining question, then, was how to achieve the best results.

Much of the advisors' preparatory work lay in figuring out how to adapt the pronatalist legal precedents they read about in Roman law and literature for the legal conditions of the France of their day. Some were clearly not practicable. The Romans, for example, had allowed adoption and punished the unmarried by restricting their ability to pass on their property in wills. Because adoption was not recognized in French law, and inheritance was regulated by local customary laws, such measures could not be adapted to France; as Le Camus wrote, "they have nothing in common with our mores, nor any relationship to the kinds of privileges his Majesty can establish at the present time."[40] On the other hand, because "the king is sovereign master of awards and penalties in his kingdom," it *was* possible to copy the program of fiscal privileges and penalties that the Roman

Empire had offered to provide incentives for marriage and rewards for having large families.[41] This was the solution that Colbert's team settled on early in the process of planning the 1666 pronatalist edict.

The debate about the specifics of the policy, carried out in 1665–66, illustrates the advisors' keen sense of how elite families weighed the prospects of procreation as a part of their overall family strategies. They thought about reproduction, first, when they planned marital alliances. Le Camus noted that young people and their families avoided marriage at an early age, "for fear of being overwhelmed by taxes and by a large number of children."[42] The resort to religious celibacy was another obvious example. "The desire to place daughters in religion comes from fathers, from their inability to provide them with suitable dowries" Colbert wrote, assuming that families placed daughters in religion primarily to conserve money, not for spiritual reasons.[43] The consequence, however, was fewer descendants, and this was not necessarily what families sought. Dowry inflation, in fact, constituted a vexing problem. According to Gomont, families found themselves financially strained by the excessive sums required for a socially suitable match, a problem compounded by the large donations they made to establish their sons. To make matters worse, families spent huge sums on suitable clothing, carriages, silver, and jewelry. This economy of display meant that families were forced to keep sons and daughters out of the marriage market. The challenge for policymakers, Gomont wrote, was to redirect family strategies, finding the means so that "fathers and mothers can marry several children, and after the marriage of all their children find themselves better off than they are at present by the marriage of only one."[44] How could elite social aspirations be accommodated without sacrificing the reproductive potential of young men and women?

Colbert's advisors reflected on the marital and fertility strategies of French elites; they also contemplated what actually constituted a large family. Colbert's scribbled notes from September 1665 suggest that, originally, the royal plan was to offer exemptions from taxation to men who had ten or more living children.[45] Le Camus, for his part, proposed that the number be set at seven living children, with some special counting rules. First, all of the children must be legitimate, because, he wrote, it was not fair to provide rewards for "the products of [fathers'] debauchery." He also proposed that children in religious orders not count toward the total, because once young men and women had taken solemn vows, "being dead to the world, they can no longer render any service to the State."[46] On the other hand, to encourage behaviors deemed more useful to the state, Le Camus proposed that any child that died while in the military or on overseas commercial voyages be counted as living. Although the number seven might appear too low, he claimed that a moment's thought would show that few people had seven living children of whom none were in religious orders. Therefore, he claimed, setting the threshold for tax exemption at seven was unlikely to become a burden to the realm's taxpaying subjects.[47]

Two points bear stressing here. First, while Colbert's advisors might have agreed that children were a blessing from heaven, they did not envision fertility as outside the scope of human control. But the fertility control they identified operating in their society was primarily social (or familial) rather than individual; it was exercised primarily by male heads of household in their quest to advance familial social and economic interests. The form of "fertility control" they imagined matches what historical demographers have termed the "European marriage pattern," the system that delayed marriages and institutionalized a high rate of permanent celibacy, thereby restraining the growth of the European population. It was this form of fertility control that royal pronatalist law sought to dismantle with incentives like tax breaks for young married households, rewards for producing large families, and limits on religious celibacy. Second, in the terms of Etienne Van de Walle, Colbert and his circle of advisors were "numerate about children": that is, they saw fertility and procreation as a focus of rational calculation—and a legitimate one, at that.[48] The aim of the law they devised was thus to redirect the tendency of male heads-of-household to exercise rational choice on behalf of their households in ways that would result in the birth of more children.

The royal edict published in November 1666 brought together the men's ideological investment in marriage and their reflections on the means to adjust their contemporaries' calculus of the economic costs of marriage and procreation. The preamble to the edict praised marriage as "the fecund source from which springs the strength and grandeur of states," promising that Louis XIV would revive the dignity that "holy and profane" laws had always addressed to this "sacred and politic union."[49]

The edict promised, first, to remedy the injustice of a tax system that taxed married men and omitted unmarried men still living in their fathers' households. For that reason, men who married before the age of twenty would henceforth enjoy tax exemption until the age of twenty-five; men who married before age twenty-one would enjoy a slightly lesser benefit, remaining exempt from taxes until age twenty-four. Those that did not marry before age twenty-one, however, would become subject to taxes as single men on their twenty-first birthday, paying their share "in proportion to their goods, means, commerce, craft, [and] employment."[50]

In addition, the edict offered a panoply of rewards to fathers of large families. These rewards were designed to help fathers face the costs of raising and placing a large number of children, and, also, to attach honor to the status of prolific fatherhood. Every taxable subject with ten living and legitimate children, none of whom had taken religious vows, was promised exemption from the duty of serving as tax collector in his parish; from the *tutelle* and *curatelle* (the civic charge of fiscal guardianship over minors);[51] from the *guet et garde* and *ustensiles* (local military obligations); and from the obligation to billet troops in his home.[52] The edict thus showered prolific fathers with privileges that seemed to proclaim fathering a public function, a service to the community and state that deserved recognition and recompense. Fathers who could establish that they had twelve living children were to enjoy, in addition to these privileges, full exemption from royal direct taxation (*"toutes tailles, taillons, subsides, et impositions"*).[53]

Noble and bourgeois fathers, already exempt from taxation by virtue of their juridical status, were promised pensions to reward their service as fathers. A tax exempt bourgeois subject could hope for a yearly pension of 500 livres if he were the father of ten children, and 1,000 if he had twelve, in addition to the exemptions from any onerous civic duties to which he might be subject. Noblemen, "the firmest support of the crown," were to receive "particular marks of our esteem" said the king's edict. They were to gain yearly pensions of 1,000 livres if they had ten living children, and 2,000 if they had twelve. For all subjects, children who had taken religious vows did not count in making up the total necessary for earning rewards; those who had died in military service, however, were to be counted as living.[54]

The royal government sent the Edict on Marriage to the Paris *Cour des aides,* or royal tax court, in early December of 1666. While the officers did register the edict, they made changes on technical grounds to ensure that the provisions of the law would not unduly complicate the process of tax collection. One of these changes was particularly significant; the Paris court observed that unmarried minor men in its jurisdiction were legally encompassed within the households of their fathers, and were presumed not to have independent ownership of property. Therefore, the plan to subject unmarried men over twenty-one to taxation "according to their means" made no sense; as minors or "fils de famille" they controlled no taxable assets unless they carried on an independent trade or leased property in their own name. They should not be placed on the tax rolls.[55] With the judges' caveat written into the law, the impact of the pronatalist law on young bachelors was blunted. The edict no longer had the power to punish men for postponing their marriage. With their objection, the judges of the *Cour des aides* checked the king's ability to pressure his subjects into youthful unions, and effectively shored up the principle of parental control over the timing of marriage.

Was the court's intervention merely a technical clarification, or did it suggest some sort of resistance? The judges' motives are obscure, but there are hints that the proposal to promote youthful marriage by taxing young unmarried men had been a particularly controversial aspect of the royal pronatalist agenda. When Colbert consulted royal provincial intendants about the proposed law, a number expressed concern. Promoting youthful marriage would harm military recruiting and push immature men into the socially vital role of head of household. Plus, the proposal to tax unmarried men implied that the king rather than their fathers should choose the right age for their marriage. This, intendant Henri d'Aguesseau predicted, would strike householders as "very harsh" and would be "nearly impossible to execute."[56]

After the court's changes, what remained of the king's pronatalist policy were the carrots rather than the sticks, the promises of privileges and benefits for early marriage and prolific procreation. The minor, perhaps technical, opposition to the Edict on Marriage from the judges of the *Cour des aides* did not compare to the determined and coordinated campaign brought to bear on the other half of the royal government's pronatalist project, the plan to raise legal barriers to monastic professions.

Limiting Religious Professions

Juxtaposed with their assignment to dream up legislation to encourage marriage and childbearing, Colbert's advisors sought ways to decrease the number of religious celibates. Discouraging French men and women from taking religious vows was a consistent and logical extension of the royal government's populationist aims. But the calculating and instrumental thinking about procreation embodied in their project collided in profound ways with the religious values professed by many French Catholics in the seventeenth century. The Council of Justice's project to restrict religious professions threatened to reignite one of the major debates of the Reformation era: that is, did the celibate life of monks and nuns offer benefits to a Christian polity? The very identity of post-Tridentine Catholicism had been built on an affirmative answer to this question. While Trent had indeed fostered a spiritual movement that valorized marriage, it did so only after reaffirming the higher worthiness of vowed religious celibacy. As the Council of Trent's canon put it, "if any one saith, that the marriage state is to be placed above the state of virginity, or of celibacy, and that it is not better and more blessed to remain in virginity, or in celibacy, than to be united in matrimony; let him be anathema."[57]

Although France harbored a Protestant minority (and perhaps in part because it did), monasticism had become a more central and visible institution of French life and French politics in the years after the Reformation. The religious fervor and anxiety unleashed during the Religious Wars of the sixteenth century fueled a wave of penitential piety that moved French men and women to choose the celibate religious life in truly historic numbers. Historians have termed the movement a "conventual invasion," noting that in Paris and its suburbs alone some forty-eight new religious houses were born in the first half of the seventeenth century.[58] In

Catholic France, vows of celibacy distinguished priests, monks, and nuns from the lay population and reaffirmed the legitimacy of their position within the political hierarchy. Ecclesiastics were the First Estate of the realm, honored with significant judicial and fiscal privileges. Monastic institutions constituted visible markers of confessional identity on the landscape that distinguished France from Protestant countries, where monasteries and convents had been closed, their property appropriated by civil authorities, and their inhabitants urged to find new lives as husbands and wives in Protestant households.

The intense post-Tridentine Catholic spiritual movement garnered the attention of contemporaries. Indeed, it is no exaggeration to claim that consciousness of the rapid growth of monasticism represented the nearest thing to a "population crisis" motivating the royal government's pronatalist legislation. Even some pious Catholics judged that the scales had tipped toward an excessive and dangerous flight of the kingdom's subjects from procreative marital households into the cloister. The plan to limit religious professions was without question a reaction to the religious enthusiasm that had taken hold in France since Trent. While the royal effort drew some of its rationales from the skeptical, reason-of-state population science that had developed in the seventeenth century, it was also a response to the intensity of the religious movement that members of the Council of Justice had witnessed in their own lifetimes.

The sense that the vowed celibate population was growing provoked curiosity and a desire to quantify. Consider an anonymously authored pamphlet printed in the 1670s. After providing numerical breakdowns of various orders and their personnel, the author estimated that France as a whole supported 261,736 religious. This represented an increase, and none more pronounced than among female religious, whose numbers had more than doubled in a century. This effort to count the kingdom's expanding celibate population was one of the few times that quantified demographic argument was used in public debate about a political issue during this period.[59]

It is important to stress that what was at issue in these debates was the *number* of monastic professions and not the monastic ideal of celibacy. By the eighteenth century, populationist discourses burned with hostility to monasticism, treating the Catholic demand for celibacy as an unreasonable imposition on human nature. No one, Enlightenment *philosophes* would later argue, could be expected to conform to such arbitrary and unnatural demands. In the mid-seventeenth century, amidst the fervor of Catholic Reform, Colbert's advisors made quite different arguments. They attempted to reconcile a perceived political need to limit religious celibacy with their own Catholic piety. They noted, for example, that the rapid expansion of the celibate population suggested that men and women were entering the cloister for reasons other than divine calling. They did not deny that such a calling existed, and even evinced humility about the law's ability to determine into which group any individual fell: "It is impossible, or very difficult to recognize whether a vocation is good or bad," admitted Gomont in the report he wrote for Colbert.[60] Nevertheless, they argued, the presence of so many religious was in the interest of neither the king nor the church, since those who did not have a calling were not given the moral strength to resist their sexual desires, and thus made bad monks and nuns. The proper response was hardly to forbid celibacy, since "that would be against religion, besides the fact that it cannot be done by the secular authority of a Christian [i.e., Catholic] kingdom."[61] Rather than an attempt to stamp out monasticism, then, royal advisors sought to bring celibacy and monastic professions back into some sort of balance that, they feared, had been lost.

What were the "disorders" inherent in the growth of monasticism? Some of the arguments rehashed in these debates were as old as monasticism itself, and were not specifically related to the rapid expansion of the celibate population: the complaint that monks and nuns did not always live up to their vows, for example, or that contemplative religious were sinfully idle while others had to work. Alongside these perennial complaints, Colbert's circle voiced complaints about the expansion of monasticism in a recognizably economic, reason-of-state language. Several, for example, complained that the property pious laypeople had donated to religious orders ended up reducing the taxable property base of the kingdom and thereby overburdening its taxpayers. The alarmist d'Orgeval wrote to Colbert to warn that religious institutions "possess more than a third of all the revenue in the kingdom" and would soon own half if royal measures did not move to protect assets from falling under the control and privileged tax status of the church.[62] Other advisors observed that the lack of secure endowments among the newly founded orders made it necessary to demand large convent dowries and entry fees from novices, which strained family budgets and diverted money that might otherwise be invested in commerce and industry. And several noted that the proliferation of religious diverted precious manpower away from trade and agriculture.[63] The rapid expansion of monastic professions also prompted observers to examine the role of monasticism in family strategies. Because some fathers placed daughters in convents so as to be able to offer larger dowries to their other daughters, Colbert asked his advisors to study measures to place sumptuary limits on dowries that would allow fathers to marry their daughters, "however many they have."[64]

In addition to their economic flavor, discussions of the problem of monasticism were distinctly gendered; members of the Council of Justice were particularly concerned about the explosive growth in *female* professions. Although post-Tridentine religious enthusiasm touched both sexes, these elite men were struck by the expansion of religious institutions for women. Their assessment is confirmed by modern historians' calculations that the population of female religious in France grew to exceed that of men sometime in the mid-seventeenth century. For the first time, in other words, monasticism was becoming a pre-dominately female phenomenon.[65]

The members of the Council of Justice did not attribute this change to God's decision to call more women to His service. They sought worldly explanations for the growth of religious institutions for women. We can follow their secret deliberations in January of 1667 thanks to a summary prepared, likely by Etienne Baluze, for Colbert.[66] As the councillors saw it, it was first and foremost convents' custom of accepting *pensionnaires*, or female boarding students, that had "foment[ed] this great number of nuns." Parents, for reasons that were temporal rather than spiritual, sent their young daughters to convents and there the girls "took the habit before ever having seen the world." Raised in the rarefied world of the cloister, these "young souls easily receive the impressions necessary to carry them toward the religious life."[67]

Although they phrased their worries in language that noted the "tender age" and impressionability of young women supposedly manipulated by the convent environment, these royal advisors were not championing a feminine right to self-determination. Rather, their analysis of the expansion of female professions highlighted the interdependence of elite families and religious institutions. Elite families, they noted, increasingly relied on convents to educate, shelter, and pre-pare their daughters for adult lives; the convents, in turn, relied on elite families for the money they needed to function. Not only did the relationship increase the number of girls who took the veil, it also threatened to undermine the proper functioning of patriarchal households. Even for daughters who later married, members of the Council of Justice worried that "the education given in religious houses is not in harmony with life in the world." Sending away a daughter as a boarder, mothers and fathers gave up the direct supervision and influence over her which was their natural right and responsibility, and the young woman that returned was not reliably prepared for the life they might choose for her. Furthermore, members of the Council of Justice complained that convent edu-cation was a form of conspicuous consumption that served mostly to free elite wives from their domestic responsibilities to care for and educate their children, activities which were their "proper" and "natural" concerns.[68]

While the Council of Justice's members favored some form of regulation to restrain religious celibacy, they were divided on how it could best be achieved. Wanting to limit religious professions, especially female professions, they never-theless recognized that convents performed a crucial social service by educating young women in discipline and obedience, "accustoming them early on to do good, and teaching them their duty." The counselors were not certain that an education of similar value could be obtained within the normal hustle and bustle of an elite household. Plus, for young women without mothers, whose mothers were Huguenot heretics, or otherwise "neither well-behaved nor virtuous," being raised in a convent was perhaps better than life at home, the sole recourse if these women were to take their place in society as Catholic wives and mothers.[69] All these factors suggested that convents were an important resource for shaping the patriarchal, domestic world the counselors hoped to reinforce.

There were further reasons for caution in regulating convents. In addition to the useful educational services that religious institutions provided, the jurists recognized that in "*le monde*"—polite society—it was customary to send adolescent children to board in convents or *collèges* and thereby free elite women from some of the domestic responsibilities they would otherwise shoulder. However they might feel about this "novelty" of their century—a lifestyle they claimed was not seen in Protestant countries, and was tantamount to an abandonment of women's natural responsibilities as mothers—members of the Council cautioned against any law that sought to end the practice. It would be inadvisable to try to mandate new child-care practices, one argued, because the law would be flagrantly violated, and respect for the king's authority would be diminished by the attempt.[70]

The elite men gathered to discuss regulating monastic professions recognized how central monasticism had become to French Catholic life in the years after Trent, and in particular recognized the impact that the wave of spirituality and monastic professions had on women and domestic life. The expansion of religious institutions had created a host of new spiritual opportunities for women, both religious and lay. Convents offered education for young women and a penitential retreat for widows. Many of the seventeenth century's newly formed female orders also offered temporary retreats for married laywomen, where for a few hours or days *mères de famille* mixed with nuns who provided spiritual counseling and education in the mysteries of the Catholic faith. In this way, the much-touted Tridentine requirement of strict cloister that ostensibly separated female monastics from lay society proved in practice far more supple. As Barbara Diefendorf has argued, the crossover between the lay and monastic paths for women compels us to reassess our understanding of the Catholic Reformation's impact on women. Not simply an oppressive movement that enabled male ecclesiastics to control the female religious population, Tridentine spirituality also served women's religious aspirations and fostered a female spiritual style in which both nuns and laywomen shared.[71] The Council of Justice's discussions recognized the dual nature of these developments: some of them reinforced patriarchal discipline and morality, while others undermined or threatened it.

Knowing that religious professions and religious institutions were central to the family practices of French elites, the Council of Justice had a difficult assignment. The first means that Colbert's advisors fixed upon to "make religious vows more difficult" was raising the age at which men and women could legally pronounce them; they formulated a proposal in 1665–66 that would have raised the age from sixteen (for both sexes) to twenty for women and to twenty-five for men.

To understand why the Council chose this plan, it is necessary to return briefly to the history of French royal legislation concerning religious vows. A century earlier, in 1560, the Estates General at Orléans had recommended to the king that the age for taking vows be raised to twenty for women and to twenty-five for men, and that religious dowries and pensions be limited. These recommendations were reflected in article nineteen of the royal Ordinance of Orléans in 1560.[72] But the Ordinance of Orléans was promulgated while the Council of Trent was still in session, and before it had issued its own guidelines on religious professions. Those guidelines, issued in 1563, set the age for profession at sixteen for both men and women. After 1563 then, French law and Catholic canon law were in conflict over the age of majority for making valid religious professions, a situation that produced thorny questions about the legal status of vows made by those between sixteen and twenty (for women) or twenty-five (in the case of men). The Canons of the Council of Trent were never fully incorporated into French law, but its spiritual principles proved highly influential. So, when the next Estates General met in Blois in 1576, it recommended that the age for taking vows be returned to sixteen for both men and women, a decision reflected in article twenty-eight of the Ordinance of Blois of 1579.[73] At that point, French laws on the age for monastic profession conformed to the guidelines set at Trent, although, in deference to the so-called "liberties of the Gallican Church," the matter could technically be said to be regulated by French statute rather than ecclesiastical law.[74]

The proposal being debated by the Council of Justice in 1666 very consciously revisited this history. The terms of the Ordinance of Orléans had emerged from the deliberations of the French Estates General and offered the Council the possibility of depicting the royal plan as a return to solid Gallican tradition rather than royal innovation. By reviving the older terms of the Ordinance of Orléans, the members of the Council of Justice were hoping to minimize outcry in France. The terms they inherited from the Ordinance of Orléans did not universally please them, however. They feared that restricting men from taking vows until the age of twenty-five might "completely extinguish monachism" (that is, male monasteries) which was far from the goal of their effort.[75]

Not only would a royal effort to make law regarding the age of majority for making religious vows be controversial, royal officials recognized that their regulation would apply only to questions of property ownership, and not to the issue of the religious validity of vows. As Gomont explained to Colbert, this legal matter was "in the power of the king, without recourse to the pope or any other ecclesiastical power, because the king is not ruling on the validity of the vows, a matter under the church's jurisdiction. He is only taking into account temporal questions of successions and of property, of which he is sovereign master."[76] The measures would complicate the transfer of property to religious institutions for any young man or woman professing before the age set out in the law, and thereby dissuade such professions. Other elements of the projected law would have allowed certain teaching congregations like the Ursulines to continue their work, but disallowed other convents from keeping boarding students over the age of fourteen.[77] In other words, the royal government's plan sought to regulate the financial relationship between elite families and monastic institutions, and to remove adolescent women from environments that, they believed, prompted them to embrace celibacy rather than to marry and become mothers.

Attempts to avoid controversy failed, however, when news of the proposed new rules leaked in January 1667, igniting virulent opposition from some of France's most powerful political and religious leaders—a list that included Colbert's rival Michel Le Tellier, the First President of the Parlement of Paris, Guillaume de Lamoignon, and the Archbishop of Paris, Hardouin de Péréfixe.[78] Representatives of religious orders were alarmed, and enlisted their supporters to lobby on their behalf. Particularly troubled were the Jesuits, who observed that their missionary work would be impossible if the long period of training necessary could begin only when candidates reached twenty-five. Papal opposition to the royal plan was conveyed to King Louis XIV's Jesuit Confessor, Père Annat, by the Papal Nuncio, Roberti, and then to the king himself. The plan's critics charged that it overstepped royal jurisdiction in a matter that was "purely spiritual." Plus, its hostility to the holy institution of celibacy was redolent of Protestant heresy. Roberti even threatened that the declaration over vows could lead to schism between Rome and France.[79]

The forces arrayed against the plan proved overwhelming. The diarist d'Ormesson reported that Colbert paid a call on the Parlement's First President, Lamoignon, an opponent to the proposal, in the first days of February to acknowledge that the king's declaration on religious vows was "a failed affair."[80] Faced with the concerted opposition of pious elites, Parlementarians, and the Holy See, the royal government scaled back its plan to regulate monastic institutions. In place of the planned increase in the age of majority for taking vows, the royal government promulgated a safer regulation focused more narrowly on the foundation of new monasteries and convents. The "edict on the establishment of religious houses and other communities," that was registered in March 1667 forbade the founding of new houses without letters patent. It also set out to remedy the "scandalous" problem of communities that had been founded without sufficient wealth to support their members, and were now being pursued in the courts by creditors.[81] Even more than had been the case with the edict to promote marriage and reproduction, the royal government was forced to accept a much weakened law in its effort to discourage monastic professions.

In Louis XIV's political memoir, the decision to withdraw the legal proposal on religious vows is depicted as the result of nagging religious scruples; the king explains that he reconsidered his original plan because "I was halted by those respectful feelings that we always owe to the church in [the spiritual matters] which are its true jurisdiction, and I resolved to legislate on this matter only in concert with the pope."[82] Whether the king's change of heart was genuine or not, the royal government's failure to enact fully either aspect of its pronatalist agenda provides an illustration of the limitations of royal power in seventeenth century France. The young king tested the waters, attempting to exercise the full measure of royal legislative authority over marriage that his jurists claimed for him. But when he met with resistance—in his pronatalist plans, over the issues of parental power to determine the timing of marriage, and over the sanctity of religious celibacy—he retrenched. By doing so, the king preserved his legitimacy as the "most Christian King" and as "the father of his people," and helped to guarantee the support of the social and political elites on whom royal power fundamentally depended.

THREE

Gendering Reproduction

When Parisian bookseller Jean Ribou brought out the second edition of his popular *Les Delices de la poésie galante* in 1667, he opened the volume with an anonymous poem entitled *L'edit de l'amour* (the "Edict of Love"). The poem's first lines proved that its author had legislation on his or her mind: they mimicked the formulaic beginning of royal letters patent, altering convention so that the edict in question originated not from "Louis by the grace of God, king of France," but rather from "Love, by the grace of nature, master of the Universe."[1] Love's power was arguably greater than the French king's and its will on "the way that we wish that one should love in the Empire of Lilies" was far different than that espoused in contemporary French royal law. The poem's nineteen articles provided rules to govern the conduct of men and women in romantic affairs, but never in the poem does the word "marriage" occur, nor does a single article suggest that love does or should produce anything other than pleasure and emotional satisfaction for the women and men involved.

Published in the months following the registration of Louis XIV's 1666 pronatalist edict, it is instructive to read the "Edict of Love" against the backdrop of royal laws regulating marriage and sexuality, and in particular, on the king's recent pronatalist legislation. Since the late sixteenth century, the French state and its judges had marked out the domestic realm as politically significant and reinforced the power of fathers and husbands to preside over it. The Edict on Marriage extended the rationale to the domain of reproduction; conjugal intercourse was the origin of royal subjects, and thus played a role in the creation and stabilization of royal authority. The "Edict of Love," on the other hand, left reproduction out as it made statutes governing relations between women and men. By doing so, it provided a trenchant reminder of what was at stake in royal efforts to regulate relations between the sexes.

The "Edict of Love" represents a typically *précieuse* treatment of the ideals of male-female relationships. To call it *précieuse*, I mean to associate the poem with the elite sociability and salons of seventeenth-century France, a cultural and literary milieu shaped to a large extent by aristocratic women in Paris. The "Edict of Love" drew inspiration from models like the *Carte de Tendre* (Map of the land of Tenderness) associated with Madeleine de Scudery's novel, *Clélie, histoire romaine* (1654–60). Scudery had offered her readers a playful allegorical map intended to guide lovers through the uncharted terrain of romance.[2] The verses of the "Edict of Love" provided similar guidance. Through devices like the *Carte de Tendre* and the "legislation" of Love, seventeenth-century writers in the salon milieu found creative ways to depict an imagined world where relationships between men and women were governed by different priorities than the concerns with social reproduction and political order that prevailed in the culture at large.

Over the past thirty years, scholars have focused on the social practices forged in salons as an important site for the development of ideas that challenged the authoritarian, hierarchical, and patriarchal norms of Old Regime society.[3] None of the challenges to prevailing social norms was more fundamental than the call emerging from the salon milieu for change in the standards governing relationships between men and women. Using their power as arbiters of taste, the women and men in this elite environment valued women's intelligence and creativity, and argued that it was necessary to increase the educational opportunities available to girls.[4] Marriages, they argued, should be based on reciprocal respect. They decried the obligation imposed on young women to marry without affection in the service of family goals, and complained about the detrimental effects of repeated pregnancies on women's health.

By 1659, when the French playwright Molière produced the play *Les précieuses ridicules,* the term *précieuse* was becoming derogatory. Over the next two decades, the very time that Louis XIV was establishing his power and reforming his government, women who imagined reforms in love and marriage were mocked as pretentious pseudo-intellectuals who lacked common sense and foolishly refused their natural duty to become wives and mothers. Yet, as feminist scholars have observed, if the female intellectual elite of the seventeenth century became targets for writers like Molière, it was not because their calls for a different model of male-female relationships were foolish. Rather, it was because they offered a powerful and attractive alternative to traditional ideas about marriage. In the traditional model, individuals were called on to subordinate their own desires in order to serve the reproductive needs of families, and, in the case of the king's pronatalist edict, the state.[5] By claiming that marriage might be different, and that women are rational individuals who deserve greater autonomy in their marital and reproductive lives, elite women in the seventeenth century were leaders in a broader evolution of ideas about marriage, and by extension, about all social and political relations.

This chapter interprets royal pronatalist policy in the context of these debates about gender roles and conjugal power. As we have seen, the 1666 royal pronatalist edict embodied a patriarchalist definition of politics, one that figured marrying and fathering children as the sources of legitimate political authority. It passed in silence over the question of whether marrying and mothering could have a similar political significance for women; indeed, the word *mère* appears nowhere in the text of the law; insofar as the women who give birth to the infants vital to the state are mentioned in the 1666 edict, they are defined relationally, as the wives of fathers.[6] The absence of mothers in a legal text proclaiming the fundamental importance of procreation to the state was not the result of any innocence on the part of pronatalist policymakers about where babies came from. Rather, their silence about mothering followed from the peculiar logic of patriarchalism, which passed over motherhood in discussions about political authority in order to focus on the relationship between fathers and children. As feminist political theorists have observed, patriarchalism thus elided the prior sexual relationship between men and women that made fatherhood possible, and rendered invisible the female reproductive labor on which fatherhood (in particular the prolific fatherhood envisioned by pronatalist legislation) depended.[7]

Defining Fatherhood and Motherhood

Far from a merely private duty, early modern culture defined fatherhood as a social, religious, and political role.[8] When French writers wanted to evoke the weighty responsibilities that went along with fathering children, they spoke of acting as a *père de famille*. The French phrase has no precise English equivalent: *père de famille* means both "father" and "householder," connecting a man's reproductive role with the exercise of authority and with fiscal responsibility for a household. According to the 1694 dictionary of the Académie Française, to say a man was a *père* meant only that he had fathered one or more children. To say a man was a *père de famille* denoted, in addition, that he had a wife and was responsible for a household (*tient ménage*). The dictionary's definition acknowledged the fact that status as *père de famille* was available to men only through the prior exercise of the man's conjugal sexual role; so it was that "when a woman gives birth to her first child, one commonly says to her husband, 'now you are a *père de famille....*'" Furthermore, being a *père de famille* implied economic empowerment and responsibility. For that reason, the dictionary explained, lease contracts specified that the lessee was bound by the contract to treat the property he leased "as a good *père de famille*," that is, as a responsible adult male accountable to the community for his behavior.[9]

If fathers played a vital role in securing social order, this did not mean that contemporaries denied mothers a fundamental role as well. The prescriptive literature of the Catholic Reformation, for example, stressed the importance of mothers as nurturers and moral examples for their children. Mothering was configured by some writers almost as a form of religious worship: "[God] wishes you to see Him in the person of your children, and that you do for Him what you are obliged by natural tenderness to do for them," wrote one writer.[10] Indeed, calls for women's education in this period often turned on the influential role that mothers played in the household. Religious orders devoted to teaching girls, such as the Ursulines, proliferated during the sixteenth and seventeenth century, justifying their mission as a preparation for women's socially significant task as mothers.[11] Even Colbert's legal advisors on the Council of Justice recognized how important mothering was in providing moral training. The period offers a wealth of evidence, including the popularity of Marian devotions, depictions of mothers in fiction, and self-expression of real mothers in their letters and memoirs, that mothering was accorded social value and that women as well as men were internalizing messages about parental responsibilities in the early modern era.[12]

Yet if early modern writers praised mothers for the role they played in the kingdom's households, they were far more reticent about connecting motherhood to public power. In contrast to fatherhood, so frequently cited to legitimize power and authority in the political realm, motherhood was rarely constructed as a civic or political role by French political theorists during this period. Jean Bodin referred to fathers as the "true images of God" endowed by nature with the power to command. But he defined the importance of a *mère de famille* in the following fashion:

> Inasmuch as every household, corporation and college, every commonwealth and in fact the whole human race would perish were it not repopulated through marriage, it follows that a family is not complete in every respect without a woman, who for this reason is called the *mère de famille*.[13]

Bodin acknowledged that mothers were crucial to the fate of humanity; indeed he grounds women's social importance purely in their reproductive role, without which "the whole human race would perish." But Bodin stopped short of making women's essential role in reproduction and human survival a source of legitimate social or political authority.

Such reticence may have stemmed from France's particular political experience. Bodin composed much of his great political tract, the *Six Books of the Commonwealth,* just after the regency of Catherine de Médicis, as civil war raged. During the sixteenth and seventeenth centuries, three queen mothers—Catherine de Médicis, Marie de Médicis, and Anne of Austria—acted as regents to their minor sons. Each of these foreign women struggled to defend the legitimacy of her authority, and scurrilous attacks on Anne of Austria during the Fronde proved that masculinity remained an important asset in French royal politics.[14] Amidst the succession crises and civil wars of sixteenth- and seventeenth-century France, motherhood was clearly not in favor as a political metaphor. Sixteenth-century political writers, in fact, tended to define the rule of women as a curse that God inflicted on the sinful.[15]

Some historians have suggested that models of physical generation may also help account for the elision of motherhood in early modern political tracts. The

Aristotelian theory of generation, influential from ancient times until the nineteenth century, held that males played the preponderant role in reproduction. According to Aristotle, the father's seed contributed the active life force and form to the developing child, while the mother's body, in a more passive fashion, furnished mere nourishment and a vessel for fetal development.[16] As a result, Aristotelians saw fathering as an ordering, powerful, and more noble role in procreation than the role played by mothers. In essence, Aristotle's theory held that a father was more the true parent of a child than a mother, an idea with obvious significance when social position, status, and political authority were passed through generation.

Aristotelian theory was no doubt attractive to those who wished to buttress particular models of monarchical succession, especially the French model that excluded both daughters and daughters' children from the crown. By the mid-seventeenth century, however, it no longer held much authority within scientific circles. The alternative, Galenic theory of reproduction had long dominated popular texts treating reproduction like Laurent Joubert's *Erreurs populaires* (1578), Ambroise Paré's *De la génération* (1579), and later, Nicolas Venette's *Tableau de l'amour conjugal* (1685).[17] It asserted that both mother and father provided "seed" that mingled at conception. The Galenic theory reaffirmed conventional sexual hierarchy (i.e., men were more "perfect" than women as physical specimens) but attributed generative power to mothers as well as fathers.[18]

By the mid-seventeenth century the scientific community was, in fact, in turmoil over the relative role of men and women in reproduction. The book published by William Harvey in 1651, *Excertationes de generatione animalium,* attributed to females the capacity to produce eggs, but to male sperm the capacity to spark human life into being. Harvey's explanation of procreation was neither Galenic nor Aristotelian in a traditional sense.[19] Work with microscopes in the 1660s, 1670s, and 1680s identified egg and sperm, provoking arguments about the qualities of each, particularly in terms of which one transmitted form to the developing embryo.[20] At the time pronatalist policy was formulated, the newest science had undermined the authority of the Aristotelian, male-dominated theory of reproduction, and raised new questions about what, precisely, mother and father each contributed to the child to whom a woman gave birth.[21]

Colbert's advisors, for their part, steered clear of science and, indeed, of conjugal relations in their discussions of the value of procreation to the state. Their writing about the political significance of reproduction is notable, in fact, for the way that it avoids any mention of the physical costs of conceiving children, being pregnant, or giving birth. The "costs" of children as calculated by pronatalist policymakers were assessed, rather, in economic terms: dowry costs, tax burdens, and the challenges of providing for many children. In other words, pronatalist policy did its reproductive "cost accounting" purely from the standpoint of the *père de famille.* He was the economic agent of the conjugal household and its representative within the metaphorical body of the *res publica.* With this fiction, the real, parturient bodies women and the labor pains of the birthing room were relegated to a world outside politics, hidden within the households over which these *pères de famille* presided.

Law and the Question of Fatherhood

From the mid-sixteenth through the early eighteenth centuries, royal legislation strengthened the legal control of fathers over the persons and property of their children. Simultaneously, royal judges assumed jurisdiction over relationships between husbands and wives, and expressed suspicion about widows' exercise of control over estates and guardianship over children. Frequently, historians discuss these related and contemporary developments together, as aspects of the increasingly patriarchal and authoritarian ideal of family life in this era. But, for the purposes of clarifying how gender ideology shaped pronatalist law, it is important to recognize that however much law and prescriptive literature may have conflated paternal power and conjugal power, control of adults over children and men over women are not identical and were recognized as different by contemporaries.[22]

Paternal power, as early modern theorists explained it, flowed from the "natural" relationship created between a man and his biological child. The power over children also engendered a reciprocal (and public) obligation of fathers to nurture and care for the children they procreated. Because children were manifestly not capable of taking care of themselves, this relationship was "sealed with the seal of nature."[23] Relationships between husbands and wives could not be justified in precisely the same way; it was not as obvious that women needed men as it was that children needed adults. Jean Bodin, for example, appealed to tradition and divine will rather than nature to justify men's conjugal power over women. He cited the customs of various ancient cultures, concluding that they showed "the authority, power and commandment that the husband has over the wife from human and divine law."[24] In Bodin's estimation, the subordination of wives to husbands did not arise in nature, but was nevertheless a principle of "all systems of law." Yet while a wife was obliged to be obedient to her husband, she was not his slave; indeed, Bodin identified treating a free person as a slave as a defining characteristic of tyranny. Following the lead of Aristotle's *Politics,* Bodin took pains to distinguish conjugal power from paternal power even as he stressed that both wives and children owed obedience to the head of the family.[25]

In the seventeenth century, natural rights theorists would go further, flatly denying that conjugal power was "natural" and ineluctable and noting that it arose from history and convention. Most, however, continued to believe that it was necessary to accord one partner—the husband—with power over the household and its resources. The English political theorist John Locke suggested the conjugal relationship might best be thought of as a contract between two rational individuals, regulated by civil laws that varied across time and culture. Nevertheless, Locke fell back upon "nature" to explain why it was that once men and women were married, it was the "abler and stronger" partner to the contract—the male—who had the superior power in what had been a relationship of free and equal adults.[26] The Cartesian François Poulain de la Barre, in his treatise entitled *On the Equality of the Sexes* (1673) posited a historical rather than natural origin for male domination in households and society. Poulain argued that male dominance had been enabled by men's physical strength, which had allowed them to overturn a primordial natural equality between the sexes. Originating in force, male domination was now sustained by prejudice and law. Poulain, in fact, blamed jurists for "plac[ing] women under the tutelage of their husbands, like children vis-à-vis their fathers." The contract of marriage was reciprocal, he noted, granting each partner equal rights in the other's body. In a passage that is surely significant for thinking about the negotiation of conjugal sexuality and reproduction, Poulain goes on to explain the limits of legitimate male power in the household:

> Since the will of the one is not the rule of the other, if a woman has to do what her husband wants her to do, then no less must he in his turn do what she tells him to. In no way can a woman be forced to submit to her husband beyond reason simply because he is the stronger. That would be the behavior of out-and-out bullies and not of intelligent adults.[27]

Poulain's argument illustrates the ways that salon culture's emphasis on civility in male-female interactions influenced philosophical debates. He implied that conjugal relations demanded negotiation and masculine self-discipline. The "will" of the husband was not sufficient justification for female submission to an "unreasonable" demand.[28]

Procreation, with its different costs to men and women, highlighted the stakes of conjugal power. As modern political theorists note, when early modern political writers sought to distinguish conjugal power from paternal power, they were forced to contend with the problem that the two have an essential relationship; it was only by having a wife that a man could become a *père de famille*. Legitimate fatherhood and the political stability with which it was associated depended on female sexual submission and wives' sexual fidelity. Placing the origins of legitimate social authority in fatherhood thereby licensed husbands' exercise of conjugal power and male (and public) surveillance of women's sexual behavior.[29]

French legal tradition insisted on defining the family as an institution built exclusively through biological filiation within marriage. French fathers were by law not allowed, as Roman fathers had been, to choose whether or not to recognize a child, nor were they allowed to adopt should biology fail to provide them with an heir. While French jurists idealized Roman-style paternal power, the liberty to define a family without regard to the marital sacrament was unacceptable.[30] Yet if paternity could not be defined by fathers' will, how could this socially vital relationship be recognized? Unlike maternity, paternity was invisible. The solution lawyers settled on was legal marriage. A marriage solemnized in a church and recorded in the parish register became *de jure* proof of fatherhood, a principle signified with the Roman legal aphorism *Pater is est quem nuptiae demonstrat* ("The father is he whom the marriage indicates"). The increasing intervention of the state in family matters throughout the early modern era helped construct fatherhood in this historically specific fashion. One of the provisions of the 1667 Ordinance of Saint-German-en-Laye, or Code Louis, mandated the submission of a copy of parish registers to local judicial archives. The registers were intended to function as a public record defining civil status, which children inherited through the paternal line.[31]

In order to function according to plan, however, this system demanded that women's reproductive sexuality be reserved exclusively for the men to whom they were legally married, an ideal that was, of course, never achieved. Unmarried women had children and, even more insidiously, in the eyes of jurists, married women sometimes gave birth to children whom the law assumed were their husbands' offspring, but who were in fact the children of someone else. Adultery committed by a woman rendered paternity uncertain, posing a threat to public order even deeper than the wife's lack of faith. As the eighteenth-century jurist Robert Joseph Pothier wrote, "adultery committed by the woman is infinitely more contrary to the well-being of civil society, because it despoils families by handing over their possessions to adulterous children who are foreign to them."[32] The emphasis on biological fatherhood as guarantor of "the well-being of civil society" provided a rationale for preserving masculine conjugal authority.

The importance of fatherhood also led to laws that monitored the sexuality of unmarried women. For example, the 1556 edict against clandestine pregnancy required unmarried pregnant women and widows to file *déclarations de grossesse* with local judges or risk prosecution should their infant die before baptism.[33] Not only were these declarations intended to prevent women from committing abortion or infanticide to protect their honor, they created a legal mechanism for women to identify the father of their child before the law, and also to obtain financial support from him.[34] The edict of 1556 also instituted penalties for the crime of *supposition d'enfant,* defined as an attempt to falsify a pregnancy and birth and thereby position a "stranger" to the family as heir to family property.[35]

Surveillance of all women's reproductive sexuality was instrumental in constructing the biological model of fatherhood that was an essential component, according to contemporaries, of a well-policed society.[36]

A case argued before the Parlement of Paris in 1675 demonstrates how the legal emphasis on biological paternity constructed different social roles for mothers and fathers and enhanced scrutiny of women's sexual behavior. The case arose from the marriage of François Fourré de Dampierre, Seigneur de Beaulieu, and Marie Charton in 1672.[37] Charton, the daughter of a butcher, married Dampierre, a man from a much higher social rank, after having lived with him for twenty-two years in concubinage. Their nonmarital union had produced sixteen children. The couple's irregular situation was explained by Dampierre's clerical status. He held benefices in two priories; because he had taken the vows for minor orders necessary to hold these benefices, he was legally unable to marry. In 1672, however, as he and Charton prepared for the birth of their sixteenth child, they married quietly and passed their eight surviving children "sous le poêle"("under the veil"), a religious ritual of symbolic rebirth intended to claim the children as Dampierre's legitimate offspring.

The couple's decision to marry, which would have required Dampierre to give up his benefices, may have indicated an awareness of Charton's failing health. She died during this sixteenth birth. Afterward, the legal status of the couple's children became a source of contention in Dampierre's family. The father's relatives wished to exclude the children from the capacity to inherit family property they would have if their legitimation were recognized.

As both sides prepared arguments, the difference between maternal and paternal power loomed as an important issue. Lawyers for the Dampierre family argued that birth and civil status were defined by public records. They cited the royal law of 1667 that required priests to keep baptismal records and turn these records over to royal courts every six months. The law designated these registers, they argued, to "guarantee the birth and status of persons," or verify their civil identity. Since Dampierre and Charton's children had been baptized under the name of Marie Charton only, they claimed, they could not simply be recognized after the fact by the Dampierre, "who is not presumed to be their father, according to law, nor according to nature, which only makes itself known by the precautions of law."[38] If such legitimations were allowed, the lawyers warned, "a man could recognize whatever children he wants, even if he is not their father, and thereby introduce among us the liberty of adoption, which our French jurisprudence cannot abide."[39]

In addition, Dampierre's family charged that Charton's status as concubine was analogous to "public debauchery" and prostitution; legitimacy belonged only to children whose parentage (that is, father) was clearly known, and a woman who gave birth outside marriage was presumed not to merit the law's trust. Only marriage could function as certain proof of paternity, they argued, albeit with provisions that allowed men to repudiate children when they could prove their wives' adulterous behavior.

Lawyers for the children concurred that biological fatherhood was vital for social order, but used this claim to argue for the opposite legal conclusion. Civil status could be regulated by means other than baptismal registers, they argued; even the king's recent ordinance on the matter made allowances for other kinds of proof. As for evidence of Marie Charton's "debauchery," the lawyer dismissed this evidence by noting that Dampierre had never expressed any suspicion of Charton in the more than twenty years that the couple lived together. In response to the charge that allowing for such legitimations would set a dangerous precedent for adoption, he responded that "it would be a more dangerous consequence that children have no publicly acknowledged father. It is to him alone, and not to the mother, that Roman laws gave authority over these children." Against the insinuation that the couple's irregular union made the children's paternity uncertain, then, the childrens' lawyers juxtaposed the specter of children who were "masterless" and constrained by no legitimate authority.

Both parties sought to ground their case by explaining why their position reflected the important principles of paternal authority as defined in French law. Likewise, both recognized that maternity was critically different from fatherhood, a natural fact as opposed to a legal (and political) relationship. Finally, the case showed that conjugal relations could not be separated from the legal definition of fatherhood; it was *Dampierre's faith in* Charton's sexual fidelity—his lack of suspicion—that the lawyer cited to bolster his argument that Dampierre was the father of the children. The length and trust of the couple's bond to one another was essential to define his relationship to these children. In the end, the court ruled that the legitimation of Charton and Dampierre's children should stand. Even though the marriage had happened long after the birth of the children, and was followed in quick order by the mother's death (which suggested what was called marriage *in extremis,* a union hastily arranged for inheritance purposes), the court agreed that clear lines of authority defining the relation of fathers and children were fundamental to public order.

Louis XIV's pronatalist law embodied a similar emphasis on a family defined by biological filiation. It addressed rewards for reproduction to fathers rather than to wives or mothers, reflecting the emphasis on fatherhood as the determinant of childrens' civil status, and by extension, of political order.

One way to see the effects of this emphasis on fatherhood is to examine the fate of widowed mothers in pronatalist law. When widowed, women assumed the status of heads-of-household in their own right, and often (but not always) became the legal guardians of their children.[40] Widowed women were explictly accorded the right to claim pronatalist tax exemptions and pensions; the 1666 royal Edict on Marriage had promised that pensions offered to fathers of large families, for example, would be paid "to the said gentlemen and bourgeois *or to their widows* for the rest of their lives."[41]

Households headed by women consistently account for a very small proportion of known households petitioning for and receiving pronatalist benefits.[42] Of eighty-four noble recipients of the royal government pronatalist's pensions in 1670, for example, only three (3.6 percent) were widows.[43] Administrative correspondence about the pronatalist program referred to these women as widows of fathers rather than mothers. It was conventional, of course, for legal documents to specify that women were widows, as this explained why they were petitioning on their own behalf. And, arguably, since noble status was passed through the male line, directing the pensions offered specifically to nobles to male nobles' widows helped avoid confusion about the noble status of the children the couple had produced.[44] In the case of blended families, composed of mothers and fathers with ten or more children from several marriages, the results of a patrilineal idea of the family become clearer. Overall, such families account, again, for only a small proportion of families receiving pronatalist awards.[45] Among these blended families, it was normal for men to count their children from more than one marriage in order to qualify for pronatalist awards. In 1668, for example, a nobleman from the Limousin, Jean-Louis de Montaignat, claimed a pronatalist pension on the basis of the thirteen children that remained to him from his marriages to "deceased ladies Gabrielle Foucaud de St. Germain, Françoise de Brousselles de Carlus, and Anne de l'Estrange, his first, second, and third wives."[46] De Montaignat's eligibility posed no conceptual problem for the royal intendant. De Montaignat was the head-of-household and the biological father of all thirteen children as recognized by law. Matters were different with another Limousin nobleman, Claude de Very, Sieur de Marillac. De Very and his wife Françoise des Asis had eleven children from their marriage. But, after discussing these children, the intendant added, "The said lady, formerly widow of the Sieur de Combort, has two living children . . . from her aforementioned first marriage."[47] The intendant noted this because he was uncertain as to whether de Very should receive the 1,000 *livres* the Edict on Marriage promised to noble fathers of ten or the 2,000 *livres* awarded to fathers of twelve. De Very, after all, was the biological father of only eleven children, while his wife was the mother of thirteen. Accounts for 1670 reveal that—at least by that year—de Very received the smaller amount, 1,000 *livres*. This suggests that the royal government chose not to see Françoise des Asis's children from a previous marriage as integral parts of the couple's family.[48] It is possible that two of the couples' children might have died between the application of 1668 and the pension award of 1670. However, the evidence of the masculine and patrilineal definition of reproductive labor at work in pronatalist law is strengthened by the fact that de Very-des

Asis are the only couple among hundreds examined for this study where women's children from prior marriages are mentioned *at all* in the records. Fathers defined the status of households, mediated their relationship with the political community, and exercised powers of command. Even if women were responsible for the reproductive labor pronatalist legislation sought to encourage, motherhood simply did not count in the same way.

Reactions to Pronatalist Policy

Nothing in the text of the Edict on Marriage suggested that pronatalist law sought to impact relations between husbands and wives; any hint of conjugal negotiations over sexuality and reproduction was hidden within the household that fell under the legitimate authority of the *père de famille*. But reactions to pronatalist policy make it very clear that contemporary observers were intensely aware that the king's legislation staked out a royal claim to the reproductive labor of his subjects, and in doing so had definite implications for conjugal relations. Consider, for example, the following lines from a verse gazette, the *Muse de la Cour,* that appeared the week after the 1666 pronatalist edict was registered in royal courts:

> For pity's sake, help me understand
> this incredible rumor.
> They're saying that all inhabitants
> commoners as well as gentlemen
> burdened with ten or twelve children
> will receive payments every year.
> If the GREAT KING so dear to us
> has decided on this initiative,
> then it's the real way to keep wives
> from sewing their nightgowns at night.[49]

The *Muse de la Cour,* authored by Adrien Perdoux de Subligny, was aimed at an elite reading audience in Paris. It fulfilled the role of newspaper and gossip column, reporting on the court, diplomatic and political events, and members of the aristocracy in verse. When the *Muse* mentioned women "sewing their nightgowns at night," Subligny was clearly alluding to the issue of husbands' sexual access. Women "sewed their nightgowns at night" either literally by sewing the bottom together, or (more likely) by working late into the night on domestic tasks like sewing or mending. The excuse of domestic tasks allowed them to avoid intercourse, and thus pregnancy.[50] In the comic terms of the *Muse de la Cour,* the king's pronatalist Edict on Marriage was designed to undermine this feminine contraceptive strategy. Not only did the edict attempt to assure men access to female sexuality and women's reproductive potential, it in fact encouraged husbands to capitalize on this opportunity by providing economic rewards for them to do so.

Evidence like the hint in the *Muse de la Cour* coincide with some of the earliest measurable instances of contraceptive practice in Western Europe. In his famous study of the Genevan bourgeoisie, demographer Louis Henry found that family size dropped from an average of 5.4 children per family in the period 1600–1649 to 3.6 children per family in the period 1650–1699.[51] These trends were not limited to Protestant Geneva. For seventeenth century Rouen, Jean-Pierre Bardet dates the beginnings of fertility decline to the 1640s.[52] And, Louis Henry and Claude Lévy's study of demographic patterns among the high French nobility underscored a clear trend toward family limitation. Among dukes and peers married between 1650 and 1699, seven out of the thirty-four married couples studied produced ten or more children in the course of their marriage. In the next cohort, couples married between 1700 and 1750, fecundity declined overall and, significantly, families of ten or more children disappeared from the sample altogether.[53] These figures attest to the early adoption of contraceptive practices among the French elite.

During the seventeenth century, such prodigious reproductive feats were not uncommon; Henry and Levy's work suggests that perhaps one in five of the wives of dukes and peers could expect to give birth ten or more times in her reproductive life. Having so many children nearly always meant experiencing pregnancies in rapid succession, a practice contemporaries considered especially dangerous to women's health. Madame de Sévigné famously begged her daughter to avoid sex with her husband after she gave birth to the third child she had conceived in as many years. The pregnancies, a miscarriage, and giving birth had taken their toll: her daughter, she said, had "suffered more than if she had been broken on the wheel." Fearing the health consequences if she were to become pregnant again, she recommended the married couple sleep in separate bedrooms and that her daughter take the additional precaution of sleeping with a chaperone to avoid any temptation.[54]

Sévigné's letters provide precious clues about how elite men and women negotiated conjugal sexuality and reproduction. The mother-in-law browbeat her son-in-law, counseling him to accept his wife's request for temporary abstinence: "You say that my daughter should do nothing but have children because she acquits herself so well of that function...But I warn you that if you do not give that pretty machine a rest—whether you do it out of love or pity—you will assuredly destroy it, and that would be a shame."[55] Remarking on an acquaintance who had recently died, "by being worn out by child-bearing," she advised her daughter not to "change for the worse"—that is, to become pregnant—and wrote disapprovingly of "husbands who get rid of their wives through excess of love and tenderness."[56] Sévigné is only the most famous of the seventeenth-century writers who bemoaned the frequent pregnancies endured by elite women. Writers from the salon milieu noted that the reproductive expectations of elite marriages constituted a particularly perilous expression of the "slavery" tyrannical husbands might attempt to impose on their wives.[57]

Louis XIV's pronatalist policy endorsed reproductive patterns that many of the king's elite subjects already considered oppressive and even dangerous. Comments on the policy in poems like the "Edict of Love" that opened this chapter, and in gazettes like the *Muse de la Cour*, establish that elite audiences in Paris understood the Edict on Marriage in a broader context of legal changes that limited women's autonomy in the household and society. As it rewarded men for prolific reproduction, the Edict on Marriage also reinforced male conjugal authority and reaffirmed that reproduction—rather than satisfaction and companionship—was the legitimate end of relations between men and women.

In September of 1668, Colbert received the following letter from a relative, the Douairière de Lavardin, announcing the birth of his grandchild:

> No one in the family, Monsieur, wanted to inform you that Madame de Lavardin gave birth to a daughter. I am the only one who sees no problem in doing so, knowing how much you love increase in the number of the king's subjects and approve when young ladies give their husbands many children. Our own young lady has come through her first business so happily that she has decided to start again soon to give us a boy. She wishes to make herself worthy of your adoption by giving you many grandchildren....
>
> I relate all these details to you, Monsieur, because you are our good papa that we respect and love dearly and because we are obliged to inform you of everything that happens in a house that belongs to you....[58]

The Douairière had good news for Colbert in every respect but one: the child was a girl. Again, the letter suggests that the gendered messages of pronatalist policy were well understood by the king's female subjects. The significant irony of a policy that gave fathers money for the reproductive work that only women could do does not seem to have been lost on the Douairière. She reported on her obligation to her family's "good papa" from the archetypal female space of the birthing room. Writing to the kingdom's most important economic minister, she referred to Madame Lavardin's birth as an "*affaire*" ("business"), a word that connoted work or occupation, and seemed designed to underscore how the young woman had accomplished the politically significant task that her father-in-law had set for the king's subjects.[59] In the end, however, Madame de Lavardin did not give Colbert many grandchildren; she died giving birth to her second child.

How much did the royal government's endorsement of prolific reproduction really matter to women and to the evolution of conjugal relations? Recent historians caution against believing that the ideology enshrined in law prevailed in everyday social reality. They argue that the real experiences of women in the early modern period prove that women played a greater role in shaping family life than the patriarchal ideals embedded in legal texts would lead us to believe. The supposed legal incapacity of women did not restrict women to passivity; on the contrary, women savvily engaged the legal system to achieve their goals.[60] Similarly, the growing prevalence of family limitation suggests that women's desires to limit births increasingly won out over tradition and incentives that pushed men to desire larger families. Finally, it would be a mistake to think of reproduction only as a contest for power that inevitably pitted men against women—perhaps a particular mistake in the case of couples that produced ten or more children together over the course of their marriage. The negotiation of conjugal sexuality and reproduction is a feature of companionate marriage as well as traditional unions. Laws that sought to reinforce paternal and conjugal power were attenuated in personal, often affectionate relationships between women and men.[61]

The royal government's determination to make the king a patron of prolific procreation was nevertheless a significant ideological statement, coming at a historical moment when both married women and political theorists were raising questions about the nature of conjugal power. Although it earned them some ridicule, *précieuses* imagined how the social relations between the sexes might be restructured along lines of affection, civility, and reason rather than domination and force. The Edict on Marriage expressed the logic of the traditional system of social reproduction they rejected. The odd elision of mothers from the text of the law, in effect, only called attention to the debate over these issues and the essential role that women's reproductive labor played in households and the state.

FOUR

Domesticating New France

In 1663, the nobleman and philosopher Philippe Fortin de la Hoguette published a work of political theory entitled *Les elemens de la politique selon les principes de la nature* ("The elements of politics according to the principles of nature"). Fortin's book offered an account of how humankind had developed government, linking this evolution to the observance of four basic prohibitions: rules against murder, theft, false witness, and adultery. Marital fidelity was necessary for social stability, Fortin claimed, because only "the purity of the marriage bed" assured that children and their fathers would know one another's identity with certainty. And, only certainty about paternity could clarify the natural lines of authority and duty on which order in the family—and by extension political order—rested. Without a family structure centered around the clear observance of this elementary sexual rule, Fortin warned, humans devolved into "a single and tumultuous family of men and women living all in confusion."[1]

Fortin's political theory painted the establishment of a specific conjugal regime as a marker distinguishing savagery from civilization. His book, published just as Louis XIV's government took direct administrative control over the North American colony known as New France, is broadly representative of the attitudes regarding marriage and sexuality that became imperatives of France's colonial government there. In the 1660s, the royal government began a concerted effort to impose French notions of social order in the St. Lawrence Valley; marriage and reproduction were vital to their plan. Royal officials believed that marriage in the French style—that is, monogamous and indissoluble unions within settled households—would promote population growth and, just as important, seal colonists into the hierarchical order that linked heads of household, or *pères de famille,* to the French king and Christian God.

This chapter explores the royal government's experiment in imposing marriage as a tool of demographic growth and social order in the colonial environment. France was not alone in trying to construct a particular family order in its colonial possessions, of course. No matter the place or time, policing marital and sexual arrangements went hand-in-hand with efforts to secure political authority and maintain economic domination over Europe's colonial outposts. Colonial policymakers inevitably faced questions about the family and sexuality: how intimately should natives and settlers interact? Where would labor come from? How would insider and outsider status be determined? Integrating distant regions and their peoples into imperial political orders forced colonial administrators to confront the reproductive and disciplinary functions served by the conjugal household.[2]

The governments of Louis XIII and XIV faced these questions during an era when marriage was particularly freighted with religious and political significance. As France built its imperial presence in Canada from the early decades of the seventeenth century, first missionaries and then colonial officials attempted to impart, respectively, Christian salvation and French political order to New France's inhabitants via the marital and sexual norms that helped to define post-Tridentine Catholicism and French state formation. The values that they brought with them across the Atlantic defined the approaches of colonial officials. Though their ultimate goals differed, missionaries and government officials both believed that the conjugal household was the irreducible unit on which social and political order depended. But, as the following pages will show, the demographic and economic realities of seventeenth-century New France rendered French notions of orderly, civilized marriage and reproduction particularly difficult to sustain.

The first part of the chapter examines the efforts of Jesuit missionaries in New France to change the marital practices of the Huron, Algonquin, and Iroquois peoples who populated seventeenth-century Canada, trading and often mixing sexually with French Catholic people. It focuses on the years between 1630 and 1660, before the royal government took direct administrative control of the colony. During this period, enduring patterns of native-French interaction took shape, and Jesuits confronted the difficulties of transplanting Tridentine marital norms to a society in which such notions were alien.

The second part of the chapter turns to an analysis of the direct interventions of the French royal government in conjugal matters between 1663 and about 1690. During this period, the government actively promoted marriage and reproduction among the settler population: nowhere in the metropole, in fact, did the government more energetically implement its pronatalist agenda. Royal officials believed that in order to implant the colony firmly in Canadian soil, it was essential to encourage the formation of conjugal households and the birth of a second settler generation. Not only would this generation born on-site relieve the chronic labor shortage that retarded economic development and threatened security, the formation of conjugal households promised to rectify the many social and economic "disorders" that had plagued the colony for decades.

The official most responsible for the implementation of this royal policy was Jean-Baptiste Colbert, the same man responsible for the creation of pronatalist policy in the metropole. New France, in fact, became the principal laboratory for Colbert's experiments with techniques for surveillance and control of population, a project in which he invested significant royal funds and administrative resources.

By the time Colbert turned colonial administration over to his son, the Marquis de Seignelay, in the early 1680s, the mixed results of these efforts was becoming clearer: although the colony had grown in population, the "civilizing process" that marriage had been supposed to promote had hardly advanced.

Marriage as Antidote to Savagery in New France

When French missionaries began to arrive in North America in the early seventeenth century, they came as representatives of a society already fascinated with the variety of marital customs practiced around the world. Metropolitan readers avidly consumed accounts of Amerindian peoples, and no description of the "savages" European explorers or missionaries met was complete without an account of native sexual and conjugal customs. The Protestant Jean de Léry accorded a chapter of his 1578 narrative about the French colonial outpost in Brazil to a description of "marriage, polygamy, and degrees of consanguinity observed among the savages and the treatment of their infants."[3] Léry contradicted the stereotype of savage promiscuity by describing the different but no less exacting sexual standards of his Tupinamba hosts. Like other visitors to Brazil, he marveled at the peaceful coexistence of wives in polygynous unions, asking his readers to consider whether—were polygamy not expressly forbidden by Christianity—European women would ever be able to display such patience and obedience to their husbands.

By the eighteenth century, a growing number of Europeans would even claim to see benefits to the sexual and marital practices of "savage" peoples, offering praise for the superior candor or fecundity they claimed to observe among these beings ostensibly closer to nature and thereby innocent of the corruption of society. Louis-Armand de Lom d'Arce, Baron de Lahontan, author of an enduringly popular travel account of North America, extolled the "tender friendships" he claimed to be the basis of Amerindian marriage. Lahontan described how couples courted with what, for European readers, seemed like astonishing sexual freedom. He praised their marriages characterized by discretion and lack of jealousy. When such conjugal peace broke down, he reported, his Amerindian hosts dissolved their marriages without rancor and moved on to seek happiness elsewhere. As a result, love and marriage caused many fewer "extravagancies" among them than among Europeans, "from whence," Lahontan wrote, "I conclude they are not altogether so savage as we are."[4]

Yet despite a persistent curiosity about alternative marital regimes, the stress French Catholics laid on marriage as a sacrament and basis of social and political order made it impossible for French missionaries and colonial officials to look with indulgent eyes upon the range of marital regimes they found among Amerindian groups. Indeed, missionaries and colonial officials interpreted the flexibility of relations between the sexes in New France as a source of the brutality and instability, which, they claimed, plagued these wild places. As they saw it, Amerindian marital practices contravened supposedly "natural" laws by tolerating infidelity, confusing paternity, and all too frequently dissolving in divorce. Such practices were consistent with people that, as they saw it, had little notion of order, beauty, or God. Native marital practices, in other words, struck the French as tumultuous and confused, characteristic of the savagery European philosophers like Philippe Fortin de la Hoguette warned about. From the standpoint of transplanted French church and state authorities, moving New France's native peoples toward acceptance of French marital norms was an essential step in improving their lives, saving their souls, and building a stable society in the colonial environment. Compromise on marital principles would only retard the development of civilization in the colonies.

Yet instituting this marital order in New France presented enormous problems, as the Jesuits would discover. From the 1630s to the early 1660s, responsibility for regulating the colony's moral order fell primarily to French members of the Society of Jesus. With only a few Franciscan friars and nuns and a handful of secular clergy to challenge their monopoly on spiritual power, the Jesuits wielded significant influence over the development of native-French relations in the colony.

Jesuit missionaries' attitudes about marriage were shaped by the French cultural environment and the training that missionaries received before they left for New France. In the metropole, the Jesuits were active promoters of Tridentine marital norms who worked to develop a theology to serve the spiritual needs of married people. Jesuits authored seven of the eleven marriage manuals aimed at laypeople published in France before 1650, and nearly half of all the marriage guides published from the late sixteenth through the eighteenth centuries.[5] In combination with their pulpit oratory and metropolitan missions aimed at the married population, these manuals attest to the special role that marriage and conjugal life played in the Jesuit mission project of the Catholic Reformation era.

Seventeenth-century marriage manuals offered a more positive assessment of marriage than had been common in Medieval Europe, one designed to counter the dour Pauline view that "it was better to marry than to burn." Jesuits writers, like other post-Tridentine Catholic theologians, elaborated an argument that marriage was both a sacrament and a spiritual calling, and that conjugal union had the potential to sanctify those who undertook it with holy purposes. Celibacy of course remained the higher path, but men and women called to the estate of matrimony and united within a valid, sacramental union could transform the natural human impulse to couple and reproduce into a calling through which they would achieve a married person's sort of spiritual perfection.[6] One of the costs of investing marital life and sexuality with formidable spiritual potential, however, was that it rendered non-orthodox marital practices and nonmarital sexuality even more threatening than they had been before. Illicit sex or alternative marital arrangements became more than mere confirmations of the natural weakness of the flesh; they were associated with heresy. Protestants, for example, denied the sacramental status of marriage, accepted divorce in some cases, and raised other challenges to Catholic marital theology.[7] Trained amidst this politicization of marital theology, French missionaries were disinclined to look indulgently on other cultures' marital practices. Indissoluble, monogamous marriage was a fundamental principle of Christianity, nothing less than the "doctrine of the Son of God," as Jesuit missionary Jean de Brébeuf put it in 1636.[8]

The *Jesuit Relations,* published between 1632 and 1673, demonstrate that French Jesuits brought these ideas about marriage with them across the Atlantic. The *Relations* contain accounts of the missionaries' conversion work written primarily for an audience of pious readers and potential donors in France. If they struggled with questions about whether rules could be relaxed for the sake of building the church among the native people of America, the *Relations* suggest that they soon arrived—in part, perhaps, because of this reading audience in France—at the conclusion that they could not. Convinced that sacramental marriage was an absolutely vital foundation of true Christian life, French Jesuits were not relativistic about sexual values, tending instead toward Augustinian rigor about the pollution and corruption inherent in the Amerindian marital norms. Jesuits interpreted sexual freedom, polygamy, and divorce as snares of the devil that prevented Amerindians from attaining salvation, and expressed their anxiety about the difficulties posed by native marriage customs to the Jesuit mission in New France: "Oh what trouble these marriages of the Savages will give us!" exclaimed Paul le Jeune in 1639.[9]

Changing Indians' marital habits became central to the Jesuit mission of conversion. The *Relations* show Jesuit writers in New France wrestling to understand the very different conjugal traditions they found in Amerindian society. As a result, they provide a gold mine of information about Amerindian customs. The Jesuits broached classic ethnographic questions about kinship and the formation of alliances, noting in some cases how native customs of premarital sexuality, polygamy, and divorce connected to developing social and economic relations in native communities. The reports of Indian marriage practices began in the earliest reports from Jesuit encounters in North America. One of the earliest missionaries, Pierre Biard, reported debating his native interlocutors about the advantages and disadvantages of the polygamy occasionally practiced by the Acadian Micmac families he encountered in 1611. His native informants argued that plural wives guaranteed them a larger number of descendants, a source of prestige and political influence in their society. Having many children was considered a blessing by many Europeans as well, but rather than stressing this similarity, Biard responded by rehearsing typical European arguments about the disadvantages of polygyny, for example the claim that it unavoidably caused arguments between rival wives and their offspring (Léry's claims about the patience of Tupinamba wives notwithstanding). Biard told his French audience that polygyny was a sign of a broader devaluation of women in Micmac society, writing that Micmac husbands "beat [their wives] unmercifully, and often for very slight cause." His comment was intended primarily to underscore the connections of polygyny to savagery, and not as an argument for greater equality between the sexes. The problem, that is, was not that Micmac husbands beat their wives, but that they did so "unmercifully" and unreasonably—that is, in savage fashion.[10]

While changing Amerindian marriage practices was central to conversion, and thus a necessary topic of conversation between missionaries and their flock, the evidence suggests that the Jesuits found communicating about sexuality difficult. The problem, admittedly, may be a reflection of the sources: frank accounts of Jesuits' sexual teaching are limited in the *Jesuit Relations*. Probably to shield pious metropolitan readers from potentially titillating knowledge, the *Relations* were sometimes oblique in discussions about sex. Consider the report that the Jesuit Father Superior, presiding at a baptism and marriage in a Huron mission village, "spoke to [the assembled] boldly of the sanctity of marriage among Christians"—without telling more about what was said—or when the writer notes having instructed the Huron that they must give up "those shameless assemblies of men and women (I would blush to speak more clearly)."[11] It is thus often necessary to infer what the conversation between missionaries and natives was actually about. The problem also reflects barriers to communication between the Jesuits and Indians who were the targets of their missionary efforts. Huron peoples, for example, frequently associated celibacy with shamanism and magical power that could be used to harm.[12] The Jesuits' celibacy was disturbing to the Huron and served to heighten the Jesuits' outsider status and even to arouse suspicion. In addition, the Huron soon recognized that French notions of propriety made talk about sex taboo, and politely adjusted their conversations and behavior, in particular when Jesuits were present, in order to avoid the subject.[13] Although these tendencies mean that the *Relations* have limitations as sources, they do provide rich detail on the confrontation between the ultimately irreconcilable ideas about marriage held by Catholic missionaries and their Amerindian hosts.

Among the practices that separated native marital practices from missionary expectations, perhaps no difference proved more troubling to Jesuits than Amerindian cultures' practice of divorce. Among Jesuits trained in Catholic Counter-Reform theology, marital indissolubility was a principle of paramount importance, serving to distinguish sacramental Catholic marriage from those of Protestant "heretics." Yet, the missionaries complained, among New France's natives, marriages were "broken more easily than the promises children make to one another."[14] Amerindians saw the situation quite differently. The mid-seventeenth century Récollet missionary Chrétien Le Clerq reported that his Micmac interlocutors "cannot understand how one can submit to the indissolubility of marriage."[15] The notion that an unhappy couple could not separate and seek other mates seemed utterly ridiculous and counterproductive, a rule likely to cause misery and violence. The early eighteenth-century writer Lahontan (himself a critic of the Catholic position) remarked that the demand of indissolubility was considered "monstrous" by Amerindians, and was, in addition, interpreted as a sign of European inferiority, since it proved that "we Europeans are born in slavery, and deserve no other condition than that of servitude."[16]

Amerindians' rejection of indissolubility suggests that they, like Europeans, saw connections between marriage customs and broader social and political norms. They intuited that indissoluble, Christian marriage was of a piece with French notions about hierarchy, order, and submission to political and patriarchal authority. These expectations sat uneasily with the personal autonomy prized in the native cultures of New France, of which the freedom to choose one's mate and to divorce if unhappy were central expressions.[17] Yet both French missionaries and colonial officials interpreted the Amerindian practice of divorce as evidence of changeability and lack of faith, qualities that did not mesh with the duties of a faithful Catholic and royal subject. At least in the early years of the mission to New France, then, Jesuits believed that native acceptance of marital indissolubility was a necessary discipline that would serve to mark definitive conversion to Christianity.[18]

The *Jesuit Relations* return repeatedly to the "barbarous" aspects of Native marital customs. Beyond divorce, particular Jesuit concerns included polygamy and the premarital sexual activity accepted for adolescents. (The Jesuits were predictably more horrified by the sexual freedom afforded native girls.) Very soon, both Jesuits and their Amerindian interlocutors came to recognize that the very different sexual and marital customs of Native culture constituted major "stumbling blocks" for Christian conversion. Indeed, one writer reported that his earliest native converts had warned the fathers that "conjugal continence and the indissolubility of marriage" constituted "the most serious obstacles in the progress of the Gospel."[19]

Jesuit writers sometimes despaired over changing these customs that proved so thoroughly imbricated with Amerindian social relations and ideas of self. In 1636, Missionary Jean de Brébeuf revealed his reluctance even to discuss Christian expectations for sexual behavior in the village of Ihonatiria, fearing his prospective Huron converts would grow "restive" and "alarmed at the proposal of purity and chastity." Brébeuf was moved to ask his French readers to pray for a miraculous transformation of his catechumens through the sacrament of baptism. Wasn't it likely, he asked, that if "the holy Spirit takes them in hand" and "impress[es] upon them so deeply, in every place and time, the respect they owe to his divine presence and immensity" then by virtue of this immanence the villagers of Ihonatiria would "be very glad to be chaste in order to be Christians, and will ask earnestly to be Christians in order to be chaste"?[20] Such a miraculous transformation seemed vital, since his native hosts had assured Brébeuf that the chastity Jesuit Catholicism demanded was simply impossible for them. One Huron man, struggling with the demands of Christian marriage, reported to his Jesuit teachers that his "heart was sad" because "it seems to me that God does not love us, since he gives us commandments that we cannot keep."[21] Brébeuf wrote of his hope that cleansing the Huron of original sin through baptism might infuse his Huron neophytes with a capacity to change their sexual behavior to meet the Jesuits' uncompromising standards.

One of the problems Jesuits confronted came from French settlers' similar difficulties in meeting Catholic standards for chastity. French male settlers and Indian women frequently formed sexual liaisons. Interethnic marriage in formal, French-style Catholic sacramental unions—the kind recorded in mission registers—proved uncommon throughout most of New France during the seventeenth century. Historians cite different figures on the exact number; one important account places the number at thirty-three. All agree, however, that the number was small.[22] Far more prevalent were informal Amerindian-style unions known as *mariages à la façon du pays* (marriages in the local style).

From the earliest days of French activity in North America, union with a native woman proved the surest route to alliance and integration into native society. Although such unions offended ecclesiastical and colonial officials, *mariages à la façon du pays* offered tangible benefits to both partners. Because French men vastly outnumbered French women in the St. Lawrence Valley until the last quarter of the seventeenth century, union with an Amerindian woman offered many French men their sole chance for domestic partnership. In addition, native women provided a means for French men to tap into native trade networks and knowledge about hunting. The special skill of preparing animal skins was considered women's work, so native women became invaluable partners to French men eager to participate in New France's lucrative fur trade. Finally, the sexual openness and freedom of Amerindian society proved attractive to many French men. Owing to the masculine and European bias of our sources, native women's interest in French men is more difficult to document. Historians speculate that French men brought native women access to valued French goods, freed them from the polygamous unions that would have been their lot due to the skewed sex ratio of the Amerindian population, and suggest that French men may have been preferred sexual partners. The Baron de Lahontan, bolder than the Jesuits about sexual matters, explained that native women liked French men because they were "more prodigal of their Vigour, and mind a Woman's Business more closely."[23] A tradition of asceticism that discouraged Amerindian men from indulging frequently in sex may also have contributed to the attraction between French men and Amerindian women.[24]

No historical source records the number of *mariages à la façon du pays,* or even provides sure footing for estimating their number. If precise numbers elude us, the reiterated complaints of missionaries and colonial officials about French men's degeneration toward savage habits provides good evidence that many French men formed sexual partnerships with native women. Some of these unions produced children, but again, the numbers are impossible to know and difficult to estimate; few métis children are mentioned in seventeenth-century historical records.[25] Although they are hidden from sight, it seems clear that the vast majority of interethnic partnerships and reproduction in the St. Lawrence Valley occurred within unions that more closely matched Amerindian norms than the exacting marital standards of the Jesuits.

Some historians have claimed that promoting interethnic marriages was a central pillar of French colonial policy during the seventeenth century, one in which the Jesuits and royal government joined forces.[26] The reality proves far more complicated. Missionaries and colonial officials no doubt grew aware of the difficulty of changing native sexual practices, and were increasingly presented with the reality of nonsacramental sexual unions between French men and native women. But both missionaries and colonial officials were, nonetheless, on the whole, ambivalent about promoting formal marriages between Amerindian women and French men.

As evidence of the ostensible policy of intermarriage, historians usually cite the words of French explorer and commander in New France Samuel de Champlain. The *Jesuit Relations* record that Champlain promised a Huron party in May 1633 that "our young men will marry your daughters, and we shall be one people."[27] But a closer look at the context of Champlain's words proves that this was not the beginning of a considered French policy to deploy intermarriage toward the goal of building a culturally and racially homogeneous society in New France. Rather, Champlain's invocations of intermarriage came in the context of diplomatic negotiation of the terms of French-Huron military and trade alliances and of Huron willingness to accept Christianity (and, implicitly, French and Jesuit authority). Champlain, adopting kinship concepts familiar to both Huron and French societies, was proposing closer relations between the two groups by using marriage as a metaphor of political and economic alliance and cooperation.[28]

Although Champlain's words should not be understood as a proposal for intermarriage, this is not to say that the French never considered intermarriage as a strategy for integrating natives into French religious and political life. The *Relations* tell us that Jesuit officials did briefly contemplate deploying intermarriage as a tool for sealing relationships between the French and Huron. No sooner was the proposal of intermarriage raised, however, than different cultural meanings of marriage asserted themselves as a virtually insurmountable obstacle.[29]

In a 1637 formal meeting between the French Jesuit Father Superior and Attignawantan (Huron) headmen, for example, a proposal for French-native intermarriage was on the top of the French agenda. The Jesuits formally proposed that the Christian conversion of the people of the village be followed by the intermarriage of some of their young, recently converted women with French men. The Huron demurred on the question of a definitive conversion, and reacted to the request for intermarriage with confusion; from their point of view, they had already accepted the marriage of many Frenchmen into their midst. They would continue to allow French men "to take wives where it seemed good to them." The Jesuits then explained that they did not wish to propose more Huron-style marriages to seal unions between the French and Huron. The French men who had entered such unions, they said, had done so with the purpose "to make themselves barbarians, and to render themselves exactly like [the Huron]." By contrast, the Jesuits "intended by this alliance to make [the Huron] like us, giving them the knowledge of the true God, and to teach them to keep His holy commandments, and that the marriages of which we were speaking would be stable and perpetual."[30]

In this exchange, different marital practices served to define cultural identity and modes of authority; as the Jesuits describe the negotiation, marriage practices became the crux of the misunderstanding that divided the two groups. The passage suggests that in 1637 the Jesuits were eager to see if the sacramental union of French men and baptized native women might indeed transform the Huron community in spiritually significant ways, "teaching" the Huron and giving them access to "knowledge of the true God." But the "spiritual considerations" attendant on the plan for sacramental unions between native women and French men, the missionary Le Mercier reported, were of little interest to the "brutal minds" of the Huron. After reflecting for several days, a Huron representative returned with a series of pointed questions about the terms of the marital contract the French were proposing: What kind of goods were on offer to mark the marital exchange? Would a native woman be expected to follow her husband to France if he returned? What would happen if "of her own free will" she chose to leave him, as was accepted in Huron society? These questions highlighted the chasm between French and native ideas of marital union.

The French tried to "reassure" the natives (how the *Relations* do not tell us) but negotiations broke down. Le Mercier summarized the impasse in this way:

> This is the situation in regards to these marriages. Some of our Frenchmen had thought seriously of going farther, and of carrying out this plan, and the thing seems indeed to be advantageous to Christianity; but some obstacles

were thrown in the way. The matter certainly deserves mature deliberation; many things are to be considered before engaging [Frenchmen] in marriage,— above all, among barbarous peoples like these.[31]

Despite Le Mercier's effort to paint the failure of the marriage plan as a result of French uncertainty about the wisdom of marital alliance among the Huron, the more reasonable conclusion is that it was the Huron who refused to accept the terms the French were offering. The questions Le Mercier reports suggest that the people of Attignawantan were tepid at the prospect of placing their daughters in indissoluble, French-style unions, especially when they saw that most of the advantages of marital alliance with the French could be gained without accepting the strict terms the missionaries demanded.

The *Relations* suggest that, for Jesuits, sexual and marital behavior were inexorably connected with genuine conversion. These convictions shaped Jesuit mission policy regarding marriage, discernible in the *Jesuit Relations* by around 1640. Native sexual and marital customs had, as we have seen, come to be perceived as an obstacle to conversion. In addition, the missionaries feared that indigenous sexual and conjugal habits posed a grave threat of backsliding and apostasy. What would happen if Christian converts faced temptations from unbelieving spouses and lovers, or were offered advantageous alliances outside the Christian community?

The requirements for valid Christian marriage could create conflicting priorities. The Jesuits' greatest fear was apostasy, a spiritual crime that they regarded as individually damning and dangerous to the entire project of conversion; they preferred not to baptize rather than to risk backsliding. But baptism could help promote chaste behavior, and—importantly—by canon law, without baptism no valid marriage could occur. Baptism was not the only hurdle; in order to be united in the marital sacrament, both partners needed to agree to accept the principles of indissolubility and "marital continence." Continence meant, principally, monogamous sexual exclusivity between partners. It might also include observance of Catholic principles about the times, places, and ways permissible for marital sex (e.g., abstinence during penitential times, modesty and privacy to keep sex hidden, no practice of contraception or abortion, etc.).[32] It is simply unclear how these demands were imposed on the longhouse societies of North America, where Amerindians lived in matrilocal extended family households and long hunting trips into the woods were common. As a result, Jesuits were reluctant to perform marriages, except between native converts involved in stable unions with other converts.[33]

The problems created a cascading series of effects on the missionaries' project of conversion. For one thing, the difficulty of imposing Christian marriage could mean delaying baptism for young people, because once baptized a Christian was

forbidden by canon law to contract marriage with anyone but another baptized
Christian willing to accept Christian standards for sexual behavior and indissoluble union. And yet the Jesuits recognized that the structure of Amerindian societies made male-female partnerships as economically and socially vital for natives
as was the case for peasants in Europe. This seems especially to have been true
for men: "To live among us without a wife is to live without help, without home,
and to always be wandering," worried one Huron deeply attuned to the implications of Catholic marriage norms for Amerindian men.[34] In the case of communities whose male populations had been decimated by war, on the other hand, a
surplus of women without partners may have made liaisons with French men
more attractive.

In effect, then, the Jesuits found their conversion efforts hemmed in by irreconcilable socioeconomic and religious demands related to marriage, with consequences that were frustrating for their Amerindian catechumens, such as the two
who demanded

> Either baptize us without marrying us, or else find maidens suitable for
> us. Dost thou wish to cause our perdition? If we should die in the woods,
> or if some accident should happen to us in hunting, what will become of
> our souls? Thou makest us tremble by thy account of the fires and tor-
> ments of Hell, and thou wilt not deliver us from this peril.[35]

Only the young men's threat that they would not march to war unless baptized,
and their solemn promise not to marry a non-Christian earned them "to their
great joy" the baptism they sought.

The Jesuits' strict standards for baptism and sacramental marriage also presented a barrier to the formalization of *mariages à la façon du pays*. The missionaries regarded any sexual union between a baptized Christian (practically
speaking, all French colonists) and Amerindian partner as illicit concubinage. Yet
transforming these unions into valid marriages was more complicated than
merely reading the banns and performing the nuptial blessing. Unless the native
partner (virtually always a woman) had already been baptized, she was technically considered an infidel and her Christian, French partner was forbidden by
canon law to contract marriage with her. Yet in order to prepare for baptism,
some missionaries and convert communities seem to have demanded natives
renounce and atone for their "concubinage," a renunciation that might require
couples to separate.[36] The proper course of action for a missionary faced with
native-style unions between French Christians and unbaptized native women was
already a matter of debate by 1648, when the Jesuit Pierre de Sesmaisons sought
a papal dispensation that would allow French Catholics to marry native catechumens before their baptisms. His request was denied, which is hardly surprising at

a time when European Catholics and the French state were adopting stricter laws governing the formation of licit marital unions.[37]

If implementing Catholic ideals for marriage was a source of problems, there is sign that Jesuit responses to interethnic unions varied by place and evolved over time. In the heart of New France, the St. Lawrence Valley, Jesuit and colonial authorities both encouraged missionaries to chastise French men who "abused" native women, to deprive both partners of the sacraments if their relationship continued, and by about 1670, in keeping with French civil laws, not to marry such couples without the consent of parents and of Jesuit superiors.[38] It also seems that by the middle of the seventeenth century, Jesuit anxieties about sexual relations between French and natives contributed to their increasing efforts to segregate native and habitant populations.[39] On the margins of French settlement, interethnic liaisons do not seem to have been subject to the same strict rules as was true nearer to centers of French population. As the French colony extended outward with French traders, marriages between French men and native or métis women became more common.[40] Few French women were to be found in these remote outposts, and missionaries apparently decided that formalizing the unions that existed was preferable to accepting the moral disorder of habitual concubinage between French Catholics and Amerindians. Nevertheless, the solemnization of such marriages was to remain controversial both in the church and among colonial officials throughout the eighteenth century.[41]

French ambivalence about interethnic marriages also showed the influence of Europeans' notions of gender. The Jesuits and the Ursuline nuns to whom they delegated the task of educating young Amerindian girls considered native women to be the most promising vectors of conversion. At a practical level, the missionaries recognized that the matrilocal extended families typically found in Amerindian longhouses gave women central influence in the religious identity of their communities, more than was the case in the patriarchal conjugal households typical of early modern France.[42] But imported notions about essential feminine qualities also played a role in their focus on women. Although the missionaries feared that native women were prone to licentiousness, they also believed that they were, due to the common characteristics of the female sex, more malleable. They hoped they could thus be transformed into pious Christian women able to bring salvation to their people.[43] Jesuits and Ursulines delighted in examples of Amerindian female devotion; native women impressed and even sometimes worried the missionaries with the ascetic intensity of their penitential practices.[44] The spiritual fervor missionaries saw in these converts made them hope that female converts would marry native men rather than French men, and thereby transmit Christianity to their households and kin much as had the Barbarian women of France's remote past.[45]

Marriage between native women and French men, then, was not necessarily the missionaries' preferred arrangement. Nevertheless, church-sanctified interethnic marriages did take place. Marcel Trudel claims they account for just 1.5 percent of the 449 marriages recorded in New France's parish registers for the period before 1663.[46] The *Jesuit Relations* sometimes mentioned these relatively uncommon marriages to provide evidence for the success of the Jesuits' conversion efforts, and to solicit support for their mission. In 1638, for example, the *Relations* reported that "a worthy and pious person has given a hundred écus for the wedding of a young Savage girl sought in marriage by a young Frenchman of very good character."[47]

Marriage reports helped elicit donations of dowry money from the metropole, part of the missionaries' strategic response to their realization that Indians were unable to amass the start-up capital necessary for the formation of the settled, French-style households they hoped their converts would form. The Jesuits and Ursulines were happy to accept the largesse of laypeople seeking to promote the formation of these settled Christian households in New France. The *Relations* observed that marriages often dissolved because of poverty: "one of the parties is not able to supply the needs and necessities of the other, which causes that other to go and seek them elsewhere."[48] Settlement was important because the missionaries considered it more likely to maintain converts in their faith. Itinerant life threatened to separate converts from the sacraments, not to mention clerical supervision. Hunting expeditions into the forests presented a host of temptations, including sexual temptations. So, as they appealed to potential donors, missionaries extolled the power of a dowry given to a native woman "married to some Frenchman or Christian Savage," arguing that the investment in such a moral example would be "a powerful check upon some of her wandering countrymen."[49] The Jesuits wrote that "certain persons of merit" had established a "perpetual foundation" to provide native couples with small gifts of money to establish their households. Ecclesiastical personnel sometimes worked together to raise money from their own foundation funds to provide dowries for their pupils.[50]

By soliciting dowries from their French readers, missionaries were extending to the colonial environment a conventional type of Catholic Reformation charity offered to support poor women in France. For metropolitan donors, the charitable gift of a dowry, whether offered to a poor French woman or a Huron convert, expressed a conviction that the Catholic sacrament of marriage had the power to convey grace to individuals and to support the integrity of the Christian community. As grateful as missionaries were to collect these gifts, however, there is little sign that French missionaries sought to use them specifically to promote interethnic marriages, as has sometimes been claimed. These dowries were intended to establish settled conjugal households, not specifically to mix "races"—

a concept not yet firmly established in seventeenth-century New France. The missionaries hoped to match native women like the young catechumen Amiskoueian with "a God-fearing man," seeming to subordinate ethnic identity to the ideal of a settled, Catholic conjugal household.[51]

Despite missionary efforts to promote settled, French-style domesticity, however, marital practices were destined to remain one of the most salient markers of cultural boundaries between the French and Amerindian populations. Jesuits had arrived with the conviction that changing the marital customs of Amerindian peoples was an essential step toward their definitive conversion to Catholicism. But, as time wore on, the disappointing results of their missionary work chastened the missionaries, who developed a pessimistic awareness that the harsh conditions and mixing of different belief systems in New France raised formidable obstacles to the marital discipline they had come to expect of their Catholic flock at home. The troubles lay both in the difficulty of transforming native marital practices and also in the seeming ease with which French Christian men, separated from the metropole, adopted Amerindian conjugal norms as their own. When the French state became more directly involved in government in New France, marriage became even more important as a marker of French cultural identity and submission to royal authority.

Marriage by Royal Mandate: Louis XIV's Pronatalism in New France

During the 1640s and 1650s France's royal government was preoccupied by civil unrest and political difficulties at home, and paid little attention to developments in New France. Day-to-day questions of government and economic control had been delegated to the pious Catholic officials of the *Compagnie des Cents Associés* in 1627, which had in its turn ceded much of its control in 1645 to the colony's male householders, or habitants. This state of affairs—a colony virtually unsupervised by the royal government—was hardly in keeping with the push for renewed royal authority that characterized the early years of Louis XIV's personal reign. The young king formally dissolved the Company of New France in 1663 and declared his intention to rule his empire in New France directly.

In practice, the shift after 1663 meant that royal power in France's North American colonies was centralized in the hands of nonvenal officials, the intendant and governor, who communicated with the king and with his minister for colonial affairs—none other than pronatalist Jean-Baptiste Colbert. During the next three decades, as colonial supervision passed from Colbert to his son, the Marquis de Seignelay, population, marriage, and childbearing remained fundamental to royal goals in New France.

As they assessed the results of a generation of colony-building in the early 1660s, French officials in Paris were neither satisfied by the results of Jesuit efforts to Christianize Amerindians nor by the economic development of the St. Lawrence region. A count of settlers revealed that only a few more than three thousand French habitants were to be found in the whole expanse of the St. Lawrence Valley. Although officials in Paris could not have known (as modern historians do) that England's Atlantic colonies were nearly twenty times as populous in 1660, they knew well enough that Louis XIV's efforts to build a settler society in North America lagged far behind those of his principal imperial rivals, England and Spain. The lack of settlers posed serious problems for the colony, as it meant a chronic shortage of the labor needed to clear land for farms and to develop industries like mining and fisheries. The small number of French settlers, surrounded by warring Amerindian peoples, were often insecure and unable to defend themselves. As a result of these factors, Colbert came to see increasing the population of New France as the key first step to making the colony successful. As a result, the history of royal administration in Canada contains one of the earliest and most intense population discourses in French history.

The urgency of numerical increase encouraged innovation. First, it led officials to create a means to measure New France's population: the first nominative census attempted by France's royal government. Colbert demanded that the intendant in New France count all the French men, women, boys and girls of marriageable age, and small children to be found in the French settlements, and then asked him to provide an annual count of marriages and baptisms.[52] Armed with the census and count of marriages and baptisms, Colbert had a snapshot of colonial society that illuminated, in particular, its marital and reproductive habits. The census permitted administrators not just to apprehend conditions thousands of miles away, but to work to change them.[53]

From the moment the king and Colbert began writing instructions for the royal intendants and governors whom they dispatched to the scene, the message of metropolitan officials was clear and remarkably consistent: setting New France on the right course meant growing the colony. In the intense first decade of direct royal control in New France, few missives from Paris failed to remind colonial officials of their duty in this respect: "a considerable augmentation in the size of the colony is the principal end his majesty desires to achieve," explained Colbert to the Intendant Jean Talon in 1665, adding two years later that "the king will gauge the service you render in this charge . . . only by this multiplication of colonists."[54] Even ten years later, Governor Frontenac was reminded that increase was "practically the sole thing you should keep continually in your mind."[55] Numbers, then, provided a basis for evaluating both the colony's success and the performance of its administrators.

The royal government's colonial ambitions were threatened by the fact that few residents of metropolitan France were enthusiastic to try their luck on the other side of the Atlantic. New France did not enjoy a good reputation in the metropole, and the *Compagnie des Cents Associés* had been consistently unable to meet the quota of indentured laborers it was contractually bound to provide. French people associated the St. Lawrence colony with frigid winters and the threat of Amerindian violence. And they were not wrong; in the mid-seventeenth century, the St. Lawrence Valley was experiencing the consequences of a shift in the balance of power between Amerindian groups. Allied by trade and missions with the Hurons and Algonquins, French settlers lived in fear of those groups' traditional foes, the Iroquois, who were expanding their territory through raids and warfare. When the Governor of the French settlement at Trois-Rivières, Pierre Boucher, addressed his plea for more direct royal support for New France to Jean-Baptiste Colbert in 1663, he dwelt at length on the way Iroquois treated their prisoners of war, describing in frightening detail the tortures that constituted "a perfect image of hell" for nervous French settlers.[56] The sense of peril continued throughout the remainder of the century, becoming more serious in the 1680s, after the fragile peace forged between the French and Iroquois in 1667 crumbled.

War and the fear of war contributed to the colony's difficulty in keeping its settlers, but economic factors also played a significant role. Simply stated, it was harder to get rich in New France than in France's island colonies with economies based on slavery. Many of the French men who came to New France did so as indentured laborers, and many of them had come unwillingly; but they were not slaves. After their contracts ended, only a minority wanted to stay and make the enormous labor investment necessary to make settler life profitable. The surest route to riches in New France was, instead, to take off into the woods as a fur trapper and trader, or *coureur du bois,* exploiting the seemingly insatiable desire of European consumers for beaver fur. After making a fortune in the woods, many of these men returned to France. Of the twenty-seven thousand French emigrants who set out for the St. Lawrence Valley in this period, demographers estimate that roughly two-thirds returned to France without leaving descendants in the colony.[57]

For those male emigrants who might have wanted to try their luck at farming or other industrial enterprises, the skewed sex ratio made the formation of a household difficult. In the early 1660s, the St. Lawrence Valley was host to between six and fourteen French men for every French woman of marriageable age. Where would a householder find the female labor, not to mention companionship, to make settler life possible and bearable? Women were such scarce and precious commodities in New France's marriage market that the average age at first marriage for French women in Canada before 1660 was fifteen, around eight years younger than was typical in the metropole. Some daughters of French families were married as early as age ten or eleven. The marriage of such young girls violated French norms—and canon law—emphasizing the competition among and desperation of prospective grooms. Faced with an inadequate supply of marriageable French women, it is hardly surprising that many settler men formed partnerships with Amerindian women, even though few of these women proved willing to leave native communities to partner with a French man in the culturally unfamiliar, backbreaking labor that characterized settler life.[58]

The royal government sought to address these challenges, first, by priming the pump of demographic growth with a significant investment in subsidized emigration from France. By far the most famous of the royal government's efforts to increase the colony's population was the program that sent 770 women of marriageable age to New France between 1663 and 1673. The women sent by the royal government, dubbed by historians the *filles du roi* or "king's daughters," were recruited from charitable institutions in Paris or from surrounding areas like Brie and Beauce. The average *fille du roi* was an orphan in her early twenties who had grown up in an urban environment. Although urban women were, perhaps, unlikely partners in the labor of hewing a homestead out of the forest, when the ships carrying the *filles du roi* arrived in harbor in late summer or early fall, they were met by hordes of men eager to form households. The arrival of the *filles du roi* precipitated a frenzied autumn of marriage contracts and wedding ceremonies. The royal Intendant's last dispatch before the winter freeze that cut off communication with Paris usually noted that the majority of them had already married; only a small number waited more than six months before pronouncing their vows in a church.[59]

The second group of emigrants the royal government proposed as an answer to New France's population problem was the 1,200 soldiers of the Regiment of Carignan Salières. Veterans of action in Turkey and elsewhere, the battle-hardened troops were sent to New France in 1665 principally to address the growing threat from the Five-Nation Iroquois Confederacy. But from early in their mission, the royal government offered fiscal incentives and land grants to convince these men, both common soldiers and officers, to stay in the colony as permanent settlers. Around four hundred of the men took the offer. After providing the men with land grants, Colbert wrote to the Intendant Jean Talon to remind him "it is necessary to work towards their marriage," since only the formation of a household by marriage and the arrival of children would guarantee that the grantee intended to stay permanently in New France and provide the return on investment that the royal government expected.[60]

The transfer of female "raw materials" from the metropole for the marriage market of New France represented significant royal investment in colonial demographic development. The transport of the Carignan-Salières regiment was a military expense, difficult to trace in the intendant's budget, but Intendant Jean Talon's 1669 account records that he had distributed some 6,000 *livres* to more than a dozen officers in order to catalyze their transformation from soldier into

Canadian householder.[61] Yves Landry calculated that the recruitment and transport of the *filles du roi* cost the royal government several hundred thousand *livres*.[62] This was precisely the kind of outlay that many colonial powers resisted, preferring to encourage the more economical solution of local concubinage, which in this case would have meant encouraging *mariages à la façon du pays*.[63] But officials of Louis XIV's nascent empire envisioned a New France composed of countable households defined by legal marriage and legitimate procreation, and French-native unions had already given evidence that they would not meet this expectation.

Promoting the formation of indissoluble, monogamous conjugal households would increase the population, but it was also intended to channel sexual desire toward orderly ends. Much like the Jesuits, colonial officials invested indissoluble monogamous union with a power to discipline individuals and mark the boundaries between civilization and savagery. When they toured the frontiers of New France, officials observed domestic arrangements that crossed the boundary toward savage behavior. These included not only *mariages à la façon du pays* between French men and native women, but other troubling domestic irregularities. Governor Louis Buade de Frontenac reported in 1672 that the shortage of marriageable women caused "a thousand disorders" in French villages. Bachelors sowed mischief in the homes of their married neighbors, creating a plague of adultery and violence. And, in the most remote villages, he found the scarce female settlers were "very at ease" about entering into polyandrous unions.[64] These households were, no doubt, adaptations of household labor needs to the colony's skewed sex ratio. But Frontenac, for his part, was not at ease about households where one woman agreed to sexual and economic union with several men. Polyandry, in seventeenth-century French eyes, was far more troubling than the polygyny practiced in some native villages, because it reversed the "natural" balance of authority in the household, and created confusion about ownership and inheritance of property.[65] Finally, while French officials were loath to name the issue, the predominantly male population of remote outposts hints that homosexuality may have numbered among the "thousands" of disorders they worried about.

Faced with the pressure to grow the population, the crown employed some of the same strategies to promote marriage and reproduction in New France as at home. For example, it promised rewards for early marriage and for fathers of large families with a special *arrêt du conseil d'état* of 1670.[66] The *arrêt* was explicitly modeled on the royal pronatalist edict of 1666, noting the king wished "inhabitants of the said country to participate in the boons His Majesty made to his people" via the 1666 law. In New France, rather than a tax exemption, fathers of ten or more living, legitimate children, none of whom were in religious orders, were promised pensions of 300 *livres,* and fathers of twelve or more 400 *livres.*

Young women who married by the age of sixteen and men who married before twenty were offered a one-time gift of 20 *livres* payable on their wedding day. The *arrêt* also suggested that fathers with more children be granted special honorific status in their parishes.

While the *arrêt* of 1670 was modeled on the metropolitan pronatalist edict of 1666, it strove to be more punitive, because it also threatened penalties for single men who refused to marry, and proposed to fine fathers who postponed the marriages of daughters who had reached sixteen years and sons who had reached twenty. Such measures were even harsher than the taxation of bachelors that Colbert had hoped to impose in France—a measure that had been effectively blocked by the royal courts. In New France, the royal government again sought the means to intervene directly in patriarchal decisions about the timing of minors' marriages, with punitive consequences for unmarried men and for fathers who resisted the royal will. The punitive power sought by royal officials was an expression of the royal government's sense of urgency regarding marriage and population growth. The bold approach also grew from officials' sense that without intermediate institutions (Quebec's administrative council had been suppressed in the colony's 1663 reorganization) or its own native customary law tradition, New France was akin to a blank slate on which the king could write whatever laws he chose.

There is reason to be skeptical, however, that the full panoply of coercive power theoretically available for pronatalist purposes was ever imposed on New France's colonists. New France was thousands of miles from Paris, and even an exchange of administrative correspondence took around six months. In their reports to Paris, intendants and governors highlight their conscientious distribution of pronatalist benefits, but they provide no specific information about penalties they had imposed on fathers reluctant to marry their daughters or sons. Although the provisions of the *arrêt du conseil* made it possible for intendants to threaten penalties, there is no evidence such penalties were in fact leveled on recalcitrant householders who denied their sons and daughters to the colony's marriage market.

The more likely scenario for implementation of the king's will involved the intendant's persuasive power, and ability to offer patronage benefits for those who acted in concert with royal goals. The intendant and governor exercised this power by virtue of the personal relationships they formed with the men and women they encountered. With a population that did not exceed ten thousand souls until the 1680s, it is likely that the royal intendant and many colonists knew one another personally. In his instructions to Jean Talon, Colbert anticipated the influence that the royal government could gain through deepening such personal ties. Talon was to visit every home in New France and to assess each family's needs by "entering into the details of their petty affairs and household matters."[67]

Talon, for his part, reported that immediately after he arrived, he set off on a journey of more than twenty miles, visiting every house along his route. While we might interpret this close surveillance of households in terms of coercion, Colbert discussed it in terms of royal beneficence and patronage. Using the language of family, he directed Talon to "do the duty of a *bon père de famille*" toward the king's subjects in Canada who were "almost like the king's own children." Talon responded in similar terms, promising that he would soon continue in his quest to personally render to all of New France's inhabitants "the most ardent expressions of which I am capable of the tenderness his majesty feels towards them."[68] His dispatch of 1667 notes that he had personally performed the house-to-house surveys of Montreal, Cap de la Madeleine, and Three Rivers, and would have done more of the count himself had his faltering health not prevented it. Rather than coercively promoting the royal agenda, then, it seems that royal officials deployed an affective language of filial obedience and tenderness, in addition to offers of the king's fiscal largesse. In these ways, the intendant tried to move the families of New France toward compliance with royal goals like clearing and cultivating land, establishing industries and trade, and marrying their sons and daughters.

Royal officials understood that their labors would be judged in relation to population figures, and their letters thus stress how busily they intervened in the conjugal affairs of New France's colonists. By 1667, Talon claimed that crowds of soldiers were asking to be provided with a wife and a plot of land to try their fortunes as settlers, and he boasted that he himself had negotiated the marriage of a lieutenant of the Carignan-Salières regiment with the daughter of the governor of the Three Rivers settlement. Eager to advocate for marriage, he reported that hardly a day passed when he wasn't present at the signing of two marriage contracts. His presence at these ceremonies was a symbolic gesture signifying the king's approbation for marriages and, also, the likely occasion for the delivery of the small marriage gifts that the intendant distributed to mark the king's paternal solicitude. Talon's budget for the period of 1665 through 1668 indicates that he had distributed 6,000 *livres* for the marriage of "poor women of this country as well as those sent from France."[69] By according dowries to poor young women in New France and to the *filles du roi* he had sent there, the king himself became a source of dotal charity, supporting the creation of conjugal households, and fulfilling from afar his role as a *bon père de famille* to his "children" in the fledgling colony of New France.

The king's largesse did not include a concerted attempt to promote interethnic marriage. French colonial history has been captive to a persistent myth that the royal government sought to integrate native women into French culture specifically by subsidizing their marriages with French men. While interethnic marriages were neither prohibited nor even discouraged at this time, there is little evidence that the royal government provided money specifically to encourage them. Confusion on this score appears to have resulted from the conflation of royal subsidies for settler marriage with the dotal charity directed toward the Christian marriage of Amerindian converts.[70]

In comparison to the mandates to promote the formation of settler households, directives to royal officials regarding relations with Christianized Indians in the 1660s and 1670s are conspicuously short on references to marriage. Marriage was a means to bind French settlers to the colony, but it was not the royal government's main tool to integrate Amerindians into closer relations with French society. Rather, royal efforts to assimilate natives in the 1660s and 1670s highlighted education (especially language training) and incentives for settlement in proximity to French communities. These were the key elements of the royal government's program of "Frenchification" designed to mold the habits of Algonquian and Iroquois-speaking Christian converts according to French standards, and thereby to incorporate them over time into French colonial society.[71] Rather than rushing young native women to the altar, the royal priority was to educate them in the Christian values and skills that might allow them one day to take up the female role in a society of settled Christian households. Significant royal funds were allocated toward this end. Whether such women found husbands among the Christianized native population or among the population of French men looking for brides does not seem to have been of paramount concern to royal officials. It was, rather, the quotidian practices and the gender roles associated with French conjugal life—settled domesticity and indissoluble monogamous marriage within French-speaking communities—that crown policies sought to replicate on Canadian soil.[72]

It is a difficult matter to assess the impact of these promarriage, pronatalist policies. The crown invested its money and administrative power to pressure the people of New France to get married and reproduce consistently for two decades. During this period, in terms of raw numbers, the population in New France more than tripled, from around three thousand in 1663 to ten thousand in 1680. Yet after the government stopped subsidizing emigration, strong growth rates continued. New France's population continued to double every generation until the mid-eighteenth century.[73]

How much of this dynamic growth can be attributed to royal activity is a matter for debate. Consider the question of age at marriage; the royal government aimed consistently to promote early marriage as means to secure population growth, offering gratification payments to women married before their sixteenth birthday. But even before the pressure from Paris, it was not uncommon for women in the St. Lawrence Valley to marry young. Marriages of young girls aged fourteen or fifteen were frequent until the arrival of the *filles du roi* took some of the pressure off the marriage market in New France. To some degree, then, early marriage was a response to the shortage of eligible female partners; the internal dynamics of New France's marriage market generated pressure for early marriage of women. During the seventeenth century, the average age at first marriage for women in New France was nineteen, significantly lower than the age of twenty-two that was the norm in metropolitan France. But for men, who were also offered payments for marrying young (in their case, before age twenty) average age at first marriage in New France hovered at age twenty-eight, a bit higher than the average of twenty-seven for men in the metropole. Overall, then, age at first marriage seems to have been driven more by the shortage of female partners than by pronatalist policies.[74]

In the case of rewards for large families, the internal dynamics of the marriage market again make it difficult to know whether pronatalist policies spurred growth rates. In part as a result of the early age at first marriage for women, bustling, fertile households were common in New France. The average couple could expect to baptize seven or eight children, a rate of procreation higher than the norm in the Paris region at the same time. Families with ten or more children were, apparently, quite common. In 1682, Paris officials asked the intendant, Jacques de Meulles, to inquire about fathers of ten or more who might be eligible for pronatalist rewards. He responded that many of the principal families had more than twelve children. This surfeit of candidates threatened to strain the colonial budget if awards of 300 to 400 *livres* were delivered as promised. Officials in Paris appear to have succumbed to second thoughts, because the awards for large families then disappear from their letters.[75] How many households actually collected such rewards is not recorded in the extant correspondence.

So, while New France's population married early and frequently had large families, historians and demographers have, in general, been skeptical about attributing this demographic regime to the influence of the royal government's pronatalist policies. On balance, they note, New France's demographic growth was not out of line with the growth of other colonial communities, like those in New England. Rather than the result of government activity, the impressive growth of the population is best explained as the result of "the encounter of pre-industrial European demographic patterns with 'New World' economic conditions."[76] Graced with a better diet and lower incidence of epidemic disease, and cursed with a shortage of marriageable women that created endemic pressure for women to marry young, New France's married couples demonstrated rates of reproduction higher than those in France.

While the comparative framework helps us to put New France's demographic growth in context, it threatens to impose a modern, scientific viewpoint that blinds us to the meaning contemporaries attached to their experiences of marrying and procreating in New France. For seventeenth-century observers, it seemed undeniable that there was something prodigiously fertile about the colony, a quality that undeniably affected the French people that went to live there. Indeed, in the letters they sent home, French people marveled that Canada's verdant plains and woods filled with game somehow transmitted their health and fecundity to all the European beings that arrived there. Governor Frontenac, for example, reported being awestruck by the size of the quickly multiplying sheep he saw on his arrival in the colony in 1672, even pulling aside a lamb from Three Rivers because he was "moved with the curiosity to measure it."[77] The health and fertility of French people in the colonial environment was no less impressive. "The French women [in Canada] are pregnant every year," Talon boasted.[78] The Ursuline Marie de l'Incarnation remarked that Canadian families were distinguished by a "superabundance" of children, a condition she termed "marvelous." And the Récollet Chrétien le Clerq made sense of the Canadian couples he met who had baptized as many as nineteen children by explaining that their fertility was "a special blessing of God."[79]

These claims about the miraculous fertility of New France should be understood as a form of religious and political argument. For a society that still believed children came as a blessing to the deserving, the fecundity of married couples in New France seemed to legitimate the colonial enterprise. It suggested that despite the endless hardships and setbacks that the colony endured, the French project in North America was growing and enjoyed the blessing of God.

If hopes were buoyed by impressive fertility, the royal government proved much less successful in its attempts to use marriage as a tool of social discipline. For one, government attempts to attract Amerindians toward the sedentary, domestic life were as much a failure as had been those of the Jesuits. In 1674, Colbert reminded Governor Frontenac (who himself experimented with "civilizing" savage children) to continue the subsidy of 1,000 *livres* to the Ursuline house at Quebec that allowed them to "take the little savagesses and instruct them," arguing that "no alms or charity should be more recommended to all the habitants of the country than this one."[80] But few of the Ursuline's graduates adopted the settled conjugal life that the royal government hoped for. The Ursuline Marie de l'Incarnation, feeling the royal government's renewed pressure to work toward the "Frenchification" of Amerindian peoples, reported to her son in 1668 that after years of effort, "for a hundred that have passed through our hands, we have scarcely civilized one."[81]

The French-born population had also failed to demonstrate the commitment to a settled conjugal life. The effort to push French men toward marriage had in part been conceived as a check against the wandering and asocial profit-seeking of the *coureurs du bois,* trappers who eschewed responsibility for the colony's development in order to amass personal fortunes in the woods. The pronatalist enticements offered by colonial officials did not dim the appeal of the forest. In 1680, the Intendant Duchesneau confessed to Seignelay that he feared sending the yearly census to Paris, as it would reveal that more than eight hundred men had abandoned French settlements for the woods and the fur trade.[82]

As they took measure of the damaging consequences of the fur trade life on the colony, royal officials came to the same negative conclusion about interethnic liaisons as had the missionaries. Just as interethnic unions had not bound native peoples to Christianity, they did not bind French men to the economic and social life that royal officials sought to foster in New France. Interethnic unions failed to generate settled, monogamous, conjugal households that the intendant could count in his census. Rather than promoting the economic and social integration of native peoples into French life, interethnic marriage by the 1680s had come to connote rebellion against royal plans for the social and economic development of the colony. Sometime in the early eighteenth century, the royal government's previous ambivalence resolved into a policy against such unions, and colonial administrators actively discouraged marriage between French men and native women. (Missionaries, for religious and moral reasons, did not always follow these directives.)[83] By the late years of Louis XIV's reign, French men's liaisons with native women became an emblem of New France's resistance to imperial domestication.

When they sought to explain why French settlers resisted organization into orderly conjugal units, colonial officials cited the temptations of quick profits, the lure of illicit sexuality, and settler men's naturally insubordinate character. These temptations made them unwilling to accept the weighty responsibilities that characterized the ideal French *père de famille*. Governor Jacques René de Brisay, Marquis de Denonville, reported upon his arrival in the early 1680s that the large number of *coureurs du bois* had "inflicted serious injury on the colony, by physically and morally corrupting the settlers, who are prevented [from] marrying by the cultivation of a vagabond, independent and idle spirit."[84] Rather than investing the money they earned from the fur trade toward householding and the improvement of colonial infrastructure, the *coureurs du bois* devoted it to conspicuous consumption. For colonial officials, this irresponsible spending created more disorder. It led to no improvement in the colony and suggested a desire to ape the consumption styles of their social betters. And, in terms of marriage policy, royal officials complained that the wealth gained by *coureurs du bois* led the haughty men to refuse to marry their daughters (probably métis women) to regular, upstanding settlers. The pattern frustrated royal goals and denied potentially valuable female labor to the colony.[85]

Even among settler families, frontier conditions challenged colonial officials' visions of conjugal order. In the 1660s, Pierre Boucher, governor of Three Rivers and an ardent promoter of New France, reported proudly that settlers in New France typically had many children, who "grow up well formed, tall and robust, the girls as well as the boys." But he also hinted at a problem with Canada's young people: "they are, generally speaking, intelligent enough, but rather idle, that is to say it is difficult to get them to attend to their studies."[86] Governor Denonville, a generation later, viewed the situation as dire: "the youth [i.e., young men] of Canada are so badly trained, that, from the moment they are able to shoulder a gun, their fathers dare not say a word to them."[87] Insubordinate to the natural authority of their fathers, colonial officials feared young men born in the colony would fall victim to the same bad tendencies as had their predecessors, abandoning their duties to become responsible *pères de famille*.

Whatever the aspirations of these children, the hard life experienced by settler households did little to advertise the benefits of French-style conjugal life. Colonial officials even came to recognize that the large families typical in New France impeded their goal of reproducing a familiar, "civilized" conjugal order there. Seeking to understand the attractions of the forest for New France's young men, Denonville noted that they were often pushed there by need as well as pulled by economic and sexual opportunity. "What can their fathers do for them?" he asked, as they "have no bread to give them, and have I know not how many children to support."[88] The Bishop of St. Vallier concurred that both the reproductive success and poverty of settler households posed a threat to ideals of domestic order, although he painted the threat in moral and sexual terms. The children of such fecund households were often forced to share beds, which promoted "frightful irregularities" he chose not to identify more precisely.[89]

French missionaries and officials had arrived in New France believing that marital and family practices were a key marker of the transformation from "savagery" to civilization. Colonial policies sought to remake domestic life in the hopes that by transplanting a social order based on monogamous, indissoluble marriage and fertile domesticity, the wilderness would become the envy of the Sun King's rivals. While the royal government believed it had succeeded, in some measure, in promoting the rapid demographic expansion of the New France colony, colonial officials were well aware that their efforts to deploy marriage as a tool of social discipline and colonial integration had been less successful. By the turn of the eighteenth century, when Paris's investments in promoting marriage had all but ended, marriage tended to show up in colonial correspondence in a different guise than it had a generation earlier. Rather than the key to the colony's success, as it had appeared in the 1660s, officials frequently bemoaned the decline of the colony's conjugal order. The intimate relations of humans never lost their centrality to the colonial project, but talk of marriage became shorthand for the perils and disorders that continually troubled the colonial enterprise, as the king's male and female subjects forged their own domestic arrangements with seeming disregard for metropolitan norms.

Implementing Pronatalist Policy

Not long after the registration of the 1666 pronatalist edict at Paris's *Cour des aides,* or royal tax court, in December of 1666, a father of twelve living children residing in the hamlet of Brinon-l'Archevêque set off to the seat of his local *élection,* or tax district, in the town of Joigny, southeast of Paris on the Yonne River. He carried with him his marriage contract, copies of baptismal documents, and sworn testimony documenting the fact that he was the father of twelve children, born in legal marriage, none of whom had taken religious vows. He made his declaration before an officer and went home the satisfied bearer of a sentence exempting him from royal direct taxation just as the edict had promised.[1]

Some years later, in 1671, this *père de famille nombreuse* experienced a tragic event all too common for parents in this era: one of his children died. Now a father of eleven, he was one child short of the twelve children he needed to be eligible for the tax exemption provided by the king's edict. The tax collectors in Brinon returned him to the rolls to pay his share. Determined to fight, the father set off yet again to Joigny to implore the *élus* to grant him a reprieve from the hardhearted numeracy of the collectors. The *élus,* venal office-owning royal officials often favorable to privilege—and, it must be said, notoriously corrupt—did take pity on this former father of twelve struck by misfortune. They ordered the collectors of Brinon-l'Archevêque once again to strike his name from the rolls.[2]

But the matter did not end there. The father's coparishioners in Brinon, many of whom were themselves fathers with children, were unwilling to accept a sentence that bypassed the precise number of living children required by the king's law. As they saw it, it was unjust to award a former father of twelve the tax exemption. The decision of the *élus* threatened to change the nature of the law by setting a precedent that would make prolific reproduction into a basis for a permanent fiscal privilege. We can imagine the resentment of the father's neighbors: By what right could this man who had fewer children than the number set out by the king's edict claim to enjoy a privilege that excused him from contributing to the parish's tax bill, thereby resulting in a higher bill for them? To be sure, this father had eleven mouths to feed, but they also worked hard to provide for their children, sometimes nearly as many. In the end, the parish judged the case significant enough to appeal the sentence of the *élus*. Their appeal forced the judges of the Paris *Cour des aides* who had registered Louis XIV's pronatalist edict five years before to revisit questions about the justice of exempting prolific fathers from taxation.

The conflict that began in Brinon-l'Archevêque takes us to the heart of questions about the day-to-day functioning of government in early modern France, in particular the tax system and the officials who operated it. This chapter follows the consequences of the royal government's experiment in using the tax system as a tool to "make all the king's subjects wish to have many children," as Colbert had put it, by offering fiscal privileges for those who married and reproduced prolifically. The benefits the king's pronatalist edict offered—exemptions from serving as tax collector, from billeting soldiers, from legal guardianship burdens, and from civic guard duty for men with ten children, and the prize of all these plus exemption from the *taille* for men with twelve—had been intended to recognize prolific fathers' reproductive service to the state, and to in some way offset the financial burdens of raising a large family.[3] But the benefits quickly became entangled in the complex local politics of tax repartition of communities like Brinon-l'Archevêque. Eventually, the problems arising from the pronatalist program became so severe that Jean-Baptiste Colbert resorted to a legal revocation of parts of the 1666 edict in order to limit pronatalist privileges. The chapter begins by discussing privilege as a tool of state formation in the Old Regime. It then explains the particular challenges posed by pronatalist policies, which generated competing interests at the local level, made tax collection more cumbersome, and inflamed endemic complaints about inequity. Finally, it explores the crown's conflict with venal officeholders, asking why they did not align with the crown in its quest to impose legal limits on pronatalist privileges. All in all, the royal government's effort to use the tax system to shape reproductive behavior foundered on the shoals of its need for cooperation from subordinate officials, a need that effectively limited Louis XIV's ambitions to extend his governing power into new realms.

Privilege as a Means for Governing

With its offer of incentives intended to control behavior, the pronatalist edict of 1666 employed a typical Old Regime means for governing. It used the offer of tax privileges as a solution to the problem of how to induce compliance with government goals. In literal terms privilege means "private law," a special dispensation that grants its holder (an individual or corporate group, for example) some concession from the laws and rules to which others are subject. Such a literal definition, however, hardly does justice to the significant role that privilege played in structuring the relationship between the centralizing kings of early modern France and the society over which they ruled.[4] With only a fledgling bureaucracy to implement his policies, the French king relied heavily on his power to grant subjects a reprieve from taxation, only one among the many legal favors his sovereign power entitled him to give in return for his subjects' cooperation. The concession of privileges was "the great means of royal action," one of the most powerful tools for governing wielded by the early modern French state.[5]

The French government relied on privilege to build the state. Most critically, the sale of privilege, attached to property in venal offices, provided a vital source of personnel and capital for the cash-depleted monarchy from the sixteenth through the eighteenth centuries.[6] Privilege also served to promote economic and social behaviors considered useful to the common good. A grant of privilege, for example, could protect craftsmen, indemnify the risk a businessman took in starting an industry, or reward those who provided civil services like mail delivery. In this way, privilege became an important tool for economic development.[7]

For the government, privileges were essential because they extended the government's capacity to implement social and economic policies through its existing judicial and fiscal institutions. For their bearers, privileges were both financially and socially beneficial; they shielded an individual's wealth from taxation, and also marked elevated status in the hierarchical social system. Paying taxes was what commoners did, while tax exemption placed one in the company of noblemen, ecclesiastics, and other groups perceived to serve the common good more honorably than laboring by the sweat of their brow. This reciprocal exchange of service and collaboration with state goals for tax exemption—"the economy of privilege"—was fundamental to the governing practices of the Old Regime.[8]

Fathers acted as mediators between household and state in this economy of privilege. Early modern law empowered fathers, as heads-of-household, to guide the fortunes of their families, so it was often to fathers that the king offered privileges, even when household subordinates might be most implicated. In the age of Louis XIV, the royal government tried in a number of different ways to use privilege to guide paternal decision making. Fathers in the city of Auxerre, for example, were offered tax exemptions if they sent three daughters to learn to make lace in the workshop Colbert's client, Madame de Voullemin, established in the city.[9] In this way, the royal government offered fathers privileges in order to recruit the young, female labor force it sought in order to animate a nascent industry. In the years leading up to the Revocation of the Edict of Nantes, the government offered privileges to Protestants for converting to Catholicism.[10] In one instance, the king granted a minor office that came with tax privileges to a Protestant Sieur Combles "if he will convert with his ten children," thereby compensating this *père de famille* with a reward that could help him better provide for his children—whose spiritual aspirations, it bears noting, were not considered to be independent of their father's will.[11] These examples illustrate that the royal government considered tax privileges valuable enough to reshape family strategies, even valuable enough to provoke religious conversions. The 1666 pronatalist edict employed a similar logic; by altering fathers' perception of the economic self-interest of their families, the government hoped to inspire fathers to want more children, and thereby to change couples' procreative behavior.

Not all privileges were equal. Privileges offered to favor industry or achieve specific goals were meant to have specific limits. They were not like the privileges that came with venal offices, which were family property that could be passed down through generations, and they did not confer nobility. This distinction did not stop some fathers of many children from stretching their pronatalist claims to imply that the king's pronatalist edict had, in effect, intended to ennoble men who had twelve children. One Sieur le Cauchois, caught in a search for usurpers of noble status, asserted that his twelve children ought to earn him the reinstatement of his title or, at the very least, a tax exemption; royal officials prudently refused to consider this claim.[12] Le Cauchois was not alone, and his claim illustrates the confusion that could grow when tax privileges were attached to questions of family and filiation.

Essential as they were, privileges created serious problems for the royal government. Most notably, they increased the complexity and difficulty of tax collection. Taxpayers quite naturally sought to protect their wealth and enhance their status by obtaining or even illegally claiming a privilege—indeed, the government depended on this desire to achieve its ends. But as privileges expanded, more of the kingdom's wealth was out of the royal government's fiscal reach. Tax exemptions also intensified the inequities of the tax system, engendering resentment and resistance to the government's fiscal policies, especially in the years before Louis XIV's personal reign. Convincing French subjects that it was their duty to pay their taxes regularly had proven especially difficult amidst the economic and political crises of the 1630s and 1640s, a problem that had left the monarchy in desperate fiscal straits.[13]

Jean-Baptiste Colbert worked throughout the first decade of Louis XIV's personal reign to bring order to the collection of taxes, and to impose taxpaying as a discipline on the king's subjects. This meant working to reduce the number of subjects exempt from taxation, or at minimum assuring that those who claimed exemptions had legal title to do so. The attempt to reduce the number of illicit exemptions inspired, for example, Colbert's project to investigate noble titles, initiated in 1665, which forced thousands of noblemen throughout the kingdom to present documents proving to royal officials that they were entitled to claim noble status.[14] From his work attempting to rationalize the system of tax collection, Colbert knew well that new tax exemptions complicated the assessment and repartition of the tax burden, and created additional opportunities for fraud and conflict. However, this did not stop Colbert from creating a range of new tax exemptions; indeed, he had little choice, because the seventeenth-century royal government, with its limited resources and fledgling bureaucracy, had few other means at its disposal to implement its ambitious policies.

Pronatalist policy offers a characteristic example of how the royal government sought to use privilege to enact social and economic policy. It also offers a characteristic example of the problems such privileges could cause. Although the privileges offered in the 1666 pronatalist edict were specific and carefully defined, minor changes to the system of tax collection could have unforeseen consequences. The possibility that a seemingly minor change in tax repartition might engender major problems came as no surprise to the king's provincial intendants, who had busied themselves worrying about the complications and subterfuges they would face implementing the new policy even before the royal seal went on the king's pronatalist edict. Without reliable demographic information, the royal government could only guess how large its new class of privileged fathers of large families might be. Henri d'Aguesseau, intendant in the generality of Limoges, conveyed his impression that it was "a very common thing to have ten or twelve children" there and that, as a result, pronatalist exemptions "would be very significant, carrying off half of the parishes."[15] Other intendants warned that pronatalist policy would inspire sham marriages and false donations to minors from families looking to shield their wealth from taxation.[16] Intendants were on guard for these maneuvers, but the decentralized process of tax repartition and collection gave them limited powers to prevent them. Perhaps in recognition of the limitations of royal surveillance, the edict of 1666 provided detailed instructions on how applicants for pronatalist benefits must document their eligibility, and threatened heavy fines and criminal prosecution for fraud.[17] But the law's threats were just that; I have found no evidence that any of the king's subjects was ever prosecuted for making a fraudulent pronatalist claim. It was clear to royal officials from the outset that using tax exemptions to promote marriage and population growth entailed risks to orderly tax collection. The sections that follow explain some of the ways those risks became realities.

Fathers versus Tax Collectors: Claiming Pronatalist Benefits

The eighteenth-century controller-general Philibert Orry complained to his intendants that the tax system of the Old Regime brought out "all the subtlety and malice of human nature," as every agent within it sought to serve his own self-interest.[18] A brief review of the major steps in tax repartition and collection will help clarify what those interests were. What was at stake in pronatalist policy for local communities and for fathers who claimed pronatalist privileges? As is typical for the Old Regime, regional differences meant a great deal. The following description applies only to the *pays d'élection,* those areas in which the royal government's network of venal officeholders supervised the collection of taxes; these areas, corresponding mostly to the north and central parts of France, seem to have been the only places where the royal government offered pronatalist tax exemptions during the seventeenth century.[19]

The process of tax collection began at the center, where government officials divided the direct tax levy among tax districts, or *élections.* Each local *élection* was deemed responsible for a certain amount of money. Officials of the *élection* divided this amount among the *élection's* parishes. The officials were supposed to be mindful of the rising and falling fortunes of each local neighborhood when they made this division. Each parish's taxpaying residents became collectively accountable for that sum.

Within each parish the residents themselves chose representatives known as *asséeurs-collecteurs* to apportion and collect the money for which their community was responsible. In the areas where the main royal direct tax, the *taille,* was "personal" these collectors relied upon the community's common knowledge about the relative wealth or poverty of particular households.[20] The collectors apportioned and collected the sum for which the parish was responsible, and then were charged to turn the money in to local receivers. Serving as parish tax collector was an unwelcome task that most men avoided to the best of their ability. Collectors had to front the money for any tax they failed to collect from their neighbors. And the responsibility of determining neighbors' apportionment was guaranteed to produce enmity, in addition to being considered "very low and very onerous."[21] This was why the pronatalist edict of 1666 had offered fathers with ten children the privilege of avoiding service as collector.

When conflicts broke out within the parish—as they often did—the parties were supposed to follow a prescribed series of judicial steps. If the conflict could not be resolved by the parish assembly, it was heard first by the officers of the *élection,* or *élus.* Appeals were possible only for sums in excess of five *livres,* and were heard by the regional tax courts, the *Cours des aides.*[22]

This was the system that hopeful fathers navigated in their quest to claim a pronatalist tax exemption. Claiming such a privilege was neither simple nor free. Although the edict of 1666 mentioned nothing about potential costs, the registration of a pronatalist claim involved payments of several kinds: fees for copying necessary documents, like baptism certificates; traveling to the seat of the *élection* to register the claim; and sometimes *épices,* or emoluments for the judges. *Épices* could be substantial. In the *élection* of Romans-sur-Isère, in the province of Dauphiné, recorded *épices* for fathers registering their exemptions were usually in the vicinity of twenty *livres,* a sum larger than most of Louis XIV's subjects paid yearly for their taxes.[23]

Perhaps because of these costs, some applicants for pronatalist privileges may have tried to avoid registration of their claims at the *élection,* opting simply to inform *asseéurs-collecteurs* that, as a result of their early marriage or prolific father-hood, royal law had exempted them from taxes. There are a few clues that this sub-rosa technique often worked. At the *élection* of Clamecy, for example, young men sometimes noted that they were registering the fact of their youthful marriage only as a kind of insurance policy against collectors who "were ignorant of, or disdained" the king's declaration that married men under age twenty-five should be exempt. By registering the claim, they sought the official document to bolster their argument. Other men showed up at the *élection* to register their claims only *after* a conflict with collectors was already underway, when they had been placed on the tax rolls against their protestations.[24]

Because pronatalist tax exemptions were registered locally (if, indeed, at all) and because the central government created no mechanism by which *élections* informed the central government about the number of heads-of-household who registered such claims, it is simply impossible to know how many of Louis XIV's subjects were granted pronatalist tax exemptions. The historian's source problem points to a more urgent problem faced by the royal government: officials in Paris could have had only limited information about the amplitude and effects of royal pronatalist policies. In the first few years after the 1666 edict, Colbert sent inquiries to the provincial intendants to gather information about how the prona-talist program was working. He directed intendants to inquire during the course of their yearly visits to different *élections* how many fathers had applied for the benefits. Jean Le Camus responded to a query in 1668 with the news that infor-mants in the *élection* of St. Amand told him it contained not a single father who qualified for the exemption.[25] Jacques Barin de la Galissonnière wrote from Rouen that "few have come forward" but divulged that he had himself discour-aged applicants, "in order not to diminish the number of taxable subjects."[26]

As Colbert must have realized, this information was both unreliable and a sign that his own officials did not share his dedication to the pronatalist program. First of all, the inhabitants of St. Amand had a vested interest in concealing poten-tially qualified applicants. By preventing their neighbors from obtaining tax exemptions, they protected themselves from additional burdens, both bureau-cratic and financial. La Galissonnière's comment suggests that even the royal intendants were dragging their feet, probably because they considered the pro-natalist program too threatening to the orderly collection of taxes. The edict of 1666 created a competing and potentially contradictory priority to the collection of taxes, and some intendants were clearly wary about implementing it.

If intendants managed to express their misgivings with respect, local commu-nities tended to hide their resistance. Why would collectors "disdain" the tax benefits offered to young newlyweds or men burdened with large families? Why were intendants told that no one qualified for pronatalist tax exemptions? The obvious answer is that the tax system gave communities an enormous fiscal interest in resisting new exemptions. An increase in the number of people exempt from taxes meant that the parish's collective responsibility for taxes fell more heavily on those still contributing. *Élus* did not automatically lower a parish's tax assessment because the number of exempt households increased. As a result, collectors were obliged to tap other contributors within the community for more money to make up the difference.

This prompts an important observation about pronatalist benefits and about the government's use of privilege more broadly: tax exemptions were not paid out through the royal treasury. When the royal government offered privileges, it was the privileged subject's neighbors, not the king, who most directly paid the bill. Thus, in the case of pronatalist tax exemptions, it was the other households in the parish—those with fewer children—who were subsidizing early marriage and rewarding prolific reproduction. Because tax exemptions were freighted with social meanings, implying increased social status for their bearers, the financial sting was often joined with significant resentment.

A case from the parish of Saint-Regnobert in the city of Auxerre illustrates the tensions pronatalist tax exemptions caused at the local level. In a 1667 petition to the *élus* for a reduction in the parish's tax bill, the residents complained bitterly about excessive and unjust exemptions of every kind. One of the prime examples they offered to dramatize the injustice of their situation involved a pronatalist privilege claimed by a merchant named Boucher.[27] The petitioners spelled out their need for a substantial tax reduction in the following terms. First, the tax base was shrinking. From 150 households in the past, the number of taxable households had fallen to around 120. Of those 120 households, approximately forty, or more than a third of the parish, could pay almost nothing: "six *deniers,* one *sol,* five *sols,* ten *sols* and other very small sums" was all that collectors could hope to extract from these poor households.[28] At the other end of the spectrum, Saint-Regnobert was home to more than twenty-four tax-exempt households which, gallingly, were "without exception the rich and opulent notables of the parish."[29] Such extreme differences in wealth were not uncommon. Studies of tax repartition in the seventeenth century suggest that the top quartile of taxpayers in most communities paid the lion's share of the bill. Pierre Goubert's examination of late seventeenth-century tax rolls, for example, showed the most highly taxed 25 percent of households paid 68 percent of the total assessment, while the poorest quarter of households paid token sums that accounted for just 2.5 percent.[30]

The merchant Boucher provided a particularly aggravating example to his neighbors. In the past, they claimed, Boucher had contributed over 300 *livres* a year to the parish's tax bill.[31] While it may be that this princely sum was an inflated figure chosen to dramatize their claim, there is little reason to doubt that a few nonprivileged and relatively well-off households like Boucher's paid the highest tax bills in the parish.[32] But then Boucher claimed the exemption due to fathers of twelve.[33] Since then the merchant had paid no taxes at all. To make matters worse, Boucher had won a legal decision that the parish had taxed him in error between 1655 and 1663 (the reasons for this are not spelled out in the records). The *élus* had decided that the parish owed Boucher a refund of all the money it had collected from him during that time, plus interest and legal costs; the fiasco left the parish with a staggering 3,175 *livres* debt.

The situation was grossly unfair, the petition from Saint-Regnobert claimed, because it subjected the parish's residents indefinitely to rates of taxation amounting to double that paid by other citizens of Auxerre. Saint-Regnobert's tax problem was so severe, they claimed, that people had simply abandoned their houses. (Property in parishes reputed to be heavily burdened by taxes lost value and became hard to sell.) This flight, the residents noted, would further aggravate the inequities unless the *élus* reduced the parish's tax bill.

The problems facing householders in Saint-Regnobert illustrate how pronatalist policy, and fiscal privilege more broadly, could aggravate the economic inequalities that fueled taxpayers' resentment. Every new privilege added to a troubling problem for middling taxpayers. Exemptions seemed to flow to those at the top of the pyramid of wealth. This flow of exemptions squeezed the middling taxpayers, especially when economic downturns increased the number of households too poor to pay anything at all. This problem, of course, was ultimately a problem for the royal government, too, inasmuch as new exemptions, like those offered to fathers of large families, hindered its ability to collect taxes, inspiring resistance and engendering litigation that competed for the revenue that did enter tax coffers.

When legal rulings and provisions piled on top of one another, the *asseéurs-collecteurs* faced ever more complicated rules. The pronatalist edict of 1666 relied on these men—most serving unwillingly, and many perhaps semi-literate—to make complicated distinctions among their neighbors. The tax exemptions offered to young married men, for example, asked the collectors to distinguish men who married before the age of twenty, who kept their tax exemptions until aged twenty-five, and those who married during their twentieth year, who were legally entitled to exemption only until age twenty-four. Not surprisingly, there is little evidence that such distinctions were ever successfully enforced. The law further specified that children who died in royal service were to be counted as living, to the benefit of their fathers, while those who took religious vows, but were still living, could not be counted. It offered different benefits to men with ten children and to those with twelve children. The list of specifics went on, and pronatalist law represented merely *one* set of grounds for tax exemption that local officials were expected to implement. To make matters worse, even when the rules were clear, once a taxpayer had acquired an exemption he was likely to resist collectors' attempts to return him to the rolls. It was possible to hold up even rightful decisions with legal maneuvers, subjecting the parish to expensive litigation, the costs of which were passed along to its taxpayers. Little wonder, then, that taxpayers frequently complained about the proliferation of exemptions and the injustice they caused.

Consider the problems of the city of Aurillac, in Auvergne. By the mid-1670s, the city was involved in legal battles with at least four *former* fathers of twelve who, like the unnamed father from Brinon-l'Archevêque whose story opened this chapter, were trying to maintain their privileges after children had either died, taken religious vows, or in some other way ceased to be countable toward pronatalist tax exemptions according to the letter of the law. Returned to the tax rolls, each of these fathers had appealed his case to the *élection*, and in each case the *élus* ruled in the father's favor. The city then appealed the *élus'* decisions to both the intendant and to the *Cour des aides* in Clermont. Copies of the town's accounts from the years 1676 and 1677 survive in the departmental archives, probably because the royal intendant was charged with liquidating the city's staggering debt.[34] From the account for 1676 it becomes apparent that the city had spent over 200 *livres* in that year alone trying to return former fathers of twelve to the tax rolls, a sum equivalent to roughly 10 percent of the town's yearly operating expenses as listed in the budget. The confusion wrought by pronatalist privileges is palpable throughout the accounts. The town council feared the long-term consequences of pronatalist privilege, especially if those who no longer had twelve children in their charge were allowed to retain it. In defense of the significant legal expenditures pursuing their case against former fathers of twelve, town officials noted that enforcing limits on tax exemptions for large families "was an issue of great consequence" to the city's financial viability.[35]

By the 1670s, authorities from parishes up to the pinnacle of the tax system in Paris had grown aware of the problems fueled by pronatalist policy. It is important to recognize that these problems did not indicate an opposition to the idea of promoting marriage and "peopling," nor did they indicate overt resistance to pronatalist policy. The town council of Aurillac, for example, did not actively resist the implementation of pronatalist law. The extant evidence does not reveal how many other fathers were at that moment legitimately enjoying the privileges of fathers of twelve, and there is no sign any of these men were troubled in their attempts to claim the benefits to which the original edict of 1666 entitled them. As was the case elsewhere, Aurillac's problems arose from enforcing the limits that had been laid out in the original 1666 edict. These limits were gradually unraveling in the day-to-day negotiations between taxpayers and local officials.

Sharing the Costs of Fatherhood

The value of the king's reward to fathers becomes clearer if we look at tax exemptions from the perspective of prolific fathers resisting their return to the tax rolls. Take the example of the merchant Boucher, from Auxerre. If we accept his coparishioners' contentions that before his exemption Boucher was paying one of the highest assessments in the parish, and that the number of those who were exempt kept growing, then it is likely that he had a strong incentive to seek a tax exemption. Until he found a way to shield his wealth, collectors would likely have looked to prosperous households like his to bear much of the extra burden that arose from the parish's declining population and poverty.[36]

It is interesting to speculate whether motivations like these might have been an impetus for certain families to alter their reproductive strategies, having extra children to gain the coveted prize of a tax exemption. Such intentions are nearly impossible to trace from surviving evidence, especially since, for a variety of demographic reasons that will be explored in the next chapter, families composed of ten or twelve children were already most likely to be found among the middling and wealthy social strata. Poor families were not only demographically less likely to have many children, but also they paid less in taxes and were less likely to take the trouble to register their claims for tax exemption or to be able to afford the fees if they did.

Yet while tax exemptions claimed by rich fathers of ten or more may have caused problems in tax repartition, it is wrong to conclude from this that average taxpayers found it unjust to consider a man's paternal responsibilities as they calculated how much he should pay in taxes. Early modern political and religious texts identified paternal authority as the natural model for legitimate political authority, and proclaimed that fathers were the keystones supporting the entire edifice of social order. It followed from such logic that fathers were performing a socially and politically vital task in raising and providing for their children. If a man had many children, the burden was no doubt greater. And because the dimensions of a man's family were not held to be the product of individual decisions, neither could they be dismissed as a merely individual responsibility.

The costs of raising and providing for children have not usually figured in historians' accounts of how taxes were apportioned during the Old Regime. But, given the enormous political significance accorded to orderly households, there is good reason to believe that consideration of a man's family obligations formed part of the usual process in which taxes were divided according to each individual's ability to pay, "the strong supporting the weak," as the saying went. Across the social spectrum, challenges faced by fathers of many children were used to make compelling arguments about why particular men were deserving of special consideration. Individual taxpayers' petitions for moderation of their tax assessments, plentiful in the eighteenth century, often mentioned the number of children the taxpayer supported.[37] In a *plaçet* addressed directly to Louis XIV, Pierre Massegres told the king the tragic story of a fire that destroyed his home, barn, livestock, and livelihood; his wife, seeing their property go up in flames, "died of fright instantly," leaving her husband a widower with seven children.[38] Massegres' large family served to dramatize the depth of his suffering and need for royal aid. Similarly, in 1673, the merchants of Aurillac fought new taxes with the argument that "because of the large families that they must support, far from making a profit, they are reduced to poverty and misery."[39] And noblemen, already exempt from royal taxes, wrote letters to Colbert citing their obligations to educate their many children and make them fit for royal service as they sought to tap into the fountain of royal patronage.[40]

Early modern society's ideological commitment to the family as an economic and political unit led by men served to justify pronatalist policies, but the logic of this ideology could be used to critique them as well. The parishioners of Saint-Regnobert, for example, recognized that heads of households with dependent children had weighty responsibilities that naturally diminished their ability to pay taxes. But to dramatize their complaints about the "opulent" rich like Boucher who enjoyed unneeded exemptions, the petitioners identified themselves as hard-working fathers struggling to get by. Those middling heads of household who ended up paying the parish's tax bill, they noted, "are only humble notaries, merchants, mercers, and artisans, most of whom have trouble getting by. [This is] because they possess very little property and have big expenses, *as much from the number of children they support* and their debts as for other reasons."[41] The men noted that they, too, bore a moral and economic responsibility to provide for children, though perhaps not quite as many children as the number the king had set out for reward. In effect, they charged that the king's pronatalist law imposed an arbitrary distinction between equally deserving fathers, and as a result unfairly shifted money from needier households to less needy ones. Rather than helping men meet their obligations as fathers, they charged, pronatalist law was making it more difficult.

It bears remembering that pronatalist policies were not the only way that the costs of child rearing were redistributed in early modern society. The most obvious instances of this redistribution were at the bottom of the pyramid of wealth. The blessing of fertility imperiled families on the margins, and local systems of poor relief often felt the effects. Studies of charity hospitals, for example, demonstrate that children tended to fill their wards. Their numbers rose in times of economic distress, when desperate parents abandoned babies or sent older children out to fend for themselves.

When parish residents saw the prospect of a household's collapse, it was both a moral responsibility and in the community's financial interest to help an over-burdened father meet his obligations. Consider the case of Pierre Dauphin, from the hamlet of Petit-Lens in Dauphiné. In 1710, investigators from the *ferme de tabac* in Dauphiné caught him selling four pounds of contraband tobacco in a public market. Dauphin could not pay the ninety *livres* fine and officials were preparing to take him to prison. But four of Dauphin's neighbors fronted the money for the fine. "His poverty and necessity is well known," they explained, "and besides, he is burdened with a large family and his wife is about to give birth."[42] Dauphin's unhappy predicament called forth his neighbors' charity, but they probably also recognized that keeping him out of jail was a practical response to a communal problem. If Dauphin went to prison, his pregnant wife and children were likely to become even more reliant on the charity their neighbors provided.

Evidence like this suggests that fathers of large families—at least those who were not wealthy—probably already received some form of consideration as taxes were apportioned. But this informal relief differed in significant ways from the pronatalist benefits offered after the king's edict of 1666. The informal system was attached to a notion of charity and economic need, while the pronatalist system attached privilege to precise enumeration of a seemingly arbitrary number of children, and offered it irrespective of wealth or need. Worse yet for the neighbors of these large families, the high fertility necessary to qualify was most often found among the well-off, so pronatalist policy tended to remove from the rolls taxpayers who paid significant portions of the parish bill. This helps explain the reactions of local communities to a seemingly minor change in the tax code; in the majority of cases where they complained about pronatalist privileges, their complaints revolved around the fact that the recipient was a rich man. The loss of his household's contribution was a financial strain and seemed unjust. It explains why communities pursued fathers without the requisite number of children in court.

Negotiating the Boundaries of Privilege, 1672–1683

When the parish of Brinon-l'Archevêque asked the judges of Paris's *Cour des aides* to determine whether the former father of twelve—now a father of eleven—should be returned to the tax rolls, as the pronatalist edict implied, or whether he should be allowed to keep his tax exemption, the court ruled in favor of the father. With this decision, handed down on August 25, 1672, the judges of the royal tax court in Paris established a precedent that would prove influential throughout France.[43] They undermined the limits that royal legislation had sought to build into the pronatalist program, creating a problem so severe that Colbert would be forced, ten years later, to seek revocation of parts of the pronatalist law.

The decision rendered by the *Cour des aides* was printed in the December 26, 1672, edition of the *Journal du Palais,* a recently established legal journal that brought precedents and court decisions to the attention of readers interested in the law throughout France.[44] The journal provided commentary, allowing a glimpse of the arguments made by both sides. The lawyer for the taxpayers in Brinon-l'Archevêque based his argument on a clear, literal interpretation of the

1666 pronatalist law. He noted that the edict specified that in order to qualify for the privilege, the father must have ten or twelve *living* children. It did not make sense that the edict specified that children who had died in the king's service were to be counted as living if *any* child who had died was to be counted as living.

The lawyer representing the father supported the opposite interpretation, claiming that the privilege to fathers had been intended to be perpetual, that is, "from the moment that one has enjoyed it, it endures forever."[45] How did he justify such a counterintuitive argument? He opened by remarking upon the particular value of the pronatalist tax exemption. Even if the interpretation he proposed seemed counter to the letter of the king's edict, this privilege merited, he claimed, a more indulgent treatment in the law, because it was "the most favorable of all exemptions." Flattering royal pretensions of generosity and justice—while arguing in direct contradiction to the king's will as expressed in law—he proposed that "there is nothing more worthy of a grand prince than rewarding the fecundity of marriages, and placing an abundance of goods where the heavens have placed an abundance of children." For this reason, the court should not limit the privilege for fathers. Rather, it should extend it as much as was possible because it was in the king's power to do so and "the favors of a prince should have no limit except for that of his power."[46]

After this flowery opening, the lawyer advanced more conventional legal arguments. The most convincing element of his case was the observation that precedents for pronatalist tax exemptions in Burgundian custom and in Roman law did not cease with the death of one child. Since both of these precedents were mentioned in the king's pronatalist edict of 1666, it was reasonable to assume, he claimed, that the king had intended his judges to follow their example.[47] Besides, he added, it was common knowledge that "in every concession of privilege, one never forgets to include the conditions under which the privilege cannot last."[48] Though the 1666 edict stated that sons who died in service would still "count" for their fathers toward earning pronatalist rewards, the edict had neither specified that a natural death would end the privilege of fathers, nor required fathers to renew their application periodically to establish that they still had the required number of children. As a result, the lawyer concluded that the intention of the king was that fathers of twelve or more children should enjoy lifelong exemptions from their taxes.

Finally, the lawyer appealed to what he called "natural reason" by questioning the justice of canceling the father's privilege when only one of his children died. Having merited the king's reward for exemplary reproductive service, it seemed "some sort of harshness" to punish the unlucky father on the occasion of the death of one of his children. It did not seem just for the king to redouble the father's loss by punishing him financially. Besides, if it took twelve children for a father to "rise" to the enjoyment of his privileged status, could the loss of only one child actually justify his fall? Finally, the lawyer claimed, it was unfair to force the father to bear the costs of the loss of his child alone. The pronatalist edict, the lawyer implied, was based on the principle that the king shared with fathers an interest in producing and raising children. This shared interest constituted nothing less than an enforceable agreement between fathers and the state:

> In the acquisition of the privilege a sort of contract without name is passed between the state and fathers of twelve children. They give their children to the republic, and it gives them in return freedom from all taxes, that is to say, it receives their children as a payment for the charges they had owed, in such a fashion that the father is only the depository [for the children], and the risk of their lives belongs no longer primarily to him but to the republic.[49]

According to the lawyer, prolific fathers entered into a "contract without name," earning their positions as privileged subjects through extraordinary reproductive service to the state. Though he argued against the letter of royal law, the father's lawyer was utilizing the very same ideas that Colbert's legal advisors had used to argue for the political value of pronatalist policies. These ideas claimed that marriage and parenthood were important political institutions, which bound men to the state and ensured their loyalty to the king. If fathers and kings both benefited from the birth of children, he added, then the death of a child ought by rights to be a loss to both.

Did the legal arguments offered by the lawyer convince the judges? A number of other factors are important to keep in mind in order to make sense of this ruling, which quite clearly defied the terms set out in the text of the 1666 royal pronatalist edict. Recall first, that the *Cours des aides* and the *élection* courts were notoriously favorable to privileges of all kinds. Historians have suggested that the judges were motivated by "anti-fiscalism" that caused them to resist the imposition of new taxes and to defend privileges once acquired.[50] Second, relations between the tax courts, Colbert, and the intendants were strained throughout Colbert's tenure as controller-general. At one point, Colbert had even contemplated eliminating the *élus'* venal offices altogether, as they were a common source of resistance to the implementation of royal policy. These venal officeholders may have had some incentive, in other words, to illustrate their power to the controller-general who would have liked to eliminate them.[51]

Whatever their reasons for deciding in the father's favor, the ruling of the *Cour des aides* set important precedents. It allowed fathers of twelve to claim that they should enjoy their tax privileges for the remainder of their lives. After the court's ruling, all that was legally required for a father to claim his tax exemption was that he have twelve living children on the day his privilege was granted. The results of this precedent are visible in taxpayers' behavior; the documents show that many fathers raced to secure their exemptions in the hours after their tenth or twelfth child was born, before the grim odds of infant mortality could rob them of their lucrative reward.

Pronatalist privilege, made perpetual, became an even more valuable strategic opportunity to fathers than before. After 1672, recipients did not lose their exemption if a child died (or more likely, *when* a child died, since even rich families were subject to the diseases and accidents that robbed them of half their children before adulthood).[52] In addition, fathers inferred correctly that they could retain their exemptions if, after having obtained an exemption, their children took religious vows and became "dead to the world." The court's ruling conveniently undermined rules that had seemed troubling to many contemporaries, including those aspects of pronatalist policy that had sought to limit fathers' free choice about the marital destiny of their children, and those that seemed hostile to religious celibacy.

While the court's ruling made the pronatalist tax exemption an even richer prize for fathers, it added to the royal government's headaches. And, because the privileges for fathers had become perpetual, it also made the policy considerably more expensive to the king's taxpaying subjects. This was to serve as the explanation for the 1683 declaration of revocation, in which the king rejected his former identity as benefactor of prolific fathers to take up the mantle of protector of tax justice. The declaration of revocation, registered in January of 1683, explained the king's action in the following terms:

> Against the spirit and the precise terms of our edict, our *Cour des aides* extends the privileges to fathers who cease to have the number of ten or twelve children, despite the fact that [the children] did not die carrying arms in our service; inasmuch as these abuses were turning the edict into a disadvantage for the masses of our other subjects, to whose relief we cannot apply too much application in maintaining equality in the distribution of the taxes necessary to support the expenses to which we are obliged....[53]

The revocation thus revealed the central government's conflict with its own venal officials as it explained the king's change of heart.

The revocation in 1683 was a candid admission of political defeat. During the ten years between the *Cour des aides'* decision in August 1672 and the partial revocation of the pronatalist edict in January 1683, Colbert had tried various tactics to impose boundaries on pronatalist privilege. First, he stopped instructing intendants to publicize the program. He later claimed to have written to the principal officers of the *Cour des aides* in 1672 or 1673 explaining that it had ceased to be the king's will that they execute the pronatalist edict.[54] By 1677, Colbert drew up plans for an *arrêt du conseil* that would place a moratorium on pronatalist privilege until the end of the war; there is, however, no sign this *arrêt* was ever dispatched.[55] In 1679, he was still clarifying to intendants that privileges were supposed to stop when a child died, unless the child died while serving in the army. As he wrote to the intendant of Lyon, "in the event that officers of the *élections* or *Cour des aides* judge the contrary, his majesty will quash their decisions or rulings."[56] Colbert's repeated injunctions, followed by the 1683 change in the law, suggest that his threats had little impact.

Between what Colbert and the intendants told them to do and the contradictory decisions of the *élus* and *Cours des aides*, communities were obliged to work out their own solutions. The evidence indicates that they negotiated with individual fathers of twelve, or, more accurately, former fathers of twelve. For such fathers, gaining a permanent tax exemption had been worth significant trouble and investment; many had been willing to go to court to protect their privileges. In Aurillac, the town council found a way to settle conflicts with its former fathers of twelve, but understandably omitted an explanation of the terms of these private agreements in the budget it forwarded to the intendant.[57] The most likely outcome was that the fathers retained their exemptions by offering some payment to offset the town's debts and legal costs.

Revocation and Beyond

The January 1683 revocation of the pronatalist edict was a formal admission of a political failure rather than a repudiation of pronatalist ideas. In the first place, the declaration of 1683 revoked the edict of marriages only *partially*. It made no mention of the pensions offered to bourgeois and noble subjects, nor of the tax privileges offered to men who married before age twenty or twenty-one. These parts of the pronatalist edict remained (at least technically) in force after 1683, although there is little evidence that the royal government—struggling to support the costs of war—actually paid any pensions in the period after 1672.[58]

Pronatalist privileges proved as difficult to end as they had been to control. By the 1670s communities were negotiating their own means to deal with the gray areas in pronatalist law, so it is hardly surprising that the revocation of the 1666 law did not immediately result in an end to tax exemptions for fathers of large families. When a series of scandals prompted a thorough investigation of tax collection in Dauphiné in 1699, royal inspectors reported among the illicitly exempt a number of fathers of twelve children. These were not all men who had earned and enjoyed the privilege for decades; officials in the *élection* of Romans had continued to grant exemptions to fathers of ten until just months before the inspectors arrived.[59] Surviving records do not indicate whether the *élus* were unaware that the privileges had been revoked, or had simply resisted the royal declaration revoking them. After the 1699 investigation, however, the king did finally succeed in imposing his will; the *élus* granted no new privileges for fathers after that date. In other places, the privileges survived openly despite the king's revocation. Throughout the province of Burgundy, for example, fathers of twelve continued to receive tax exemptions throughout the eighteenth century on the basis of the preexisting Burgundian custom that the 1666 edict had mentioned. The idea, once launched, that prolific fatherhood could be a basis for tax exemption would prove to have a life of its own.

The complexity of tax codes and the written word both helped ensure its survival. Well into the eighteenth century, books published to help local officials navigate the tax system still mentioned the 1666 law, noting its partial revocation in 1683. Printed copies of the 1666 edict, made when it was new to publicize it and instruct officials on its terms, continued to be in circulation.

This information continued to be relevant because fathers of large families still applied to claim the benefits promised in the king's legislation.[60] And, even if the privilege for fathers of ten or more had been officially revoked, the central government continued to help prolific fathers informally on an *ad hoc* basis. In 1714, for example, the royal intendant reduced the taxes of Matthieu Chavagny, a silk worker in Lyon whose goods had been seized after he was unable to pay a fine levied for illicitly selling wine. Having fathered a twelfth child since this unfortunate incident, Chavagny included a printed copy of the 1666 edict with his plea for royal clemency.[61]

Chavagny was not alone. During the period between 1683 and 1760, fathers throughout France invoked the 1666 edict in all sorts of claims for tax reductions, pensions, and charitable aid and—according to royal officials—many of these requests met with success. In 1764, the intendant of finance Lefèvre d'Ormesson would remark that the informal practice of aiding fathers of large families, when finances allowed, had always been the practice of the council of finance. The 1683 revocation had been necessary, he claimed, due to abuses, but the royal government had never strayed from its intention to favor its prolific citizens.[62] Rather than a retreat from pronatalism, then, the revocation of 1683 is best interpreted as a change of tactics. The revocation used the monarchy's sovereign legislative power in a quest to assure that agents of the central government, rather than venal officials, had the authority to determine the boundaries of pronatalist benefits. It placed the mechanism for offering pronatalist aid more firmly in the hands of the growing nonvenal bureaucracy.

Colbert's seventeen-year experiment in using tax privilege as an incentive to alter reproductive behavior provokes two important conclusions. First, it underscores the dangers of using tax privileges as a tool to encourage compliance with royal policies. Privileges were vital to the survival of the Old Regime, but they proved an imperfect means to extend the monarchy's power over social and economic life. In the case of pronatalist policy, officeholders in the fiscal system were not reliable partners in implementing the king's will that *only* men with twelve living children should be exempt from taxation. The vicissitudes of Colbert's pronatalist experiment illustrate what revisionist historians have written about how government actually functioned in seventeenth-century France. Despite the extensive powers the monarchy claimed (the basis for Louis XIV's so-called "absolute" power), the French king's ability to implement his policies was limited by the cooperation he did or did not receive from subordinate officials.

Communities and even, it seems, provincial intendants feared the pronatalist program because of the threat this seemingly minor change in the tax rules posed to the orderly collection of royal revenues. With the 1683 partial revocation the royal government allied itself with those communities, using the king's ultimate authority as legislator to force his judges into line—or, at least, to try to do so. The episode illustrates the barriers that stood in the way of king's ability to enforce his laws, and highlights the opportunities for negotiation at every level of government.

The royal government's difficulties in implementing pronatalist policy, or, more accurately, enforcing the *limits* on its pronatalist policy, also draw attention to the limitations on the monarch's powers to influence family strategies. Pronatalist policy had been crafted in the faith that fiscal privileges were so valuable to France's households that they had the power to shift calculation of interest, displacing parents' incentives to control family size through late marriage, birth control strategies, or the placement of children in religious institutions. If anything, the experiment with pronatalism suggests that this belief was true; fiscal privileges *were* valuable enough that fathers clearly went to great lengths to gain and keep them. It would be difficult to prove that couples purposely aimed to have twelve children so as to secure a pronatalist privilege—few were in a position to perform such heroic reproductive feats—but we might wonder about households that already had eight or nine children; why not a few more? We do know that the option of a privilege was on their minds, for fathers generally claimed their privileges quickly once their tenth or twelfth child was born. Once they had acquired pronatalist privileges, fathers fought tenaciously to keep them. They ignored the tenets of the law that restricted their freedom to place children in religion. Rather than complying with royal will, fathers, it would seem, used pronatalist privileges in their own family interests, taking advantage where they could of the king's expressed interest in their fertility to improve the fortunes of their households.

SIX

Inside the *Famille Nombreuse*

In August of 1735, the Auxerrois merchant Pierre Germain Robinet and his wife Gabrielle Robert celebrated their fiftieth wedding anniversary. The painting commissioned to commemorate the event (figure 6.1) was not quite a traditional family portrait. It featured the prosperous couple standing before the altar of their parish church of Notre-Dame-là-d'Hors. As light streams in the church's windows to shine on the wedded pair, the priest gestures toward heaven, reminding them—as well as the viewer—the divine origins and significance of the marital sacrament.

Thirty-four years before, in 1701, Robinet, then in his sixteenth year of marriage, had claimed the pronatalist privileges offered to fathers of ten or more living children. Six years later, in 1707, he registered his claim for the more lucrative benefits offered to fathers of twelve children. Over these long years, the Robinet-Robert household had been remarkably lucky against contemporary odds of mortality, managing to raise twelve of the fifteen children to which Gabrielle Robert gave birth to adulthood. The painting carefully arrayed their large brood behind them, the children's various adult statuses—prosperous laypeople, a Jesuit, a Carthusian monk, and two nuns—indicated by their dress.

With its deliberate display of the couple's *famille nombreuse,* the painting made a visual connection between the church, marriage, and fertility. Perhaps the priest's homily echoed the celebrations of marital fertility that proliferated in the Catholic Reformation era: "Marriage not only gives heaven a husband and wife," wrote the seventeenth-century Jesuit Thomas Le Blanc, "it makes them trees of life in the center of the earthly paradise of the church, producing fruits worthy of the eyes, hands, and mouth of God."[1] Or, as another cleric put it, "Fertilized with sacramental grace, watered with the blessings of God . . . [marriage] produces the fruits appropriate to it and those that the Great *Père de famille* expects of it."[2]

This chapter turns from consideration of the political significance of French couples' reproductive behavior in order to look inside the households of the *familles nombreuses,* or "large families," identified by royal pronatalist policy. What can we discern about the meaning of marital fertility to French men and women like Robinet and Robert? Pronatalist policy makers left us a record of their thinking, and placed reproduction within what historians and demographers call

FIGURE 6.1   Unknown artist, "Noces d'or de M. et Mme de Pontagny." © Musée Carnavalet/Roger Viollet.

"the calculus of conscious choice." It is more challenging to understand how matters looked from the perspective of the couples who were responsible for procreating, raising, and launching into adult life the large number of children declared desirable to the king. To what extent is it possible to understand the dynamics of couples' actions regarding marriage and childbearing, or the meanings these families attached to their own reproductive lives?

The experience of such couples is difficult for many of us to fathom.[3] The practice of birth control has radically altered ideas of normative family relations. Modern, Western conceptions of marriage rarely contemplate the relationship between men and women that grows from the experience of repeated pregnancies spread throughout a woman's reproductive lifespan. Similarly, relatively few people in the modern West grow up in a household containing many children separated in age by more than a decade. These, however, were common experiences of marriage and family in the age before deliberate family limitation, and attempts to understand the advent of fertility control need to take such experiences into account.

Several generations of patient historical work and overwhelming evidence prove that the fertility regime of early modern France produced relatively few families as large as that of Pierre Germain Robinet and Gabrielle Robert. Historical demographers have shown that the assumption that, before deliberate family limitation, the "average" French woman gave birth to a baby every year or so betrays a fundamental misunderstanding of other kinds of checks operating in the regime. In their zeal to debunk the myth of the large families of the past, however, historians and demographers may have created another false impression, because while far from the norm, *familles nombreuses* were hardly unknown, especially among seventeenth- and eighteenth-century urban dwellers and social elites. This chapter proposes to investigate such families by adapting tools and concepts from historical demography and social history to put the very large families who claimed pronatalist benefits into context. By examining parish registers of birth, marriage, and death and notarial documents such as marriage contracts, wills, and probate inventories, it is possible to compare these unusually large families to the wealth of information we have about French families during this era. These comparisons allow us to understand *how* these couples managed to have so many children; while they cannot tell us precisely *why* they did so, they do illuminate some of the meanings attached to high fertility in an era when growing numbers of French men and women were deliberately choosing to have smaller families.

In order to do this, this chapter focuses on a sample of sixty-two *familles nom-breuses* who lived in the vicinity of two mid-sized French cities between 1666 and 1760. Seventeen of these families claimed their exemptions in the tax district (*élection*) of Romans-sur-Isère, between 1667 and 1699. Romans is located in Dauphiné, southeast of Lyon in the modern French *département* of Drôme. Perhaps best known to historians as the site of the bloody sixteenth-century riot investigated by Emmanuel Le Roy Ladurie, late seventeenth-century Romans was a city of approximately six thousand people with an economy based on trade and manufacturing.[4] It was also the seat of a tax district, or *élection* with a population of perhaps fifty to sixty thousand people.[5] *Élus* in Romans began offering exemptions to fathers with ten or more children in the late 1660s, and continued passing sentences awarding such exemptions until 1699, when royal investigators, noting the revocation of the 1666 pronatalist edict in 1683, forced them to stop doing so.

The other forty-five families in the sample lived in or near the city of Auxerre, located halfway between Paris and Dijon on the Yonne River. Auxerre was nearly twice as large as Romans, a city of between ten and twelve thousand souls around 1690. It was an ancient regional capital, seat of a religious diocese as well as two lower-level royal courts (a *prévôté* and a *bailliage et sénéchaussée)*. It also served as a transport station on the Yonne River, where Burgundian products were loaded on barges headed toward Paris.[6] Auxerre was attached, in legal terms, to Burgundy, so its fathers of large families invoked the "ancient usages of the province of Burgundy" exempting fathers of large families from taxation, a practice current in the Parlement of Dijon since the late sixteenth century, which local documents claimed had been "confirmed" and elevated into royal policy by the pronatalist edict of 1666. After the royal edict was revoked in 1683, Auxerre's prolific fathers invoked the preexisting Burgundian custom, continuing to seek and receive tax exemptions from town officials on its basis until the royal government reinitiated its own pronatalist program in the 1760s.[7]

Other places might serve just as well to provide a sample to study, and indeed many other communities in Louis XIV's France boasted fertile households and fathers eager to claim pronatalist awards. Auxerre and Romans are not demographic anomalies, set apart from the rest of France by a particular attitude toward fertility or by any unusual concentration of very large families. I have drawn examples from these two areas purely for reasons of expedience; in both places, local records were preserved and catalogued in such a way that applications for pronatalist tax exemptions proved readily identifiable amid the mass of mundane administrative business that occupied local officials on a day-to-day basis.[8]

While Romans and Auxerre were not extraordinary in demographic terms, there is an important characteristic of the sample to note: although Old Regime France was a predominately rural society, nearly every father claiming a pronatalist award in this sample lived in an urban area or practiced a profession or trade. The skew toward urban dwellers and professionals is illustrated by the following statistics: the city of Romans accounted for only about ten percent of the population of the *élection* of Romans, yet twelve of the seventeen recorded recipients of pronatalist rewards in the *élection* were residents of the city of Romans. Of the five fathers of large families claiming rewards, but not living in the city of Romans, recipients included two notaries, a merchant, a lawyer, and one man described as a *bourgeois* of the town of Serres (population ca. 1,000). And just one man among the sixty-two families claiming rewards in Auxerre claimed an agricultural occupation: Charles Gounot, a *laboureur,* or yeoman farmer, who lived in the hamlet of La Croix Pilate.[9] The predominance of urban dwellers, it turns out, is less a bias of the sample than the predictable result of the demographic patterns operating in the late seventeenth and eighteenth century. Some fathers of large families lived in France's rural villages; but large families were simply more common in urban areas, a result of specific urban customs of marriage, labor, and child care.

Social and Demographic Origins of the *Familles Nombreuses*

It was a common cliché in the seventeenth century to assert that "children are the riches of the poor." But large families, at least those receiving pronatalist tax exemptions, were most commonly found among the middling and elite segments of urban society. Overall, pronatalist award recipients were most likely to be fathers from their cities' middling ranks and to be socially tied to the artisanal and mercantile sectors.[10] Families from the lowest ranks of urban society, those who earned their living as day laborers, are totally absent from the group who claimed pronatalist awards in Auxerre and Romans.

The dowries recorded in marriage contracts confirm these families clustered in the middling ranks of the urban social hierarchy. In Romans, the brides who went on to become prolific mothers in the second half of the seventeenth century brought dowries ranging between 500 and 4,000 *livres* to their marriages. Marie Ogier, daughter of a deceased merchant, used her inheritance to constitute her own dowry of 1,500 *livres* in 1669 when she married Leonard de la Balme, a "*practicien*" (or small-town lawyer) in the town of Vizille, not far from Romans.[11] Marguerite Sautes married François Lambert, a merchant stocking maker, in 1657 and brought 600 *livres* to their union.[12] Romans was a center of textile trading, and the brides of its cloth merchants, as well as their daughters, were dowered with around 3,000 to 4,000 *livres.* Claudine Golin, daughter of a barrister in the court at Vienne, received 3,000 *livres* from her natal family when she married the merchant Barthelemy Michel in 1671.[13] In Auxerre, the social profile of fathers claiming pronatalist tax benefits reached somewhat higher into the urban hierarchy to include men who owned offices, such as Edme François Precy, chief clerk at the local salt-tax bureau or Edme Leclerc, a judge in the presidial court.[14] As a rule, however, the men claiming pronatalist privileges were a cross section of their cities' middling ranks: master artisans, merchants, notaries, innkeepers, and lawyers, for example.

Middling-rank urban families dominate for several reasons. First, such families had the wealth to make the trouble and expense of claiming a tax exemption worthwhile. Second, in demographic terms, these families were simply more likely to qualify for pronatalist rewards. Middling and elite urban families in seventeenth-century France adopted habits of marriage and childcare conducive to the production of very large households: they married relatively young and employed wet nurses. As a result, large families were likely provided both spouses survived through the woman's childbearing years. Marcel Lachiver's pioneering study of the town of Meulan between 1660 and 1739, for example, showed that among couples who married before the woman was twenty-five and whose marriages were not broken by death before the woman reached menopause, nearly half—49 percent—sent ten or more infants to the baptismal font.[15]

In the late seventeenth century, the average age at first marriage for France as a whole hovered at twenty-three or twenty-four for women and twenty-six for men. Age at first marriage tended to be even higher in urban areas than in rural ones (around twenty-six or twenty-seven for women and twenty-eight or twenty-nine for men).[16] Against this background of French brides typically in their mid-twenties, the mothers of large families in the sample stand out. For those whose age at first marriage is known, nearly all married while relatively young, usually between the ages of eighteen and twenty-one; one was only sixteen.[17]

The postponement of marriage was one of the linchpins of the "European Marriage Pattern" that tended to restrain population growth in preindustrial Europe. In general, demographers explain it as the combined result of social expectations and economic pressures; young people did not marry until they could set up an independent household, and doing so often meant that brides whose families were unable to dower them worked for as much as a decade in order to amass the necessary funds. For our purposes, it is important to recognize that the expected demographic dynamic was reversed in the situation of large families. If belated marriage meant women spent more of their fertile years unmarried, early marriage exposed women to early and frequent pregnancies.[18]

Among the families who qualified for pronatalist awards, brides' natal families usually provided their dowries, and, we might assume, exercised some influence over the timing of their marriages and, potentially, the choice of their husbands. Jeanne Corré, for example, was not quite nineteen years old when she married Edme Tangy on January 14, 1734. Her father was a master *charcutier* (maker and seller of pork products) and an alliance with Tangy, a butcher, suggests her match may have been made within her family's occupational network. In other cases, it was the death of parents that help explain the timing of an early marriage. Françoise Marie's father had died, but she was accompanied by her uncles on the day in 1665 when she signed a marriage contract. The prospective bride, aged twenty, promised all the money she had inherited or might inherit as the dowry for her marriage with Christoffle Devalloys, a merchant and the son of a notary who lived in her home parish of St. Barnard de Romans.[19] Each of these youthful marriages would produce families of more than ten children.

Despite the women's relative youth on their wedding day, these were not cases of child brides claimed by older, more established men; when men's ages could be determined, they were younger than average, too. Claude Lesserré, who went on to become a surgeon at the Hôtel Dieu in Auxerre, was twenty-three when he married Magdeleine Guilbert de la Tour, just shy of her twentieth birthday. Their union produced at least twelve children. Christophe Nombret, a master pastry chef from Auxerre, was twenty when he married nineteen-year-old Anne Bourdeaux; the couple had fifteen children together in the next twenty-one years. In general, then, the fathers in these households were slightly older than their wives, but in no case of first marriage was the groom more than five years older than his bride. This pattern matches French marital norms of the day which, in general, disfavored major discrepancies in the ages of partners, especially for first marriages.[20]

It was more than youthful marriage that allowed these couples to enter the ranks of those rewarded for their fecundity; it was also simple luck against the grim reaper. Those couples who claimed pronatalist awards typically experienced long marriages unbroken by the death of either partner. In Romans, couples who claimed rewards for having ten children had been married for an average seventeen and a half years at the time they made their claim. Data from nearby Lyon in the eighteenth century shows that only 34 percent of marriages lasted more than fifteen years, and that the mean length of union was twelve and a half years; for France as a whole during this period, only about half of marriages would survive twenty years.[21]

The likelihood that marriages would end due to the death of a spouse worked to make large families far less likely. Surviving partners usually remarried, but even the temporary interruption of conjugal life usually meant that fewer children were born. In 79 percent of the households (forty-nine households out of sixty-two) that claimed pronatalist awards in Romans and Auxerre, all the children in the household were the product of a single marriage and shared the same mother and father. Households with ten or more children born in successive marriages account for only ten out of sixty-two cases, or 16 percent, in part due to the administrator's unwillingness to count children from widowed women's previous marriages among the ten necessary to qualify for tax benefits.[22] A long-lasting, stable union was the most usual source of very large households.

A steady reproductive rhythm typified these households. In most cases, wives gave birth to their first child around a year after the marriage.[23] Then, among these couple, babies followed one after another every year to year and a half for fifteen or more years. Fecundity did not make the households immune to the ravages of infant mortality, however; their children appear to have suffered rates of child and infant mortality about average for urban environments of their era. As a result, in order to claim the award offered to families with ten living children, most women had given birth on average thirteen times before the day when their husband registered a claim for a pronatalist award.[24]

A closer examination of one family can help illustrate how the demographic patterns that characterized these *familles nombreuses* translated into the real experiences of individual couples. Nineteen-year-old Marguerite Dormoy married Claude Prevost, a medical doctor, in June of 1675. A prompt ten months later, in April of 1676, she gave birth to their first child, a son named Jean after Marguerite's father, who became godfather to the child. Dormoy was pregnant again by the fall, and the next spring, in May of 1677, thirteen months after Jean was born, she gave birth to a daughter, Barbe. Pregnant again the following fall, she gave birth in May of 1678 to another son, Edme. The reproductive rhythm slowed only slightly after this third child. Babies followed every fifteen months or so: Claude, Charles Basille, Pierre Charles, Marguerite, André, Nicolas, another Marguerite (her sister, the first baby Marguerite, had died since then), Jean Baptiste, François Germain, and Jean Florentin. On October 2, 1691, at age 35, Marguerite gave birth to the fourteenth baby, a girl named Marie, who was baptized at the parish church of Notre Dame-là-d'Hors.

In just over fifteen years of marriage (184 months) Marguerite Dormoy had been pregnant for 126 months, over two-thirds of her conjugal life. Although it was Dormoy's fourteenth delivery, the birth of daughter Marie in 1691 marked the first time she and Prevost had been the parents of ten children living simultaneously, as they had already buried three sons and the first Marguerite. One son had died at two days old. The three other children died between ages two and three, during what was, statistically speaking, a dangerous transitional period after children were weaned, when many succumbed to disease. Recognizing the fragility of infants' lives, on the day after Marie was baptized, Claude Prevost claimed the privilege offered to fathers of ten children. Though it is very tricky to read intentions from demographic evidence, it appears possible that the couple tried to stop after Marie's birth. One last child—their fifteenth—was born to Dormoy and Prevost almost five years later, in 1696, when Dormoy was forty years old.[25]

It is difficult to consider Marguerite Dormoy's life without being stunned by the demands that reproduction placed on her body. Her story was not the norm, but neither was it especially rare among the urban women of her day. Contemporaries recognized health dangers in repeated pregnancies, and believed that women were likely to suffer from complications when births followed one another in such rapid succession. Such fears would seem to be borne out by the statistics demographers have assembled about the mortality risk faced by women in preindustrial societies, which suggest that giving birth ten, twelve, or more times did pose significant risks. A first birth posed a 1.8 percent risk of death to a mother. The danger then fell to below 1.1 percent for successive births, only to begin to climb again from the seventh birth. Twelfth births and those afterward were, statistically speaking, the most dangerous, causing maternal death approximately 2.6 percent of the time.[26] Such figures refer only to mortality risk and do not take into account chronic health problems, not to mention the emotional demands associated with repeated childbearing and child rearing that extended over decades.

Wet-Nursing and the *Famille Nombreuse*

More than any other factor, the practice of hiring wet nurses holds the key to understanding the reproductive history of couples like Dormoy and Prevost. Wet-nursing has a statistically observable effect on childbearing patterns. The hormone prolactin, secreted by breast-feeding women, inhibits ovulation and works to increase the average time that elapses between births. When early modern French women turned the care and feeding of their infants over to others, the demographic evidence plainly shows that they became pregnant again more quickly, and—as a result—had larger families.

In his study of Rouen, Jean-Pierre Bardet found records that allowed him to distinguish women who fed their own children from those who paid others to do so. He found that the average birth interval (that is, time between successive births) among women feeding their own infants was 27.2 months. For women using wet nurses, the average interval fell to 20.6 months.[27] Among the *familles nombreuses* of Auxerre and Romans, intervals were often even shorter; the average interval between births among the eleven households whose entire reproductive history was reconstructed from parish registers was 16.5 months. Other data strongly suggests families who collected pronatalist rewards hired wet nurses to feed their infants. In several cases we know that a child was born because of an entry for the baptism in the parish register, and can assume the child died because his or her father did not list the child as living in his application for a pronatalist award; yet there is no entry in the family's home parish register recording the child's death and burial. Given the quality of the registers, which do record infant deaths with regularity, the likely explanation for these omissions is that these "missing" children died while in the care of a wet nurse and were buried outside the family's home parish.[28]

The *familles nombreuses* of Romans and Auxerre were far from unique in choosing to have their infants fed and cared for by others. An ancient custom, wet-nursing somewhat suddenly took off in late sixteenth- and seventeenth-century France. By the eighteenth century, it was a typical practice among many urban social groups. Historical demographers estimate that half the children born to middling and elite families in Paris were fed by someone other than their biological mother during the first year or two of their lives.[29]

Wet nurses sometimes moved into the family home, but it was probably more common for parents to send infants to live with wet nurses in rural villages. The economic ties that linked urban families with the rural communities that provided their food and domestic laborers, in this sense, stretched to include the exchange of urban newborns. Prescriptive literature exhorted parents to choose wet nurses carefully, and there is evidence that parents did so when they could. None of the families in Romans or Auxerre left direct evidence of their relationships with wet nurses, but evidence from seventeenth-century fathers' *livres de raison*—family diaries and account books—can help fill in the picture. Near seventeenth-century Limoges, François Bastide's wife gave birth to ten children over the course of fifteen years. He mentions in his *livre de raison* that a wet nurse for his seventh daughter, Anne, arrived in his house just two days after the child's birth in 1676, and stayed until the child was twenty-one months old. But the next two children born in the Bastide household were sent out, to be nursed by the wives of men to whom Bastide leased rural land. That is, Bastide and his wife entrusted their infants not to strangers but to families below them in social status to whom they already had economic ties. The children's presence on land Bastide owned suggested a desire to find nurses whom the couple knew well and trusted.[30]

Bastide noted that the fee he paid to one of these nurses was twenty-four *livres* per year. By the mid-eighteenth century, fees for wet nurses ran to perhaps seven or eight *livres* per month; for a journeyman artisan household, this sum would have made at least 20 percent of a monthly budget.[31] Middling and elite families were, of course, better able to afford these costs. At the other end of the business arrangement, wet-nursing offered an important source of income for rural women. Travelers and government officials sometimes noted that wet-nursing was a common industry in particular rural areas, where peasant families supplemented strained household budgets by taking in nurslings.[32] Proximity to a town was an important benefit. Wet nurses who lived near an urban area with parents seeking care charged more. Parents who could not afford these elevated prices had to choose between sending their child farther away—making surveillance of the child's care more difficult—or placing them with women who cared for more than just one child in addition to their own. When infants received inferior care, death rates soared.

Like other parents, the mothers and fathers in our sample of large families chose to send their infants to wet nurses for a variety of reasons. For some families, paying someone else to feed and care for children was an economic necessity. In many cases, securing care for infants was the only way for women to continue working, and their labor was often necessary to the household's economic viability. Urban women provided crucial labor to family enterprises, making the choice to hire a wet nurse a rational economic decision. Work needs probably motivated the decision to use wet nurses among some of the large families in Auxerre and Romans; fully one-third of the large families in the sample from Auxerre and Romans (twenty-one out of sixty-two) made their livings in artisanal occupations, including food and clothing trades where both partners' labor was essential.[33]

But household labor needs were not the only reason to hire a wet nurse, and cannot on their own account for the dramatic expansion of the practice in the seventeenth and eighteenth centuries. Demographers surmise that another reason for the growing popularity of the practice may be the Catholic Reformation church's strict demand for conjugal fidelity. As is true in many cultures, early modern Europeans believed that sexual activity when a woman was nursing posed dangers to the infant. Medical texts argued that sex drew blood away from the breasts, diminishing the quality of the lactating woman's milk. Moreover, if the woman conceived again while nursing, her pregnancy might cause the loss of her milk, a situation that gravely threatened the infant already born in an era when no safe alternative to breast milk existed. But the taboo on sexual activity during breastfeeding placed difficult demands on couples. Religious reform movements closed brothels and railed against nonreproductive sex, emphasizing that the conjugal bed and potentially fertile intercourse were the sole legitimate way to quench the fires of the flesh. They reminded both partners of their solemn obligation to provide this licit outlet for their spouse. Wet-nursing may have risen in prominence in part as a means to negotiate these contradictory demands. By hiring a wet nurse, a couple solved the dilemma by placing the physical demands of nursing and the burden of abstinence elsewhere.[34]

This is not to say that Catholic moralists universally accepted wet-nursing as a good solution. Their complaints fell with unequal weight on women. Some writers complained that the custom of employing wet nurses signified that women were unjustly refusing their maternal duties. The Jesuit Claude Maillard, writing in the mid-seventeenth century, observed that noble women's habit of sending their children away "cannot be without great prejudice to the love that ought to exist between the mother and the child."[35] In addition, because nursing was believed to ruin a woman's figure and sap her beauty, some writers assumed that women chose to send their baby to a nurse out of vanity rather than economic or moral necessity. These sorts of indictments, associating wet-nursing with a corruption of women's natural, maternal sentiments, reached fever-pitch in the mid-eighteenth century. Writers under the heady influence of Rousseau decried sending one's child to a wet nurse as a "cruel and unnatural act" in which women "fail . . . in their duties as citizens, as wives, and as mothers."[36] But, it is important to note, moralists did not condemn wet-nursing in all cases. In the case of a wife, "Jeanne" who wanted to nurse her own child, for example, the eighteenth-century Catholic writer Fromageau determined that she could refuse her husband his conjugal rights and thereby protect her milk supply—but only "if, on account of her poverty, she cannot have it fed by another woman."[37] In cases such as Jeanne's, clerics advocated hiring a wet nurse as an expedient solution to the problem of balancing a woman's obligation to her husband and to her child.

From the standpoint of modern Western society, where infant formula is available at every grocery store, wet-nursing may seem like an unusual transfer of a physically intimate task to a stranger and outsider to the family. At very least, it suggests some of the potent differences in the ways family and privacy were constituted in early modern Europe. Wet-nursing thrived in a society where both middling and elite families were accustomed to domestic servants performing intimate tasks such as emptying chamber pots and aiding with dressing and bathing; even sharing a bed with a servant was not uncommon. Sending a child to a nurse was in many ways little different than the array of other services that these groups relegated to their (generally female) social inferiors. Ironically, rather than being a sign of an absence of privacy, it is possible to argue that the practice of hiring wet nurses fostered greater privacy and intimacy within the conjugal household, by removing small children from the parental bed and reinforcing the primacy of the intimate sexual bond between husband and wife.

In the eighteenth century, those concerned about population matters would add their voices to the outcry about wet-nursing. Given that fact, there is some irony in the fact that the level of fertility rewarded by the royal government's pronatalist policy was unlikely unless couples hired nurses to feed their children. If we look at wet-nursing in terms of labor supply and demand, it seems clear that it was only by farming out their progeny to the rural hinterlands that so many seventeenth-century urban elites managed to produce families of ten or twelve living children. The *famille nombreuse* was based on a division of labor in which urban women's sexual and reproductive work was separated from their nursing and caregiving work. Wet-nursing outsourced the care burden to an underemployed rural female labor force. These rural women's work enabled the reproductive output and—perhaps—fostered the monogamous, companionate marital sexuality of their urban neighbors. The development of wet-nursing was in this sense a kind of shadow of the government's efforts to encourage a particular form of orderly and productive conjugal life; as the royal government rewarded men with large families, it was unwittingly subsidizing a rural child care industry that provided employment to—but, it might be added, probably suppressed the fertility of—poor, rural women.

Contemporaries were aware that age at marriage and the use of wet nurses affected family size. Consider the explanation the noted playwright Jean Racine offered to his son, Jean-Baptiste, then aged twenty, about why he had refused an eligible heiress as a match for the young man. The girl's parents were young, so the couple stood not to inherit for some time. "You run the risk of having only 4,000 *livres* of income, and being burdened with perhaps eight or ten children before you are even thirty years old," the father warned.[38] Racine's estimate was an expected fertility-versus-income projection that argued for postponing marriage in his son's case. The playwright was not opposed to a large family, necessarily, but feared his son would be responsible for one before he had the resources to support it. Similarly, it was generally known that breast-feeding had an impact on fertility; the royal intendant in New France, Jean Talon, for example, had once suggested that a way to increase the colonial population might be to prohibit Indian women there from the extended breast-feeding that diminished the number of children they bore.[39]

Seventeenth-century men and women, then, realized that marrying young and using wet nurses might increase the size of their families. The fact that they did not always or immediately act on this knowledge in order to limit births should not be surprising. Parental and child mortality meant that calculation was still uncertain. The possibility of planning family size was weighed against other factors: an opportune match, the demands of work, and the convenience of childcare. In the welter of everyday decision making, limiting family size did not always rise to become the highest priority.

Fertility, Procreation, and the Catholic Reformation

The Catholic Reformation, in particular in its teaching about marriage and the family, shaped attitudes toward fertility in complicated ways. The reform promoted, in general, a more positive view of marriage that sought to enlist the conjugal household as a stronghold of reformed Catholic life. Recognizing that the majority of Catholics were married men and women, reformers like François de Sales worked specifically to address their spiritual needs. While maintaining the doctrine that virginity and celibacy were more exalted than married life, in the first century after Trent, Catholic reformers amplified their praise for matrimony. Seeking to distinguish Catholic views from Protestants, they reiterated that marriage was not only a holy institution but a sacrament that conferred grace on those who were called to participate in it. Reformers urged the faithful to view marriage as a vocation in which men and women might earn their salvation, and reiterated that to perform the work of a good husband, wife, father, or mother was to do God's work in the world.[40]

But alongside the more positive assessment of marriage, French Catholics remained haunted by the carnal implications of married life, and it was in an effort to redeem this aspect of marriage that fertility became important. In the fourth century, Augustine had explained procreation as the natural purpose of marriage, an account that offered grudging acceptance of the necessity of sexual activity at the same time it embodied deep mistrust of sexual desire and pleasure. Agnès Walch's impressive study of post-Tridentine marital teaching documents changing emphases of Catholic theology. In the late sixteenth and early seventeenth century, Catholic writers attenuated the Augustinian focus on the procreative purpose of marriage. Inspired by Humanism, they elevated the "mutual aid" offered to one's partner—in other words, companionship and affection—to rank as the first "good" of marriage. But, the Augustinian tendency returned and became dominant as the influence of the austere spiritual style known as Jansenism took hold in French dioceses in the late seventeenth and eighteenth centuries. As a result, in the words of John Bossy, "couples were advised of their duty to breed more Catholics with an insistence which left little or no room for the refinements of conjugal gratification."[41]

Most of Louis XIV's subjects received religious instruction that taught them to regard sexual desire as a reminder of humanity's fallen, sinful nature. It exhorted them that the only licit outlet for that desire was intercourse within marriage, capable of producing offspring, and at an appropriate time (not, for example, when a woman was menstruating, or during Lent). Insofar as it was possible to reconcile a positive view of the marital state with the austere, Augustinian attitude toward sexuality, Catholic writers did so through the argument that procreation redeemed sexuality by fulfilling a providential plan. Consistent with the logic of this argument, married couples with many children were told that they enjoyed the particular approbation of God and that their fertility served to populate heaven and earth.

The new teaching about marriage and the related attitudes about fertility reached parents via the pulpit and in catechisms written by reformers. It circulated in books aimed at laypeople, and in material culture, such as the engravings and paintings like those found in the Romans household of Françoise Robinet. Robinet married the merchant Pierre Gaudo-Paquet in 1647, and, over the next twenty-four years, gave birth to seventeen children; the Gaudo-Paquet-Robinet household was able to claim the tax privileges offered to fathers of ten in 1671.[42] In the aftermath of Gaudo-Paquet's death, Robinet and three of her grown sons became embroiled in a dispute over the estate, and, as a result, the court in Romans ordered a thorough inventory of the Gaudo-Paquet-Robinet family home. The court's inventory offers us a tour of a comfortable seventeenth-century merchant household, with closets full of linens, at least seventeen chairs, mirrors, and the like.

The religious objects in Robinet's home strongly suggest her allegiance to the family-centered piety of the Catholic Reformation. The household was adorned with paintings of religious themes, including a Madonna and Child, a painting of Mary Magdalene, and the grandest, a "large painting in its gilded frame showing the Holy Virgin, Saint Joseph and the infant Jesus that the said Madame Robinet says belongs to her because she bought it since the death of her husband."[43] Robinet also owned books, including a collection of Saints' Lives and a four-volume life of Christ.

The mother of ten owned a copy of one of the many religious guides addressed to Catholic laypeople, the Abbé Cerné's *Pedagogue des familles chretiennes,* which the clerk noted to be "fort vieux" (that is, either "very old" or "well-used"). Cerné's book, popular enough to merit four editions between 1662 and 1684, is an example of an important Catholic Reformation genre: books aimed at providing spiritual guidance to married laypeople, in particular women. It advertised itself as a short and easy presentation of "the principal mysteries of our faith and things necessary for salvation," in clear and simple terms. Organized around the sacraments, the section on marriage began with a definition that adopted the traditional, Augustinian view emphasizing marriage's procreative function: "marriage is a holy and legitimate alliance of a man and a woman, instituted by our savior Jesus Christ for the generation and education of children."[44]

Cerné's text unambiguously argued that reproduction was the principal purpose of Catholic marriage, and offered a spiritual hygiene intended to promote fertility. In order to bring the blessings of God on their marriage, Cerné recommended that couples abstain from sex—though only by common accord—during the major solemnities of the religious year, on Sundays, and Fast Days. He also endorsed the custom, recommended by François de Sales, that couples celebrate their wedding anniversaries through sexual abstinence and prayer. But if these recommendations betray clerics' continued ambivalence about sexuality even within holy matrimony, Cerné soon returned to the importance of reproduction. In answer to the question "Can married people grievously offend God in that which regards conjugal duty?" Cerné's first response was that they might offend God in "refusing it unreasonably" or by preventing, in some fashion, the generation of children.[45]

Cerné further emphasized the essential relation between procreation and marriage with the two sections immediately following his pages on marriage: "Important messages for pregnant women" and "Friendly instruction for midwives."[46] For expectant mothers, he advised a regime of physical moderation and intensified spiritual devotion. Although he recommended nursing one's own children if possible, he also offered suggestions on how to choose a nurse of good moral character. The cleric's section about midwives proposed a system of parish-based surveillance of midwives that was clearly designed to make sure that midwives could not be a conduit of potions to procure abortion. Spiritual guides like Cerné's offered practical guidance and rules for avoiding sin; in relation to marriage, this meant the acceptance of childbearing as a sacred duty.

In their treatment of marriage, some clerical writers invested marital sexuality with spiritual power and encouraged their pious readers to interpret the conception of children as a sign of God's blessing on their conjugal union. Couples with many children might be praised as heroes to the faith. Thomas Le Blanc provided a list of martyred saints who had been prolific parents: Saint Felicity, a Roman mother of seven sons; Saint Sympharosa, another martyr blessed with seven sons; and a married couple, Saint Martial and Saint Nona, parents of eleven who were martyred as Nona carried the twelfth. These saints, of course, had distinguished themselves not just by conceiving many children, but also by raising their offspring to die as martyrs. Still, Le Blanc implied that all Christian parents were potentially contributing to God's providential plan. Fertility was even connected to eschatology in popular understanding. One fertile mother in Clermont, where Parisian Esprit Fléchier traveled in 1665, remarked that the wondrous fertility of Auvergne, where having many children was common, meant that "the day of Judgment would not arrive at our place until long after it had reached the rest of the world."[47] With these stories of the martyred *familles nombreuses,* or the anti-apocalyptic power of a pious Catholic couple's fertility, theologians imaginatively constructed a heroic role for married people and parents in a church where sanctity had long been closely associated with celibacy.

The church and laypeople cooperated to develop rituals celebrating marital fertility, including a custom referred to as the *droit de dîme* (tithing obligation) in which families made a special offering of their tenth child to God. Typically, the child was presented to the parish priest for baptism, who, acting as God's representative, assumed the responsibility of choosing the godparents who, in turn, would give the child its name.[48] The notion of donating a portion of one's children to God recalled the obligation to present a tenth of the harvest to the Church as a gesture of thanksgiving for the blessings of fertility. Strong hints of participation in such a ritual exist regarding at least one of the families who received pronatalist awards. When Etienne Feydel and his wife Magdeleine Monot's tenth child, Claudine, was baptized on October 23, 1678, her godparents were Charles Delconne, the abbot of a prestigious local abbey, and Catherine Garnier, the widow of a local nobleman. Claudine's godparents were from an elevated social status in comparison to the kin and local craftsmen who stood as godparents for her siblings, suggesting that this tenth birth was marked by family and community alike as a occasion worthy of special celebration.

While clerics encouraged parents to welcome the birth of large families, they were not blind to the problems that faced parents of many children. On the whole, however, many more pages of marriage manuals were devoted to instruction and consolation for sterile couples than to those who were blessed with too many. Celibate writers tended to recycle Christianity's stock of traditional comments about the earthly cares that afflicted conjugal life "whether [a couple] have children or not, whether the children are well behaved or not" to conclude that infertility and excessive fertility were just variations on a theme: "unfortunately for them, married people are never without troubles."[49]

For those few writers who addressed the difficulties of the very fertile, the health consequences of prolific fertility were a primary concern. The learned, humanistic Claude Maillard cited Aristotle, as well as "reason and experience" for his conclusion that "animals who make many little ones do not live a long time." For both women and men, he warned, "the too frequent use of carnal pleasures" could cause them, like the biblical Solomon, to age beyond their years.[50] Even in his relatively indulgent treatment of matrimony, the cleric counseled ascetic moderation in terms of sex.

Maillard also appreciated that the burdens of fertility fell unequally, affecting women more profoundly than men. It was women who bore the brunt of frequent pregnancies that "upset the entire economy of the body" only to be followed by the excruciating pain of birth, which all too often caused their death. Once a child was born, it was women who were charged to "clean it, nourish it, swaddle it, clothe it, put it in the crib, rock it, feed it, sing to it, lull it to sleep, and prevent it from crying," all of which meant that "the poor mother is busy night and day, without being able to think or do anything else, and often without any rest at all." The physical challenges of prolific reproduction were joined with emotional trials, and again Maillard seemed to imply that it was women who bore the disproportionate burden. A woman "died a thousand times" from worry over her family's well-being, experiencing her children's afflictions as her own. Her exposure to such dangers increased, he noted, the larger her family grew.[51] Of course, in enumerating the physical pains and emotional vulnerability that afflicted mothers of large families, writers like Maillard were not suggesting that women should avoid them. Rather, their aim was to figure prolific motherhood as a spiritually sanctifying sort of suffering, through which a pious married woman might deny the self in order to serve Christ, represented in the form of her children.[52]

Clerical writers throughout the seventeenth and eighteenth centuries were almost unanimous that the Christian response to fertility was not calculation, but resignation and faith in God's providence. The author of *Christian Instructions for people who aspire to marriage or are already engaged* (1730) thought that one of the benefits that those who married with holy intentions might receive through the marital sacrament was "the grace . . . not to complain that they have too many or too few children, [as children] are the fruit and blessing of marriage itself and . . . it is from God that Christians must expect to receive them." It was unquestionably a sin, he wrote, to prevent children's birth "on the pretense to not have enough wealth to pay for their education and establishment."[53] Although there was variation in the details, the clerical position on marital sexuality remained mostly consistent throughout the late seventeenth and eighteenth century: contraception or sex that could not result in pregnancy was unquestionably sinful. Abstinence had to be agreed upon by both partners, as entering into marriage meant accepting a sacred obligation to provide for the partner's sexual needs. The desire to avoid additional pregnancies on one spouse's part did not relieve her or him from conjugal duty, unless pregnancy literally threatened the mother's life. Even the health of a breast-feeding infant came second to the insistence of casuists on the necessity of either partner to protect the other from sexual sin.[54]

Did couples even try to live by these strict rules? Historians have justly questioned the efficacy of the clerical proscriptions against family limitation, since demographic evidence shows that from the mid-seventeenth century forward an increasing number of couples in France were limiting the size of their families. It nevertheless remains possible that many did so through technically licit means; abstinence and *coitus interruptus* leave more or less the same lack of evidence in parish registers. Further complicating the picture, historians note that many clerics evinced considerable reticence about discussing sex with the married members of their flock. Some religious writers argued that it was more prudent for priests and confessors to avoid sexual topics so as not to introduce from pulpit or confessional the idea of sins penitents had not imagined for themselves. Others noted that their penitents were offended when confessors tried to question them about their sexual behavior. This was a sign, perhaps, of the Catholic Church's success in promoting the internalization of sexual discipline after Trent, but it may also signal the development of a zone of privacy around married couples' sexuality that complicated confessors' attempts to impose sexual discipline. All these factors contribute to our difficulty in interpreting the influence of Catholic strictures regarding the control of fertility.[55]

For some French Catholics, true piety entailed obligation to live one's reproductive destiny as a manifestation of God's will. Avignon's Jean-Baptiste Joseph de Sudre, who fathered eighteen children between 1662 and 1688, cast himself as pious and resigned regarding the size of his family in his *livre de raison*. After a child's death in 1684, he wrote, "the Good God is my master; He gives children, He takes them away, and He knows why." In 1691, when the economic burdens of providing for his large family proved especially difficult, he wrote "never has a year been more miserable for me . . . but, finally, it is necessary in everything to conform to God's will, and since he has given me an enormous family, I must try to the end to raise and support it as honestly as I can."[56] In this semi-public venue (*livres de raison* were often passed on to heirs) Sudre depicted his position as *père de famille nombreuse* as his personal cross to bear, a Job-like test of his faith. His reflection about his large family does not suggest that he was ignorant of things he might have done to avoid fathering eighteen children, but rather that he had chosen for spiritual reasons to reject the worldly calculus that Louis XIV's pronatalist policymakers embraced as they sought to encourage large families.

In an era when conscious choice about reproductive behavior was slowly becoming the norm among France's urban populations, having many children was coming to be seen less in terms of blessing, and more as an example of piety, devotion, and sacrifice. Contemporaries like Sudre believed that parents of many children were frequently tested in their patience and faith. Writing for an increasingly literate lay audience, authors of religious texts argued that pious fathers and mothers who raised large families contributed something of high value to the community of the faithful and, eventually, to the nation. This was an idea with lasting significance; the idealized *famille nombreuse* retained many of these connotations among certain pious groups in France well into the twentieth century.[57]

Managing Fertility: Inheritance and Family Relations

Historians have often assumed that economic motivations drove the trend toward family limitation: parents (specifically fathers) saw opportunity for social advance in concentrating limited family resources toward a smaller number of offspring. These arguments begin from the assumption that large families were an insurmountable economic burden, and that consequently, when strictures on contraceptive behavior weakened, couples increasingly chose to limit the number of births. In a scheme like this, family limitation is depicted as a rational economic strategy that reflected the desire not to divide family assets among too many children.[58]

For all its appealing logic, this explanation glosses over the complexity of the economic and legal situation facing parents and leaves out the cultural and religious factors that also shaped notions of ideal family size in early modern France. In terms of legal possibilities, France featured a patchwork of different legal and customary rules, some granting parents more flexibility than others in their ability to determine how their estates would be divided among their children. Second, not all kinds of family capital were equal; some (like investment capital) could be more easily assembled and divided than others (for example, a noble estate or a venal office). Among the nobility, the customary *droit d'ainesse* ("right of the eldest") allowed parents to give the lion's share of the family patrimony, including the principal residence, to the eldest male child so that he would be able to continue to "live nobly" from the revenues. This rule ensured that noble parents with large families could preserve the lineage's status, if only by permitting them to sacrifice the fortunes of younger sons and daughters to that goal. On the other hand, non-noble parents throughout much of the northwest of France were required by law to divide the patrimony in equal shares for each surviving child. We might suspect that these different systems created different pressures on couples' ideals of family size. Yet ferreting out the relationship between variable legal rules, the practices families actually chose, and parents' complex motivations poses enormous research challenges that explain why little is known about the subject for early modern France as a whole.[59]

With the extraordinary diversity of rules and possibilities, the small number of property settlements from seventeenth-century Romans examined here can only provide a hint of how French parents attempted to solve the dilemma of providing for a large family. Unlike in some other parts of France, the customary law of Dauphiné, where Romans is situated, granted parents significant freedom in determining how their estates would pass to heirs. The law did reserve a specific portion of the estate that had to be divided equally among the surviving children. In the case of families with five or more children, this portion was half the total estate. This half, divided among all surviving children, amounted to the guarantee known as the *légitime*. The *légitime* was meant to ensure each child the chance of establishing himself or herself. But the more children a family had, the smaller the *légitime* would become. For a family with ten surviving children, a *légitime* would be only five percent of the total estate, a slim guarantee that a son or daughter could found a household on a par with the one in which he or she had grown up.

So how did parents behave when they sought to provide for a large family? The evidence suggests that parents with large families did not generally use all the freedom the law offered to "invest" in the greater status of a small number of their offspring. Rather, following contemporary norms of parental obligation and affection, they strove to provide for all their children "according to their condition," and struggled to maintain the family's status without unduly sacrificing the fortunes of the younger children or girls.

The wills of Antoine Sabliere and Marguerite Saligny provide a characteristic example of how parents of many children in the city of Romans coped with the challenge of providing for a large family. The prosperous Sabliere-Saligny family was wealthier than most of the *familles nombreuses* in the sample, but the strategies they chose to accomplish their goals were not especially different than those adopted by less wealthy households.

Sabliere and Saligny married in 1674 and baptized fourteen children over the next twenty-five years. When Sabliere applied for a pronatalist privilege in 1698, the couple had just baptized their eleventh child. In 1707, the couple "in perfect health of body and mind as apparent to all" signed a joint will (*testament reciproque*).[60] After stipulating their wishes for their funerals and pious bequests, each named the other as universal heir. The will then specified legacies for each of their children.

At the time Sabliere and Saligny composed the 1707 will, their household was still composed of parents and ten living children.[61] They had five boys and five girls between the ages of nine and thirty for whom to provide. The destinies of four of the children had already become clear. Two daughters had married other merchants in Romans and a third was a nun at the convent of the Visitation in nearby Crest. Their twenty-year-old son, Joseph, had taken preliminary vows in the Cathedral of St. Barnard of Romans and was on his way to becoming a priest.

The other six children, ranging from twenty-four-year-old Jean-Baptiste to nine-year-old Laurence, were still minors and yet to be "established." Should their father die, leaving their mother as his universal heir, each was promised 4,000 *livres* from their father, 3,000 when he or she reached majority or married, and the rest after their mother's death. Sabliere enjoined his widow to pay for an apprenticeship "if any of the said children wishes to learn a trade before his or her majority."[62] The will also granted the eldest married daughter 2,000 *livres* in addition to what she had received in her marriage contract, and the other married daughter an additional 50 *livres,* to be paid after the death of both testators. The will does not specify what the original dowries promised to these daughters had been, but it is likely that these bequests to married daughters represent efforts to equalize their shares with those of their siblings. Finally, the two children who had taken religious vows were not forgotten. The cleric, Joseph, was promised 3,000 *livres* when he turned twenty-five, as well as the lifelong use of several rooms in the Sabliere family house located "in the large square of this town."[63] The nun Marguerite was promised a token annual pension of nine *livres* (worth a capital sum of about 180 *livres*) "for her own use preventing the monastery from claiming any of it."[64]

Should the children's mother, Marguerite Saligny, predecease her husband, she made provisions to divide the much smaller part of the estate under her direct control (probably about 2,000 *livres*) among the children in very similar proportions, making gifts of 100 *livres* to each of the six children yet to be established as well as Joseph, with smaller gifts to the three established daughters.

The joint will signed by Sabliere and Saligny had a number of legal purposes. First, and most importantly, it sought to guarantee that the surviving partner would have control over the couple's estate. Secondly, by means of the legacies, it designated a minimum inheritance for each child. The legacies balanced the control given to the surviving partner, limiting his or her freedom to designate the way the entire estate would finally pass on to the next generation.

The 1707 will adopted a strategy in the middle, somewhere between the extremes available to Sabliere and Saligny, namely the choice to advantage one heir and a strict equal division among all children. Though the shares given to children appear to have been roughly equal, the couple decided to leave the surviving partner significant freedom to decide the ultimate division of the patrimony. The total size of the estate is not specified in the will. At the same time, it appears that the 4,000 *livres* promised to each child was more than the *légitime* their father was legally obliged to give them. We learn this from the threat the couple leveled near the end of the document:

> And if one or more of the said legatees named above is unhappy about the said bequests and they decide to trouble the heirs of the said Sabliere by forcing an inventory of his assets or by any other means, in that case the said Sabliere reduces to their *légitime* and revokes from that moment the bequest in so far as it is found to exceed the *légitime* for each [legatee] that causes trouble.[65]

The will thus sought to enforce peace among heirs, while maintaining the financial privacy of the estate and leaving a surviving spouse flexibility to meet problems and opportunities that might arise after his or her partner's death.

Antoine Sabliere, it turned out, died before his wife, so Marguerite Saligny played her role as universal heir. In 1729, aged around seventy-six and still "in perfect health," she made a new will reflecting the changed situation of the family and estate. Her first act was to double the pious bequests specified in the original will; as universal heir she was now in control of money that permitted her to have a funeral equal to that of her "beloved husband," alongside whom she wished to be buried. In her new will, Saligny directed additional sums to all her children and to some of her grandchildren; after twenty-two years, the trajectory of each of them was clear. The fourth daughter, Jeanne, had followed the path of several elder sisters, marrying another merchant from Romans. The youngest son and daughter, Antoine and Laurence, are not mentioned in this will; it is likely that they had died in the intervening decades.[66] Of the four surviving sons, Joseph was now "priest and treasurer of the Cathedral of St. Barnard of this town." Another son, André, had married a daughter from one of Romans' other merchant families and set himself up as a merchant in the Sabliere boutique. In the most important clause in the new will, Saligny named as her universal heirs her two eldest sons, Jean-Baptiste and Pierre Louis Sabliere, both of whom were married with children by this point (Jean-Baptiste was forty-seven years old). The will notes that both had already received *préciputs,* or preferential legacies in advance of their inheritance. Both had used these gifts of between 8,000 and 9,500 *livres* to found a merchant company with their eldest sister's husband.[67]

In what appears to be the final disposition of property for this generation, the two eldest brothers inherited shares of the parental estate that appear at least twice as large as those of their non-ecclesiastical brother and sisters.[68] In that sense, as things finally ended up, the Sabliere-Saligny inheritance seemed in some limited ways to follow the strategy of advantaging eldest sons that has long been associated with a "patriarchalist" perpetuation of male right. There are other signs of the tendency to favor sons over daughters, such as the direction of Marguerite Saligny that sums she designated for her grandsons go upon their death "to one of [their] brothers or sisters by order of primogeniture males preferred."[69] Still, the division is hardly the extreme solution to advantage eldest sons that was legally possible. The dowries and gifts totaling around 4,000 to 5,000 *livres* directed toward each of three daughters enabled the women to make favorable marriage alliances, and was more than their mother had brought to her own marriage. Indeed, far from treating its daughters as a liability, and seeing its need to dower them as a frustration of family goals, this large family formed alliances with other merchant families through them. The formation of economic partnerships with brothers-in-law suggests how daughters might play a role in expanding family fortunes. In addition, the final disposition of the estate testifies to the formidable legal power exercised by the widow Marguerite Saligny. The *préciputs* Saligny had given to her sons and presumptive heirs, as well as the still substantial sums she doled out in her 1727 will, attest to the influence she had within the family enterprise after her husband's death.

What, then, can we conclude about the family strategy of the numerous Sabliere-Saligny family? Was there anything about this strategy that specifically addressed the needs of a large family? The first observation to be made is that timing played a very important role. Two factors made timing of decisions especially critical for large families: the pressure of providing for many heirs, and the reality that in a large family, eldest children and youngest children reached maturity at periods separated by fifteen years or more. What seems most notable about the strategy, then, is a choice to postpone final division of the estate. Doing so preserved the ability of the surviving spouse to adjust parental plans to a situation inevitably in flux.

The pattern set by the Sabliere-Saligny family closely resembles the inheritance strategies chosen in more modest homes. When Etienne Mantin, a launderer (*blanchier*), grew ill and made his will in 1714, he left three *livres* to each of his eleven children, who ranged in age from thirteen to thirty-five years old. He then named his wife, Catherine Chavanne, his universal heir.[70] Seven years later, when she in turn fell ill, Chavanne left each of nine children a legacy of fifteen *livres*, citing as the reason for the small gifts the "contracts and debts she has been obliged to undertake for the care, apprenticeship and education of her aforementioned children."[71] Chavanne's will claimed that the fifteen *livres* gifts amounted to each child's *légitime* from both paternal and maternal lines. The remainder of the parental estate she left to the other two children, in this case not eldest sons but her youngest daughters, Marie and Elizabeth, aged twenty and twenty-two years old. Again, surviving documents do not allow us to know precisely how large was the parental estate, or how much each child received. But Mantin, like Sabliere, entrusted his widow with the capacity to manage the ultimate division of the patrimony. Chavanne had assumed responsibilities as universal heir to her husband at a critical moment in the family's generational cycle, when the youngest children were adolescents. Naming her as heir rather than providing individually for these children in his will indicates that Mantin believed the family's interests were better served by allowing his widow to oversee the younger children's education, apprenticeship, and marriage and to make decisions about remaining assets.

While mothers gained significant authority as widows, this does not mean that expectations of appropriate gendered behavior played no role in property divisions. The effort to postpone final decisions about the devolution of property between generations by naming a wife rather than a child as heir could exacerbate underlying tensions as male children were obliged to accept their mother's authority over family assets and wait in uncertainty to know their financial situations. This was the case in another of Romans' very large merchant families, that of Pierre Gaudo-Paquet and his wife Françoise Robinet. Like Antoine Sabliere, Pierre Gaudo-Paquet made his wife his universal heir before he died and expressly forbade the making of inventories in his will. But, unlike Sabliere, Gaudo-Paquet did not make substantial gifts to his children. Leaving each of three sons a small gift of 400 *livres,* he left his wife even more flexibility than had Sabliere. Some seven years after Gaudo-Paquet died, these three sons, with the aid of their "lawyer and curator" (because they were still legal minors) initiated a court case against their mother.[72] Claiming that their father's estate was worth more than fifty thousand *livres,* they charged that the 400 *livres* legacy left to each of them by their father was much less than their *légitime.* Plus, they charged that their mother was poorly managing the patrimony, in league with their brother André, a priest who lived in the family home. In this case, a couple's choice to preserve the flexibility surrounding property division became a source of conflict. The quarrel between Robinet and her sons demonstrates, again, that timing was an important factor in parents' difficult decisions about how to divide their estate. Parents strove to find the right moment to establish children, and meet the minimum expectations of each child about what was fair. Balancing financial interest and children's emotional and material expectations, testators strategized not just to place children appropriately when the time came, but (as Marguerite Saligny had noted in her will) "to prevent the difficulties which could arise in [the] family after [the testator's] death."[73]

Evidence from a very different source, godparenting patterns, provides another subtle indication that the effort to maintain harmony among brothers and sisters may have constituted a particular concern of large families. In general, the patterns of who was chosen to act as godparents in these large families resemble those found in other middling social groups: kin from both paternal and maternal sides as well as occupational colleagues were frequently called to hold infants over the baptismal font. A major exception to this expected pattern comes in the frequency with which older brothers and sisters were called to act as godparents for their younger siblings, a pattern seen in many of the families from both Auxerre and Romans. Sometimes the pattern might involve just a single child acting as godparent to a younger brother or sister, such as Marie-Anne Nombret, who became her brother Guillaume Eusebe's godmother when she was twenty-one years old, or François Mantin, who at age sixteen held his infant brother over the baptismal font and gave him the name "Joseph." In other cases, the pattern was much more elaborate, involving multiple sisters and brothers acting as godparents for younger siblings; the tanner François Bourdillat chose his own sons and daughters, aged from six to eighteen, to serve as godparents for six of his sixteen children.

Historians normally analyze the choice of a godparent as an effort to strengthen relationships between parents and the kin, friends, or patrons they called on to serve in the role.[74] The choice of an infant's siblings as godparents, on the other hand, places the focus squarely on the relationship between godparent and child. Forging these relationships within the nuclear family itself may have been designed to instill a particular sense of responsibility for younger siblings in older brothers and sisters who were on the verge of leaving the parental home and thus not growing up alongside the family's newest arrivals. The eighteenth-century writer Edme Restif de la Bretonne noted that his father used a similar strategy to forge ties of obligation and affection between children born of different mothers: "with a view to creating as many bonds as possible between his first and second families," Restif mentions, "he made the older children godfathers and godmothers of the younger ones."[75] The choice may also have been made in anticipation that an elder child might be charged with parenting, or dividing assets among, his younger siblings. For example, Joseph Marie, the eldest son of a merchant in Romans, served as godfather to five out of ten of his younger brothers and sisters. These godparenting relationships seem intended to bolster the cohesiveness of large families, as if they were insurance against the demographic likelihood that parents of large families might leave minor children behind when they died.

Contemporaries, including Louis XIV's advisors, often charged that parents of large families resorted to monastic professions to "unburden" their estates; the Edict on Marriage had even declared that sons and daughters who had taken religious vows could not be counted toward the number necessary to qualify for pronatalist awards. Local officials showed little interest in or ability to enforce this rule, and in fact many of the families who received pronatalist awards in both Auxerre and Romans placed several of their children in religion. Antoine Sabliere, the merchant from Romans, had eight children who lived to adulthood. One of his sons became a priest and a daughter became a nun in one of the newer Counter-Reformation orders, the Visitandines. Of the ten children of Guillaume Pillard, a "dancing master and player of instruments," in Auxerre, three sons became country curates in smaller towns in the region.[76] The Auxerrois merchant Edme Liger and his wife Jeanne Loyset were awarded a tax exemption as parents of twelve in 1686. They set a record among families receiving the award for large families. Seven of their children took religious vows: two sons became priests, two sons became Maurists, two daughters entered Auxerre's Benedictine convent, and one daughter professed as a nursing sister at the Hôtel-Dieu in Auxerre.[77]

But while many of the large families from Romans and Auxerre placed children in religious orders, there is no reason to believe that they did so primarily as an economic strategy. The common image of children sacrificed to preserve family wealth is far too simplistic. For one thing, theologians insisted that it was illegitimate to force religious vows on anyone; a calling was necessary. This prescription was sometimes echoed in wills. When Pierre Bon, a merchant in Romans, made his will in 1710, for example, he provided an inheritance made of cash, debts, land, and jewelry for his daughter Helaine, then aged twenty years old. But, "in case the said Helaine Bon wants to become a nun," the will guaranteed she would be provided with a "spiritual dowry" in cash instead.[78] We do not know, of course, what pressures Helaine Bon may have faced inside her family, but the will suggests that her father sought to protect her free choice. Also, evidence from wills does not fit the stereotypical image of surplus children being disposed of through religious professions and then forgotten by their families. Daughters in convents were commonly granted small annual pensions in wills. Their parents gave these gifts in addition to the religious dowries they paid to the convent, and directed them specifically for the young women's use. While they were modest sums, they speak to continuing bonds of affection between nuns and their families.[79] Plus, in both the Gaudo-Paquet and Sabliere homes, sons who were priests were granted lifelong use of specific rooms in the family home, showing that children who took vows of celibacy could remain closely tied to the lives of their parents, brothers, and sisters.

Dominique Dinet, who has studied religious professions in the region around Auxerre, employed family reconstitution to ascertain whether larger families were more likely than others to place children in religion. His results demonstrate that family size did not determine from which families professed religious would emerge. In families of similar size and social background, Dinet found some had several children enter the religious life while others had none. Moreover, patterns of religious recruitment were often replicated across generations. Families with few children in religion followed this pattern for generations, as did families with many professions. Dinet argues that instead of functioning as an outlet for families overburdened with children, monastic professions represent a sort of family tradition among devout urban families inspired by certain forms of Catholic Reformation piety.[80]

Evidence from the large families receiving pronatalist awards in Romans and Auxerre support Dinet's thesis that factors other than family size determined which families would give children to the church. There is no evidence, for example, that the artisan families who received pronatalist benefits regularly placed children in religion. Rather, apprenticeship seems to have been their chosen method of accommodating numerous progeny.[81] Religious professions were just one of a number of possible strategies for coping with a large family, and the attractions of various options depended on families' social status, the nature of their business and the depth and style of their religious commitments, not to mention the personality and desires of the children in question.

The small number of inheritance strategies analyzed here provide a limited base from which to draw conclusions; nevertheless, it is clear that they do not fit some of the assumptions that have guided thinking about the relationship between fertility strategies, and the economics of family life in early modern France. Having many children did not inevitably force parents to choose between advantaging one child over his brothers and sisters or accepting impoverishment for all their offspring. Plus, it is not clear that having many children was a terrible disadvantage in certain sectors; among merchant families like the Sablieres, having many children seems to have helped amass the personnel and capital to build a thriving business.

This chapter has argued that a broad range of considerations—not just economic, but also religious, and affective—shaped married couples' responses to fertility in early modern France.[82] Families of ten or more children were hardly the norm in Louis XIV's France, but neither were they shockingly rare. Even with so many children to raise, parents found ways to provide for their offspring and some, it would appear, embraced and celebrated their abundant fertility for reasons beyond the financial benefits that the Edict on Marriage had promised. These observations about large families cannot tell us why an increasing number of couples began to practice family limitation, of course. They do suggest, however, that we cannot assume that all couples sought to have fewer children, or that overburdened parents simply forced their children into religious professions in order to protect family fortunes. Neither decisions about family limitation nor the complex motivations shaping patterns of religious recruitment can be reduced to mere rational calculation.[83] This is not to say, however, that parents did not face difficult decisions in raising, educating, and providing for large families, or that skill, maneuver, and strategy were not part of the picture. Contemporaries knew that mothers and fathers of many children were likely to be beset with cares as they sought to make ends meet, fulfill their children's expectations, and maintain harmony and happiness within their families.

SEVEN

Depopulation and the Revival of Pronatalism in the Eighteenth Century

Novelist Nicolas-Edme Restif de le Bretonne's *My Father's Life* (1779) was a nostalgic account of his youth on a farm in the eighteenth-century Burgundian countryside. The author described how his stern but loving father, Edme Restif, became one of the thousands of French fathers to receive a version of the pronatalist tax benefits decreed by Louis XIV. In 1746, Restif the son tells us, the prosperous farmer complained that his neighbors had set his taxes at an exorbitant level. When the royal intendant, Feydeau de Brou, disovered that Edme Restif headed a large family of fourteen children, he reduced his taxes to a token sum of 6 *livres* annually. A few years later, de Brou's successor Berthier de Sauvigny asked Edme Restif to appear at a gathering so that he might show off this paragon of fatherhood. There, his son reports, the intendant "spoke affectionately to him, and, patting him on the shoulder, congratulated him on his happy fatherhood."[1] The message of both acts was clear: Edme Restif's prolific fatherhood made him a valuable and esteemed subject of the king.

Fathers like Edme Restif were all the more valuable to government officials because they seemed ever rarer. In the years following Louis XIV's death in 1715, the conviction that France enjoyed a population advantage over its rivals faded and a new, pessimistic orthodoxy gradually asserted itself: France was depopulating. Population was understood as a measure of national strength, so contemporaries interpreted population decline as a harbinger of national doom. It was a symptom of a hidden sickness that afflicted France, a "malady of declining" (as the philosophe Montesquieu would put it) that demanded a response.

Anxiety about France's national reproductive crisis was the backdrop against which the royal government renewed its program to reward fathers of large families like Edme Restif. Because most people had come to believe that reproduction responded to human—and thus political—intervention, it followed logically in the minds of contemporaries that their government was at some level responsible for the decline and also accountable for finding a solution.

Did rewards for prolific fathers offer a solution? This chapter examines the revival of the royal government's pronatalist program in its height, the period from 1760 until 1789. It begins by exploring the changed intellectual context in which the idea of rewarding fathers with many children rose once again to become a priority of royal government. Early in the eighteenth century, population was recast as a national weakness rather than a signal strength. By the middle third of the century, concern about the ostensible decline in France's population promoted intensive reflection on the motors of demographic growth, particularly the economic conditions that made marriage and childbearing attractive and possible. At the same time, fears that France's population was declining justified indictments of royal leadership and of changes in marital and sexual behavior. Much of the anxiety came to rest on the supposed corruption of conjugal mores, which caused both men and women to shirk their duty to become fathers and mothers. The government responded to these anxieties by identifying fathers of many children as ideal husbands and fathers, and exemplary servants of the king, who merited royal favor and protection.

Population Crisis and Enlightenment Political Critique

The great irony of the depopulation crisis, decried by hundreds of eighteenth-century writers, was that it turned out to be an illusion. As historical demographers have shown, the population of France was actually growing throughout the eighteenth century. The roughly twenty million French subjects over whom Louis XIV assumed power in 1661 would grow to twenty-eight million French men and women on the eve of the Revolution.[2] Throughout the eighteenth century, France remained the demographic powerhouse of Europe, even if its rate of growth was less stunning than that experienced by England and the German territories.

Despite this trend, most educated contemporaries believed as an article of faith that France's population was declining. Reflecting on the problem, its multiple causes, and possible solutions became something of a national obsession during the height of the Enlightenment. Contradictory conclusions, arguing that the population was in fact growing, published in the 1760s and 1770s by early practitioners of the science of demography, or "political arithmetic," mattered surprisingly little for this anxious public debate. Louis Messance, the Abbé Expilly, and Jean-Baptiste Moheau attempted to apply empirical methods to the problem, assembling a wealth of demographic data that refuted the depopulation thesis. But they failed to convince many of their contemporaries, who pursued their intense interest in population matters because the charge of depopulation was a potent political weapon; reformist writers "had in the back of their minds that the population of France must be declining, because France was badly governed."[3] During the eighteenth century, discussions of population were almost always pleas for political and social reform.

As historians have noted, the significance of the illusory population crisis for political and intellectual life of the Enlightenment era can hardly be overestimated. The specter of depopulation inspired a voluminous outpouring of books and pamphlets that analyzed the problem. Numbering in the thousands, these works addressed population from many angles, proposing social and political changes of every stripe. The attempt to address France's population "problem" pushed both moral philosophy and political theory into radical new territory that the confidence of an earlier age could never have justified.[4]

The first great oracle of France's population crisis was Charles-Louis de Secondat, Baron de Montesquieu, one of the eighteenth century's most influential writers and thinkers. His anonymously published 1721 epistolary novel, *Lettres persanes (Persian Letters)* initiated the depopulation panic. *Lettres persanes* imagined contemporary Europe as seen through the eyes of Persian visitors, urbane outsiders from a polygamous culture who were curious about Western history and social mores. Visiting Venice, one of these visitors, Rhedi, notes being struck in his travels that the West's formerly great cities seem "quite deserted and empty." Rhedi's reading and calculations lead him to a conclusion that had been voiced before Montesquieu's work, namely that Europe's population had decreased precipitously since the glorious days of the Roman Empire. But Rhedi goes further, predicting that without meaningful changes, an "inward defect, a secret and hidden poison" that afflicts the entire world will spell the end of human existence on the earth in less than a millennium.[5] Rhedi and the other Persian visitors go on to catalog the reasons for this impending human extinction, which included religious prejudices (such as the Catholic predilection for celibacy) and a civil government that failed both in its efforts to encourage fecundity and in its responsibility to nurture the children that were born. Under the cover of anonymity, Montesquieu's novel offered an indictment of the Catholic Church and French royal government for negligence that, the author suggested, had squandered France's once redoubtable population advantage.

Lettres persanes set the tone for discussions of population in France for the next two decades. But Montesquieu indeed came to surpass himself, when he returned to the theme of population in 1748's *De l'Esprit des loix (The Spirit of the Laws)*. It was this later work that would be recognized as Montesquieu's masterpiece and become a "master text in the intellectual formation of the mid-eighteenth century enlightened elite."[6] *The Spirit of the Laws* was an encyclopedic attempt to synthesize knowledge about the world's diverse cultures. Montesquieu organized this burgeoning store of information into an argument about how distinct climatic and cultural patterns influenced political regimes. "Many things govern men," he wrote: "climate, religion, laws, the maxims of the government, examples of past things, mores and manners; a general spirit is formed as a result."[7] So complex were the motivations shaping human behavior that changing this "general spirit" was difficult. Montesquieu tackled population questions in Book 23, "On the laws in their relation to the number of inhabitants." His all-embracing consideration opened with a long tribute to Venus, goddess of fertility, from the epicurean philosopher Lucretius's poem *De rerum natura*. He then sought to distinguish humans from the natural world. While animal species were locked into nature's plan for reproduction, Montesquieu catalogued the influences shaping procreation among human beings: "the way of thinking, character, passions, fantasies, caprices, the idea of preserving one's beauty, the encumbrance of pregnancy, that of a too numerous family, disturb [human] propagation in a thousand ways," he asserted.[8] Human reproduction surely responded to the influence of culture and governing institutions; but to what extent would it submit to the will of the legislator?

By the time Montesquieu published *The Spirit of the Laws* most of his readers were probably unaware that the royal government had experimented with pronatalist law nearly a century before; since the revocation of the 1666 pronatalist edict in 1683, the episode had been largely forgotten.[9] In Book 23, however, the author included a terse paragraph reminding his readers of Louis XIV's pronatalist experiment. The philosophe dismissed the Sun King's attempts to encourage fecundity as utterly failed and useless. "Louis XIV ordered certain pensions for those who had ten children and larger ones for those who had twelve," he wrote, "but [turning population decline around] was not a question of rewarding prodigies."[10]

Placed as it was in one of the Enlightenment's most influential works, Montesquieu's brief mention of Louis XIV's 1666 edict served to rescue France's seventeenth-century pronatalist experiment from historical obscurity and to inject awareness of it into an ongoing debate about the kinds of governmental reforms that might address France's contemporary population crisis. Most eighteenth-century writers on population would follow Montesquieu in their belief that measures like rewards for fathers with many children were useless; the rewards could not change the "spirit" shaping reproductive patterns, and were simply no match for the demographic crisis that France now faced.

By the time Montesquieu wrote, the ideas that had made the 1666 edict logical had lost much of their legitimacy. First, Montesquieu pronounced confidently that rewards to fathers of large families were not effective means of growing the population. When he called the large families envisioned by the 1666 edict "prodigies," he reflected his culture's changing reproductive norms; producing ten or twelve children was so uncommon (at least among the aristocratic circles in which he traveled) that a policy structured around such behavior seemed absurd.

At a deeper level, Montesquieu was inclined to reject the holistic king-as-father ideology that had inspired pronatalist law. Indeed, the notion of a "mystic paternity" uniting a beneficent, paternal king with the fathers of his realm was out of step with the philosophe's assessment of Louis XIV's reign. The source of France's depopulation, as Montesquieu saw it, were mistakes the grand monarch himself had made. France's common people had been "desolated by despotism," and "the excessive advantages of the clergy."[11] If French men were avoiding marriage and fearful of having large families, Montesquieu was not inclined to lay the blame primarily upon immorality or a lack of discipline among the king's subjects. Rather, the causes were economic and political. Population was declining because French people lived under a harsh and corrupt government that harassed them with taxation: France's potential husbands and fathers "cannot even nourish themselves," Montesquieu wrote, so "how could they dream of sharing [with a wife and children]?"[12]

What was needed to restore population growth, Montesquieu would conclude in the penultimate chapter of Book 23, was a massive redistribution of land from the nobility and clergy toward the rural poor. This was a radical suggestion, one that undermined fundamental tenets of Old Regime government and of the system of privilege that sustained it. The jurist knew it was impossible for the monarchy to take such a radical step, and the suggestion was little more than a provocation meant to underscore the failures of centralized, interventionist royal power, of which pronatalist policy had been an example and depopulation was a telling symptom. Given the devastating critique of royal government that forms the subtext of Montesquieu's population theory, it is little wonder that he saw rewards for fathers of large families—measures that symbolically reaffirmed the connection between the king and fathers—as ineffectual and even abusive.

However, if Montesquieu's view of the potential solution to population decline was radical on some fronts, it remained deeply traditional on others. The most striking example of his conservatism in matters related to population was his staunch defense of the populationist benefits of the traditional patriarchal family. Aligning himself with ideas that stretched back centuries, Montesquieu held up legitimate fatherhood defined by marriage as the *sine qua non* of civilization. Among animals, he wrote, the female of the species met the needs of the young, and fatherhood was therefore meaningless. But the unique nature of humans was defined by reason, a capacity acquired slowly under the guidance and protection of adult males. Nature had made fatherhood invisible; so human societies had thus been forced to create institutions to make it known. Among "well-policed" peoples, Montesquieu wrote, the institution of marriage served this function. Borrowing in this case from seventeenth-century natural law theorists, Montesquieu implied that the recognition of paternal (and conjugal) authority was an essential feature of civilized existence. Whether in a republic or monarchy, clear links between men and the children they fathered, made visible by the law of marriage, served to guarantee the inculcation of virtues necessary for the preservation of social order.[13]

Montesquieu recognized that other cultures defined legitimacy differently, but went on to reaffirm that the monogamous, patriarchal family was in fact the best arrangement to promote the multiplication of humanity, at least in the temperate climate of Europe. Only legitimate marital procreation could truly contribute to population growth, he asserted, because women who bore children outside marriage faced "thousands of obstacles" that limited their ability to raise children themselves.[14] The philosophe even suggested that the superiority guaranteed to men over women in many European legal traditions promoted fecundity. For example, he argued that inheritance traditions that excluded daughters encouraged larger families, because "the man who has children of the sex that does not perpetuate [the family] is never content until he has those of the sex that does."[15] His population theory also affirmed traditional conceptions of paternal power, including the father's right to arrange marriages of his children.

The role of males in engendering and raising children helped distinguish "well-policed" peoples from their savage inferiors. Neither motherhood nor women's personal aspirations enjoyed much positive appraisal from Montesquieu. The writer insinuated that bearing children was the natural destiny of female nature, or, at least, the sole destiny girls were allowed to imagine for themselves. Men had other options, so it was perhaps worthwhile for governments to dream up ways to get men to the altar; but since only marriage gave women "pleasure and liberty," the philosophe considered it unnecessary to encourage women to become mothers. In sum, then, Montesquieu's demographic writing implied that he continued to see traditional marriage as the linchpin of the social and demographic system; to encourage propagation, it was best not to tamper with the "spirit" of European laws according powers in this system to the *père de famille*.

But, as is often the case in the wide-ranging and idiosyncratic *Spirit of the Laws*, Montesquieu's positive evaluation of paternal authority in Book 23 is contradicted by some of his comments about marriage and gender relations in other sections in the work. When his focus turned from reproductive output to other considerations, the philosophe seemed to endorse an ideal of love, companionship, and free choice as the basis of marriage. Indeed, even in the book on population, when Montesquieu commented on Spanish colonial laws that had forced young people to marry, the philosophe deplored the tyranny of such a policy, asking his readers, isn't marriage "the action that should be the freest in the world"?[16] It was legitimate for a father to force his child to marry, but quite another for a king to do so.

The tensions in Montesquieu's position about "liberty" in marriage and procreation highlight common faultlines in the great effusion of eighteenth-century writing on population. Writers hesitated between a social order represented by the traditional patriarchal household and indissoluble marriage, and one defined by individual liberty and freedom in which men and women might couple for love and pleasure's sake in freely chosen, perhaps temporary unions. Which model, they asked, was likely to produce the most fertile results? Implicit in most of their arguments was the notion that the conjugal and family pattern that produced the most offspring was that which nature desired and which was solely capable of guaranteeing a flourishing and stable nation over the long term.

Montesquieu exercised tremendous influence over the population debate in the middle part of the eighteenth century, but his views were certainly not shared by all his contemporaries. David Hume and Voltaire, for example, were skeptical about the claim that the ancient world had been more populous than the Europe of their day.[17] Other writers would undermine his notion that Europe's traditional patriarchal family was most likely to ensure a flourishing population, arguing that innovations in domestic life including marital freedom, divorce, or increased sexual liberty were vital to release procreation from the stifling limitations that had caused the current crisis.[18] Yet if contemporaries continued to argue about what political and social program might provide the best conditions for remedying France's demographic decline, they were, for the most part, agreed that the measures used by the government of Louis XIV were doomed to failure. Most, like Montesquieu, dismissed France's pronatalist precedent as the error of an ignorant age.

Representing the economic theory that would later be known as physiocracy, Victor Riqueti, the Marquis of Mirabeau, expressed frustration with traditional legislation designed to encourage population. In his 1758 *Ami des hommes, ou traité de la population,* Mirabeau concluded that legal efforts to reform morals, encourage marriages, and reward large families were destined always to be fruitless, like "treating an illness without understanding its cause."[19] Physiocrats argued that only a revival of agriculture—a regeneration of France that began with reinvestment in the fertility of the land—could spur the fertility of its people. From a totally different point of view, Augustin Rouillé d'Orfeuil, a disciple of Rousseau, rejected pronatalist policies even more vehemently: "these laws revolt me," he wrote.[20] In his 1773 *Alambic des Loix,* he catalogued the failures of the French monarchy's traditional policing of sexuality. The habit of abortion, for example, "only too known and too practiced among us," helped to explain depopulation, as well as to illustrate, "the poor constitution of our government . . . and how much it is indispensable to reform it as soon as possible."[21] But laws on the order of those attempted under Louis XIV were not what Rouillé d'Orfeuil had in mind. Measures encouraging youthful marriage, penalizing celibacy, or rewarding fathers contradicted natural liberty and were "attended by a thousand disadvantages." These stock pronatalist techniques, recycled from Roman precedents and adapted by Colbert, were "very ridiculous and very absurd."[22]

In order to reignite population growth, conjugal relations needed reconfiguration. It was essential to remove barriers to prolific reproduction like indissoluble marriage, which kept men and women chained together long after they had ceased being sexually attracted to one another, and dowries, which made marriage expensive and introduced concerns of property where only desire should hold sway. To that end, Rouillé d'Orfeuil favored a kind of elemental sexual liberty that approximated as closely as possible the state of nature. Specifically, this included eliminating women's property rights so as to promote the natural dependence of the sexes upon one another. Rouillé d'Orfeuil's writing represented the radical wing of population thought, in which writers concluded that the natural reproductive process had been hopelessly corrupted by human meddling. The only remedy for was to sweep away the entire tradition of Catholic marriage and French family law and begin from new premises.

The edict of 1666 received bad press even from the empirically guided political arithmeticians who rejected the depopulation thesis altogether. Using baptismal and tax records, authors like Louis Messance and Jean-Baptiste Moheau sought to convince their readers that France was no less populous than it had been in the age of Louis XIV. But they did not credit growth to royal government measures designed to promote reproduction; quite the opposite. When Louis Messance, in 1766, reflected on the pronatalist law put in place under Colbert in 1666, he found nothing to praise. Even if France's population had grown in the intervening century, he saw no reason to believe that Louis XIV's intervention had played even the smallest role in making that happen. The pronatalist edict had long ago lapsed, and that was good because, Messance asserted, the fecundity of marriages was controlled by nature, and simply not subject to the kind of facile meddling Louis XIV's edict had envisioned.[23] A little more than a decade later, Moheau's *Recherches et considérations sur la population de la France* (1778) also rejected the old-fashioned pronatalist method of encouraging marriage and providing pensions to men with large families. As an admirer of Colbert, Moheau admitted he felt "pain and surprise" when he realized the great minister had resorted to such useless expedients.[24]

Few, then, were the voices like F. V. de Forbonnais (1758) or Jean-Louis Murat (1767), who praised the 1666 pronatalist edict and called for its revival.[25] Even Colbert's most famous eighteenth-century encomiast, the banker, neomercantilist, and future controller-general Jacques Necker, felt it best to remain silent about Colbert's 1666 pronatalist plan. His prizewinning 1773 oration, *Eloge de Jean-Baptiste Colbert,* had much to say about means to make France's population flourish. He focused, however, on the populationist benefits of commerce and industry, avoiding any mention of tax exemptions and pensions for fathers of large families like those that his hero had masterminded.[26]

By the mid-eighteenth century, then, population thinking had evolved significantly from its seventeenth-century roots. The practices of the Romans that held such intellectual authority among Colbert's advisors in the 1660s no longer seemed like monuments of political wisdom. Although the ideal of a flourishing, densely populated France remained the same, eighteenth-century thinkers increasingly concluded that stewardship of the monarch's human resources demanded deeper and more fundamental changes to the economy, family, and political system. The irony of this nearly unanimous rejection of the logic represented by Louis XIV's 1666 pronatalist edict is that it coincided with the royal government's revival of the very policy in question. Indeed, not long after Necker championed commerce and industry as the true means to make population grow, his was one of the signatures adorning stacks of administrative documents distributing rewards to fathers with many children.[27]

Why revive a measure that few considered effective? When we turn from the critical perspective of the philosophes, and imagine the situation from the perspective of those responsible for governing, the disjuncture between pronatalist theory and practice is not difficult to understand. In the late seventeenth and early eighteenth century, population had ceased to be a secret of the king and become a subject of public inquiry. Amidst much confusion and many radical suggestions, traditional pronatalist measures like rewards for fathers with many children, for all their limitations, were among the few practicable responses for a government that was under increasing public pressure to do something to demonstrate its stewardship of population.

Locating the *Père de Famille Nombreuse*

In his terse dismissal of Louis XIV's pronatalist policy, Montesquieu noted that France's depopulation crisis could not be turned around "rewarding prodigies." The writer's choice of words marked significant changes in French demographic norms. The word "prodigy" in early modern French denoted that which "went against the normal expectations of natural events." It had been far from "prodigious" among seventeenth-century elites for a couple to baptize ten or even twelve children. Claude Lévy and Louis Henry's landmark 1960 study of the French high aristocracy found that nearly one in five brides of the high aristocracy married between 1650 and 1699 gave birth ten or more times. But by the time Montesquieu wrote *The Spirit of the Laws,* such high fertility was becoming very uncommon, especially among the highest social elites. Whereas only thirteen percent of the seventeenth-century elite couples studied by Lévy and Henry limited themselves to one or two children, by the mid-eighteenth century, more than forty percent were doing so.[28] Indeed, over the course of the eighteenth century, the social location of large families changed definitively. What had, in the past, been a reproductive pattern most likely to occur among the well-to-do became increasingly associated with the urban working classes.[29]

Taking note of these changes in the relationship between demographic behavior and social status helps bring eighteenth-century population anxiety into sharper focus. For example, one reason that educated writers held tenaciously to an erroneous belief in depopulation was that the depopulation thesis made sense of changes that they saw with their own eyes; many noticed that large families were less common among their own social circle. Observing Paris high society in 1750, Madeleine de Puisieux noted, "Families have never been smaller than in the last few years. Couples are limiting themselves to one or two children." Madame de Puisieux indicated that only lower class women (*femmes du commun*) had many children anymore—a sure sign that fecundity was not in style.[30]

The mathematician André-Pierre Le Guay de Prémontval concurred, and wondered what had happened to provoke such a change. "Why is it," he asked, "that during twenty-five year unions contracted in the flower of youth... we see only two, three or four children born at most and sometimes just one?" He noted that couples who had more children, say seven or eight, were regarded "as very rare singularities."[31] Prémontval sought to evaluate with numerical precision what constituted a large family, a project that suggests the growing prevalence of "numeracy about children," that sense of reproductive norms with the capacity to shape expectations and behavior.[32] For Prémontval, the threshold of a large family fell at around five or six children, a line above which a couple's fertility became "singular" and "rare."

By the 1760s, political arithmeticians were quantifying France's dearth of large families, rendering norms of family size ever more visible to the reading public. Louis Messance's 1766 *Recherches sur la population* argued strenuously against the depopulation thesis by providing evidence that the total population had increased slightly over the past sixty years. However, in a chapter devoted to the subject of *familles nombreuses,* the author seemed to confirm the growing rarity of large households. His estimations also confirmed Le Guay de Prémontval's sense of norms; Messance also defined "large families" as households with six or more children.

The problem of how to promote large families held little interest for Messance; the author addressed *familles nombreuses* as part of his project to assess the norms and ratios that might be used to provide a more accurate estimate of France's total population.[33] The author's statistical information was drawn from censuses about the number of families with six or more children in the *généralités* of Lyon, Auvergne, and Rouen; it demonstrated that such families were spread somewhat unevenly across France's landscape. In the *généralité* of Rouen, he claimed, families of six or more children were far less common than in Auvergne or Lyon.[34] These variations illustrated the difficulties of finding a stable ratio between, say, marriages and the total population; the data showed that in some places, marriages were less fertile than they were in others. Messance did not offer an explanation for why this was the case; indeed, he implied that the causes might be environmental, for he himself claimed that marital fertility was beyond the control of human actors.[35]

It is worth considering how more casual readers might have made sense of Messance's tables. Isolated from the scientific debate about fertility and accurate calculation of population for which they were designed, the tables very clearly told another story; they illustrated that the large family of the kind specified by terms of Louis XIV's pronatalist policy was something akin to an endangered species. In his table for the *généralité* of Lyon (table 7.1) the author enumerated nearly a hundred families with six children: one in every twenty-five families could meet that bar.

But above that number, large families quickly moved from singular to the prodigious where Montesquieu had put them; families with ten or more children were as rare as the proverbial hen's tooth. Messance's data noted only five in the entire *généralité* of Lyon, statistically the most fertile of the three he studied. Taking into account all three *généralités,* Messance's data enumerated only twenty-three families of ten or more children in his sample of more than twenty-two thousand households—statistically, it seemed that those very large families accounted for just a little more than one family in a thousand.[36]

Why were there so few large families? Contemporaries offered a range of often contradictory answers. Some blamed changes in marriage. Couples were not getting along as they once had; or alternatively, they were getting along *too well,* and selfishly choosing their own ease and pleasure over their religious,

Table 7.1 Messance's Survey of Large Families in the Generality of Lyon

We counted in the Generality of Lyon, within 3,820 families, those composed of six or more children and found 179 comprising in total 1,224 children.

THAT IS TO SAY:		
Number of Families	Number of children of which each family is composed	Total of children in the families mentioned in first column
97.......of	6 children.....	582
40.......of	7	280
26.......of	8	208
11.......of	9	99
2........of	10	20
2........of	11	22
1........of	13	13
179 families composed of..	.....	1,224 *children*

The number 179, the number of families with six or more children is equivalent to 1/ 21 1/3 [4.6%] of the 3,820 families out of which they were selected.

Louis Messance, *Recherches sur la population des généralités d'Auvergne, de Lyon, de Rouen* (Paris, 1766), 145. Author's translation.

familial, and political duty to produce offspring. Other contemporaries claimed the trouble was economic, following Montesquieu in their claim that the dearth of large families was the result of parents' poverty and inability to provide for a large brood. Still others took the opposite economic position, claiming that modern parents were too rich. These writers plotted the decline of large families against the rise of luxury consumption, leisure, and other "sterile" pleasures. By the terms of this explanation, falling birthrates were the result of parents' greed and ambition, which made them unwilling to sacrifice their own desires for an easy and comfortable life in order to raise a large family.[37]

Whatever parents' motivation, nearly everyone implicated deliberate contraceptive behaviors for the observed rarity of large families. "Fooling nature" (the contemporary euphemism for efforts to avoid conception, perhaps *coitus interruptus)* was the cause. It was most often a practice that characterized a rich man "proud of his grandeur, drunk with his opulence," writers thought.[38] Sometimes, they complained, married couples practiced abstinence, quenching the first fires of desire after the wedding, and then retiring into a "sort of clandestine separation" that ran counter to the traditional purposes of marriage.[39] Eighteenth-century writers were not likely to interpret abstinence as laudable "marital continence," a sacrifice of carnal pleasure for the purpose of closer union with God; men's and women's motives for avoiding reproduction were worldly, selfish, and corrupt. Nowadays, Jean-Henri Marchand lamented, "when he has one or two children, the *grand seigneur* or his imitator thinks he has the right to rest himself beneath the myrtles of a love faded by marriage. His wife becomes indifferent to him, and he doesn't bother [with sex] except, for a bit of air, with the wife of someone else...." Marchand, like many of his fellows, associated this behavior with corrupted elites and urbanites. Both men and women of these classes had become dangerously alienated from their true physical natures and the gendered obligations that nature decreed as laws: "we live in a refined age when men wish to digest and women to give birth by proxy," he mourned.[40]

Nearly all of these contemporary lamentations took for granted the idea that family size was volitional; that is, smaller families were the result of human choices, rather than a result of an environmental or biological condition outside humans' control.[41] Strikingly, however, rather than seeing the exercise of reproductive choice as a mark of human progress, a victory against superstition and religious prejudice that would allow men and women to fashion more satisfying lives for themselves, writers of the Enlightenment era expressed grave concerns about the consequences of human meddling in the procreative process. In the context of the widespread belief in depopulation, the notion that married French men and women were choosing not to address the nation's demographic crisis was troubling, of course. But the dangers of contraception were perceived as individual dangers as well as an aggregate threat. Contraceptive behaviors that in previous centuries had been proscribed by the church were reimagined by the philosophes as offenses against "Nature" that could not fail to render human beings unhappy in this world.[42] One way they expressed this was by singing the praises of the *famille nombreuse,* a form of family life that everyone agreed was on the wane. During the 1760s and 1770s, as sentimental literature blossomed in France, French audiences indulged in a wave of nostalgia for large families. *Familles nombreuses* were imagined as embodiments of the rustic, innocent family life of a mythic past, the antithesis of the overly refined, luxury-loving, and depopulating present.

The philosophe Denis Diderot would prove to be one of the most important purveyors of this nostalgia. Diderot's 1762 account of the country evening he spent with a prolific tenant farmer in the village of Maisons struck many of the common chords. The story he told in a letter began like this: finding no other lodging, the philosophe and his stylish traveling companions found themselves sharing bed and board with a peasant, fortuitously named Monsieur Bled (Mr. Wheat). "This man is fifty, and his wife is forty-two," Diderot wrote, "They have twelve children, and they hope to have more."[43] After a wine-soaked evening, he reported, "the good farmer became gallant with his wife, and propositioned her." Madame Bled demurred, saying they had run out of godparents in their tiny hamlet. When Diderot and a woman in the group offered to serve, the couple promised to get to work on the godchild right away. "I assure you," the writer confided somewhat naughtily to his correspondent—who happened to be his adulterous lover, Sophie Volland—"that these healthy and vigorous people kept their word twice rather than once." Diderot related his story in the genre of a bawdy comedy, in order to regale his correspondent, but this did not stop him from drawing a sincere moral lesson: in comparison to Bled's rich landlord, shut up in a mansion, the tenant farmer in his thatched-roof house, surrounded by his numerous progeny, was truly happy. His large family denoted virtue, domestic satisfaction, and generosity of spirit that Diderot, an unhappily married father of one, found idyllic.

The Bled family was just one of the large, happy rural families that dotted the literary and visual landscape of the period. The 1762 French publication of Swiss writer Hans Kaspar Hirzel's *Le Socrate rustique (The Rural Socrates)* created a vogue among French readers for the wisdom of the peasant philosopher Kliyogg, a hardworking and stern *père de famille* who presided over a dual household composed of eleven children, six from his marriage and five from that of his brother. The book describes Kliyogg's farming practices in some detail, answering to the contemporary interest in agricultural techniques and reform. But the book's success also owed much to the supposed moral wisdom of the prolific father. Hirzel complimented the morality of the peasant, whose refusal to adopt contraceptive practices was implied by the writer's claim that "[Kliyogg] considers his children presents that the Divine has given him, in order that he put them on the right path." True to his austere values, the peasant philosopher made it his first priority to inculcate reason and virtue in this brood. He kept corrupting society at arm's length, in order to "prevent false ideas and destructive passions from slipping into [his children's] tender souls."[44] *Le Socrate Rustique* embodied the "natural" paternal and reproductive virtues that eighteenth-century readers idealized.

Sentimental paintings, particularly those of Jean-Baptiste Greuze, also catered to contemporary nostalgia for the *famille nombreuse*.[45] Among Greuze's popular works of the 1760s were heartwarming scenes of fertile, rural domesticity. The author populated these canvases with as many rosy, healthy-looking children as the composition allowed, an aesthetic of fertility whose message was not lost on viewers. Diderot, for his part, responded enthusiastically to the 1769 exhibition of *The Beloved Mother* (figure 7.1). The painting, copied in the engraving here, depicted a father returning to his family and hearth. He enters to find his still lovely wife smothered with the love of six adoring children, aged from infancy to adolescence. Diderot interpreted the father's excited gesture as an expression of masculine pride in his large family. He also believed the painting had a didactic impact on the viewer: "this preaches population," he wrote.[46]

But no artifact from these decades better exemplifies the nostalgia for the virtuous, fruitful family life of a regretted past than Nicolas-Edme Restif de la

FIGURE 7.1 Jean Massard, "The Well-Loved Mother." Harvard Art Museum, Fogg Art Museum, Gift of William Gray from the collection of Francis Calley Gray, G2584.

Bretonne's 1779 *La Vie de mon père* (*My Father's Life*). Restif is best known as a prolific cataloguer of his own sexual eccentricities, the so-called "Rousseau of the gutter." Among many other libertine tendencies, the author documented his supposed capacity to populate the world with daughters conceived in hundreds of casual sexual encounters, to completely ignore any responsibility for these children, and then to return in later decades to make these same daughters his sexual partners.[47] Amid a torrent of works that describe Restif's adventures in the sexual underground of Enlightenment Paris, Restif's *My Father's Life* stands out. In it, the writer nostalgically recounted his own childhood in the home of Edme Restif, a father of fourteen children.[48]

Restif offered his father's burgeoning household as an example for his troubled, depopulating generation. "Fellow-citizens," he wrote, "I shall paint a picture of an everyday kind of virtue, an easy and amiable virtue which provides the only solid foundation for happiness in this world and for one's reputation after death."[49] The "easy and amiable virtue" of Edme Restif included acceptance of the authorities and duties of the sexually active male adult. The author considered his father's reproductive success to be a meaningful symbol of his virtue as man and citizen. Edme's embrace of his paternal duty differentiated him not just from his dissipated son, but also from the selfishness that supposedly characterized those who limited the size of their families. Yet while Restif's book highlighted the intensity of Edme's paternal commitment through the sheer number of his children, it also implied that his virtue showed in the distinct, traditional way he exercised paternal authority.

The supper table scene in *My Father's Life* provides a classic depiction of Edme Restif's gentle patriarchal regime. Twenty-two souls gathered around the table, first father, then mother, then children arranged hierarchically by their ages, and then farm and household servants, with the lowliest members, the servant girls, at the bottom end where the lady of the house could keep her watchful eye on them. After supper, the author recalled, his father read aloud from the Bible, communicating to the whole family "a mood of goodwill and brotherly love."[50]

The clarity of the household's class and gender hierarchy was reinforced not just by the strictly defined position of each family member at the table, but also by what each person consumed. Restif is very specific, noting that only Edme drank mature wine, albeit in small quantities. His wife drank wine mixed with water, the children pure water, and the adult male servants, in keeping with their less refined tastes, "a wine that rasped their throats." But if the table ritual enacted his father's supremacy, Restif took pains to show that Edme's patriarchal authority never strayed toward despotism. His father's privileged consumption of good wine (along with his Bible reading) gave the table scene a distinctly eucharistic cast, and symbolized Edme's pastoral role in the family. But the writer notes that everyone in the household, regardless of rank, ate the same daily bread, "for in this house, the odious distinction between those who had white and those who had black bread did not exist." The scene idealized the harmony and camaraderie of the world where Edme presided as "venerable patriarch at the head of a large household."[51]

Restif's treacly picture of the happiness that fertility and traditional family life could bring was consistent with a broader contemporary trend to sentimentalize paternal power, a movement that sought to reconcile the potential abuse of paternal power with its importance as a guarantor of social order and stability.[52] The writer depicted his father's authority in the household as simultaneously absolute and benign. Edme led by example, working hard and showing tender concern for those below him. He enjoyed, his son claims, the work of driving his plough himself rather than leaving such hard labor to his servants. And he took pains to plan recreations for the family amid their labors.

If these details strained to show that the authority of fathers over children and masters over servants was natural and a source of long-term happiness, *My Father's Life* also offered a justification for the traditional gender order, linking it, too, to happy, large families. The work makes Restif's father a spokesman for the notion that a clear distinction of sex roles is essential to the proper functioning of household and society. The writer claimed that the happiest relations between the sexes came by maintaining a certain distance and reserve between men and women, even within the intimate confines of the household. In sharp contrast to the writer's own incestuous tendencies, his father, he claimed, never even spoke to his daughters "in the familiar manner." Even legitimate marital affection was subdued, as Edme worked to preserve "a certain marital dignity" in exchanges with his wife.[53]

Restif depicted his father affirming this traditional way of life in the face of modernizing tendencies that were undermining it. The story he told about his mother, Barbe Ferlet, made the point. The author was the eighth of Edme Restif's fourteen children, and the first from his father's second marriage. Ferlet, the author writes, was a "vivacious" soul raised in an indulgent household. Predictably, she came to her second marriage after an unhappy first union. Restif reports that his father quietly pulled her aside to teach her how to avoid the modern plague of marital discord. "It is only by obeying nature that we can be happy," Edme instructed his new wife, "the natural role of the stronger sex is to govern. . . . I know from experience that wives who play at being husbands are the unhappiest of all."[54] Restif claimed that his mother bloomed within the strictures of this patriarchal regime. The writer "was able to witness the touching spectacle of my mother bringing to life again the wifely conduct of a bygone age"—conduct which, not incidentally, included bearing seven children in this second marriage.[55] In the context of Restif's novel-memoir, Barbe Ferlet's rebirth as fertile farmer's wife symbolized the redemption that traditional rustic patriarchy might offer French society as a whole.

What impact did this nostalgia for a regretted, fertile past actually have on those who consumed it? The conduct that Restif extolled in his father was, of course, the antithesis of his own. And, not surprisingly, viewers and readers of the mid-eighteenth century had varying responses to this idealization of large families. Where some saw an idyll, others saw dangerously frequent pregnancy, endless child care, economic burdens and worries, crowded houses, and outmoded notions of conjugal relations.[56] The salonnière Madame Geoffrin, for example, is said to have loathed the "fricassee of children," depicted in the paintings of Greuze, due to her "aversion...for marriage and large families."[57] To judge by population trends, few of the reading and art-buying public who appreciated works celebrating large families sought to reenact this prodigious fertility in their own households. The vogue for looking nostalgically at large families—placing them, as it did, in a rustic "elsewhere" for the reader—may have been little more than a comforting story to help eighteenth-century French men and women negotiate their anxiety about the contraceptive practices and new norms of family and sexuality that were becoming standard in their own social milieu.

Rewarding *Pères de Familles Nombreuses*

Although most provisions of Louis XIV's pronatalist 1666 edict had been officially revoked in 1683, the government's interest in fathers with large families had never completely waned. Throughout the eighteenth century, royal administrators continued to respond to the petitions of fathers like Edme Restif on an ad hoc basis. Beginning in the 1760s, however, the practice suddenly increased in scope. Royal administrators again advertised to the king's subjects that the king intended to reward prolific fathers. In some cases, provincial intendants even directed their subordinates to search out those supposedly rare families with ten or more children.[58] For the next three decades, until the Revolution, providing tax relief and charitable aid to men with large families became a routine part of provincial administration.

No royal edict stood behind the renewal of the royal government's rewards for *pères de familles nombreuses,* so we must look elsewhere for explanations of the royal government's motivation for reviving the pronatalist program. Administrators habitually referred to the aid for fathers of large families as a measure undertaken to favor population. And yet, at the same time, these administrators revealed that they, too, were skeptical that the rewards they were offering could actually inspire French people to have more children. The pronatalist grants the royal government offered were, they indicated, intended to be symbolic rather than effective, a sign of the government's concern for a noteworthy social group of useful subjects. The labor and sacrifice to raise France's next generation merited prolific fathers the king's "particular protection," intendants wrote.[59]

The lack of any edict or legal declaration announcing the revived pronatalist program was part of a new administrative strategy intended to keep pronatalist awards in a legal gray area. Aware of what had happened in the 1660s and 1670s, officials in Paris were intent on excluding venal officials from any power of administration over the pronatalist awards. So rather than renewing the edict of 1666, administrators carefully avoided making rewards for prolific fathers a matter of law or legally enforceable right. Time and again, administrators stressed that the 1666 edict had been "entirely revoked" and that "the intention of the king [was] not to reestablish it."[60] At the same time, officials in Paris informed provincial intendants that rewards to fathers with large families were to be promoted again, as they said, "in conforming to the spirit of the edict of 1666." The new rewards, however, were matters of "pure grace," that is, "entirely voluntary [on the king's part] and having no legal force."[61] The new strategy allowed the crown simply to refuse to pay fathers when money was short; it also enabled it to direct the benefits to fathers of its choice, according to criteria beyond the mere number of children in the household.

The revived pronatalist initiative took shape within a tax system that had grown significantly beyond its seventeenth-century contours, one in which the dangers of tax privilege were foremost in administrators' minds. The wars of the late years of Louis XIV's reign had forced the ever-penurious royal government to introduce new universal taxes, such as the *capitation* and the *vingtième,* that were levied on all subjects of the king, noblemen included. Assessment and collection of these new taxes was designed to bypass the local mechanisms through which the *taille* had been collected, which had effectively blocked efforts to extract taxes from the wealthy and powerful. This evolving tax regime introduced important new concepts into the French political vocabulary. One of these was the notion that taxation was not a mark of low social status, but rather a contribution to a collective national project. Accordingly, all subjects had a duty to contribute as their means allowed. This ethic undercut the ethos of privilege that had traditionally justified the exemptions received by noblemen, the clergy, and royal officers.[62] Yet if taxation was a contribution to the polity, it was still possible to argue that other meaningful contributions to national well-being—royal service, for example—deserved recognition and compensation, too. As a result of this new logic, thousands upon thousands of royal subjects petitioned every year for "justice," and a lower tax bill claiming that their services merited it.[63] Once the royal government made it known that it was going to offer its protection to prolific fathers, men with many children joined these petitioners. They were, as the intendant of Bordeaux, François Fargès, put it in 1768, "a class of citizens who, in raising a large family, deserve without question to contribute less than others to the charges of the state."[64]

How significant was the king's largesse to large families? Unlike the seventeenth-century royal government, eighteenth-century provincial administrators kept extensive (if incomplete) records of the pronatalist rewards they doled out, and sometimes produced lists or accounts of these expenditures. These records suggest that funds available to men with large families varied significantly from one region to another. The variation seems largely to have reflected the provincial intendant's interest in devoting his discretionary budget to the pronatalist cause. François Fargès thought that fathers of many children were "without question" deserving, and distributed tax reductions to 136 *familles nombreuses* in his *généralité* in 1768. The number rose to 147 in the following year, and cost him nearly 8,000 *livres* from his budget. Tables prepared for Rouillé d'Orfeuil, intendant in Champagne, suggest that 323 *familles nombreuses* received benefits between 1768 and October 1772.[65] By the 1780s, the *généralité* of Caen was among the most active in allocating aid to fathers of large families. Accounts suggest that, between 1785 and 1787, intendants and subdelegates in the *généralité* approved approximately three hundred tax reductions annually to men with ten or more children.[66] Some of the other provincial intendants were less generous to the cause. Nevertheless, judging by these numbers, the number of large families who received pronatalist tax reductions or grants in the last three decades of the Old Regime ran into the thousands.[67]

A common source of the benefits distributed to fathers of large families was the *fonds libres de la capitation* (free funds of the *capitation*), a pot of money skimmed from the takings of the *capitation* tax and retained for use at the local level.[68] Intendants used the free funds in a variety of ways. It served to pay local administrative costs, supplement salaries, and also to support a dizzying variety of charitable and public works projects. These included the maintenance of roads and public buildings, support for the blind, compensation for farmers whose crops had been damaged, even rewards for hunters who shot troublesome wolves. In the second half of the eighteenth century, the free funds available to intendants expanded appreciably, rising to more than a million *livres* split among the twenty-one intendants in the *pays d'élection* for 1772.[69] The free funds was not the only means used to funnel aid to fathers of large families, but it provides the best means to estimate the weight of these benefits across France.[70]

Provincial intendants had significant influence over how the money was allocated, and the proportion of these funds that they redirected to fathers of large families varied considerably. In Caen, awards to *pères de familles nombreuses* quickly outpaced spending on other causes vying for the free funds. For 1785, small grants to 323 prolific fathers mounted to 20,470 *livres,* a sum equivalent to 22.4 percent of the free funds of the *capitation* available that year. This means that the intendant, Cordier de Launay, directed more money to fathers of large families than toward the prevention of epidemics, toward veterinary education, or to supplement the public works budget (the *Ponts et Chaussées*).[71] In the *généralité* of Limoges, however, the intendant did not open his wallet as wide. Although he gave a larger sum to each of the fifteen to twenty lucky fathers he chose to reward annually during the 1780s, his expenditure was, on average, just 2.7 percent of the annual free funds he doled out, less than he spent to foster industry (3.8 percent) or to refurbish the building where he and his secretaries worked (10.4 percent).[72] This effort to limit expenses by doling out just a few awards was probably closer to the norm. An account from the Archives Nationales in Paris suggests that, across the *pays d'élection,* approximately 2.3 percent of the annual payments from the free funds were allocated to fathers with large families. The figure rises to 5.3 percent if we consider just the part of the free funds used for nonadministrative purposes. In other words, about one out of every twenty of the half million or so *livres* that provincial administrators in the *pays d'élection* reallocated to worthy causes every year ended up in the pocket of a father of many children.

Although political arithmeticians counted few *familles nombreuses* of ten or more children, such families seemed all too common to France's provincial administrators. Administrative correspondence suggests that keeping within the budget for pronatalist awards was difficult; intendants soon had more applicants for aid than they could accommodate. By the 1780s, the pressures of meeting the need became intense. The intendant in Rouen exaggerated that large families were "infinite in number," despairing, like his colleagues, of meeting the claims of so many.[73] Rouillé d'Orfeuil, in Champagne, noted that he had identified more than five hundred families of ten or more children in his *généralité,* far more than he was able to help as he would have liked. Even reducing the aid he granted to the most modest sums, the expenses rose, he claimed, to 38,000 *livres* per year.[74]

How do we explain the conflicting claims about the prevalence of large families? The likeliest answer is that the methods of political arithmetic led to an undercount of these prolific households, while the government's offer of aid led many who were not technically qualified to come forward in the hopes they might secure some benefit. Evolving administrative practices suggest this was the case. In 1784, Feydeau de Brou, the intendant in the *généralité* of Caen wrote a punctilious letter to his subdelegates bemoaning the rising costs of aid provided to fathers, and prescribing strict adherence to set standards for qualification. The criteria that he set out were as follows: the families receiving the king's aid must indeed have ten living children, all of them still dependents in the household, and each family who received the aid should actually need the grant to get by. For the most part, it seems, recipient families did have at least ten living children—or at least are recorded as having that many—although families with nine or fewer occasionally slipped through the net. Feydeau de Brou's directives recognized that the subdelegates were the gatekeepers most responsible for determining to whom the aid would be allocated and suggests these men may have abetted fraud for reasons we can only guess at.

Note that the intendant also asked his subdelegates to evaluate families' need. Feydeau de Brou was not unique in this demand. The activation of this nebulous and complicated concept of "need" served to distinguish the revived eighteenth-century pronatalist program from its seventeenth-century antecedent. Officials wanted to know which houses needed government assistance because they hoped to control expenditures, and to use limited funds most effectively. But with the added criterion of need the royal pronatalist program ceased being a recognition of reproductive service based on the objective standard of the number of living children a man had fathered. Administrators' effort to assess need forced them to develop normative standards of what was required, economically and morally, to raise a family. It also encouraged them to sort "deserving" fathers from those who were not, a process that transformed the exchange between applicants and officials from a simple affair of counting children to an exercise in economic and moral surveillance.

Some administrators tried to standardize and bureaucratize this evaluation, but their efforts were largely unsuccessful. In order to more fairly evalute prolific fathers' requests, for example, Feydeau de Brou devised and printed a form. It asked for details on children's ages and health as well as information on household revenue and taxation. Recognizing that this method of evaluation increased the workload of his overburdened subordinates, Feydeau justified his demand by reminding the subdelegates how it felt to say "no" to a needy man with many children: extra bureaucratic care would alleviate this problem. "I cannot remind you enough," he wrote, "not to cede to importunity, and to consider that aid accorded without real and obvious necessity puts the administration in the position of being unable to grant justice to some other truly worthy request."[75]

If Feydeau tried to promote the labor-intensive bureaucratic form as a means to sort through too many applications, it is likely a sign that his subdelegates were under pressure from fathers seeking to secure tax reductions and royal aid. The most common way for fathers to do this was to write a petition. A glance at the petitions submitted by these fathers of large families illustrates that aspirants did offer poignant stories of distress in order to lay claim to pronatalist aid. Like other tax petitioners, these men skillfully spun tales of the insurmountable hardships they faced. Often, they placed the burdens of raising their large families alongside myriad other sources of economic distress: harvests damaged by hail or flood, business reversals, health crises, lost court cases, high housing costs, and crushing tax bills.[76] Prolific fathers explained how these chains of misfortune left their large households in danger of hunger and homelessness despite their consistent and virtuous efforts to make ends meet.

A couple of the hundreds of stories contained within prolific fathers' petitions will illustrate the style of such documents. The Norman farmer Jacques-Louis Le Grand explained that he had ten children, and owned only eight acres of mediocre land. The eldest of his children was crippled, the others were too young to work, and his wife had recently broken her leg. To make matters worse, one of the walls of his house had collapsed. As a result of these trials, "no matter how assiduous [the petitioner] is, he cannot draw from his land all that is necessary to nourish, take care of and educate his large family and also to satisfy his annual charges."[77] Claude Duter, from Champagne, wrote that he barely eked out a living repairing shoes. He owned nothing, not even the house where he lived with his family of ten children; he was so poor that he was forced to send four of his little children out to beg. Several of the children had health problems, including four-year-old Marie-Magdeleine, born with two thumbs (the extra had been cut off by the local surgeon). Duter, like many other petitioners, adopted the humble posture of the supplicant to ask for mercy and help in reconciling his paternal obligations and his responsibilities as a royal subject: "Because the suppliant is unable to feed his wife and his children and also to pay his *taille* and *capitation,* he resorts to the authority of your grandeur."[78]

Centuries later, the stories can still evoke the reader's pity. Administrators were hardly immune themselves; they sometimes noted that they had been moved by a father's story as they forwarded documents from one desk to another. Some of the recipients of pronatalist aid were desperately poor, like René Bellois, a fifty-year-old day laborer living near Avranches, in Normandy. Supporting ten children, the youngest of whom was only three months old, Bellois owed taxes that barely topped one *livre;* the intendant's records suggest he gave Bellois a payment of fifty *livres* from the free funds to help him feed his family.[79] In 1768, when seven fathers of large families from the subdelegation in Marmande in the *généralité* of Bordeaux forgot to attach certificates recording their *capitation* to their applications for pronatalist awards, further inquiries by the subdelegate revealed that four of them had omitted these certificates because they were simply too poor to owe any *capitation* at all.[80] Such families were in all likelihood living in misery.

But these poor fathers of large families were the exception rather than the rule. Despite the conventional language of neediness, a survey of available data on families who received pronatalist awards shows most of the recipients were not poor, relatively speaking. In Champagne, for example, recipients' recorded occupations were most commonly *laboureur* (that is, yeoman farmer), but the group included master artisans, lawyers, and noblemen. In the *généralité* of Bordeaux, among 130 fathers listed as recipients in 1768, five of the fathers with large families (3.8 percent) were judged too poor to pay any *capitation,* but nine of them (6.9 percent) paid more than fifty *livres* of *capitation* annually, which suggests they were quite well-off. Michael Kwass has estimated that a poor household in the 1760s might have paid, altogether, around twelve *livres* in taxes annually. Households in the *généralité* of Bordeaux who received pronatalist aid had an average *capitation* bill of nearly twenty *livres* (19.55 *livres*). This does not include what they paid for the *taille* and other charges. In other words, most of the large families claiming pronatalist tax aid were far from destitute.[81] Matters were similar two decades later in the Caen subdelegation of Avranches. Seventeen households are recorded receiving aid for large families between 1784 and 1788: ten of the heads-of-household were *laboureurs,* five were craftsmen, one was a widow who kept a farm, and one was a day laborer. The day laborer and one of the craftsmen, a carpenter, were poor; each was noted to pay less than two *livres* annually in total taxes. But the average total tax burden paid by the other fourteen men and one woman was approximately sixty *livres* per year, a healthy sum that underscores these households' relative comfort.[82] In sum, recipients of pronatalist awards ran the gamut from the desperately poor to the wealthy, but middling to well-off households were more numerous than destitute ones.

Petition writers crafted their requests with some understanding of the criteria that were used to evaluate need. They noted the number of children they had as well as the number they currently supported with their labor. The petitions suggest that by the time children were in their teens, it was expected those children would be working to help support the household; if they were not, fathers were expected to explain why—a fact that helps to explain the frequent, harrowing accounts of childrens' chronic illnesses, injuries, and handicaps.

For fathers higher in the social hierarchy, expectations for childrens' labor were different, however. Parents who were craftsmen or professionals often mentioned the costs of education and apprenticeship to explain why they nevertheless qualified by "need" for the king's aid to fathers of large families. In other words, even when royal officials evaluated potential recipients in terms of need, pronatalist aid took wealth and social status into account. Despite changes, the eighteenth-century pronatalist program continued to support the reproduction of a social order in which status was defined by birth. So it was that even wealthy noblemen could tap into royal pronatalist largesse when fertility threatened their ability to provide their children those things necessary to maintain a noble lifestyle. Indeed, nobles accounted for a larger proportion of the families receiving royal pronatalist aid than one might expect. In the *généralité* of Bordeaux in 1768, seventeen of the 136 recipients were noblemen, or 6.6 percent—a number that surely overrepresented the proportion of nobles in the population at large.[83] Even more important than their numerical representation among recipients, however, noble fathers soaked up a larger proportion of the available funds. In the *généralité* of Caen, average taxpayers commonly received grants from the free funds of the *capitation* of forty or fifty *livres* per year, whereas noblemen often received hundreds. The Duroset d'Entremont family, for example, probably had fewer than the ten children theoretically necessary to qualify, as the number of children in the family is never specifically mentioned in their correspondence.

Nevertheless, they received a 1,200-*livres* grant in 1765, 1,800 *livres* in 1767, and 500 to 600 *livres* annually from 1768 to 1773.[84]

Petitions from prolific noble fathers are fascinating documents featuring rhetorical strategies that veer from extremes of supplication to haughty entitlement. Some, for example, told tales of ancient lineages fallen on hard times. In 1762, Gérard Dupleix Cadignan wrote on behalf of his household. He and his wife Serène de Secondat had thirteen children, making them prodigies of fertility according to the standards of Secondat's kinsman, the philosophe Montesquieu. Dupleix reported that, although his family's history stretched back into the mists of time, most of the wealth reported in the history books was now gone. Dupleix and his progeny, which included several sons serving in the military, were left with just one chateau to their name. It was "a very vexing situation" for the property was inadequate to "support [the family] in a manner matching their status."[85] He hoped the intendant would see fit to help preserve this grand family in distress.

Intendants clearly paid special attention to such requests, recognizing that noble fathers were socially obligated to provide their children more costly educations, to amass large dowries in order to marry their daughters, and to outfit their sons for military careers. When a nobleman had many children, the burden was heavy. Rather than face this distress, contemporaries feared that noblemen were choosing to limit the number of their offspring. Pronatalist grants were, in this sense, a response to the anxiety that nobles were even more likely to practice birth control than others. More immediately, the grants also served to build a cadre of loyal nobles within the military: intendants were instructed to tell families like the Duroset d'Entremont that "this gift (*grace*) from the king has as its object the maintenance of their son in the service [as well as] the education of the other children."[86]

While pronatalist aid implicitly accepted the reproduction of a hierarchical society, correspondence about pronatalist benefits for nobles did occasionally reflect Enlightenment debates over the changing position of the nobility in both society and the state. Noble petitioners sometimes alluded to contemporary questions about whether nobles should be allowed to practice trades without *dérogeance;* most, however, expressed a preference for placing their children in social roles that were more traditionally considered appropriate for nobles. The nobleman Demothes de Labesiade, for example, reacted with confusion to the Bordeaux intendant's suggestion that he provide for his sons by getting them land grants in the lowlands outside Bordeaux. "Depite my wish to procure bread for my children," he wrote, "it would be impossible for me to acquiesce to this plan, first, because no matter how much they desire to earn their living and are ready to lead an austere and hardworking life in order to do so, they have not been accustomed from childhood to use the tools of a farmer and wouldn't begin to know how to work the land."[87] Could the intendant help them get commissions in the imperial forces instead, the father asked? The suggestion that noble fathers place their sons in the service was, in fact, more common than the Bordeaux intendant's proposal that noblemen participate in agriculture. Gérard Dupleix evoked this traditional notion of noble honor and duty in his request for a pronatalist grant, hoping that "the affection of the king for the military nobility of his kingdom" had not changed.[88]

Writing a petition was only the firt step in securing the aid intended for fathers of large families. Royal administrators investigated the facts of each case, consulting with village officials and parish priests. Applicants who exaggerated their claims of poverty or whose conduct received poor reports were likely to find their request summarily refused. Surveillance of behavior appears to have been most important at the upper reaches of the social hierarchy where financial "need" was a more nebulous quality. For example, royal officials rebuked a small-town lawyer and father of nine known to sow discord in his community with lawsuits and to treat workers poorly. Investigation by the subdelegate led the intendant to conclude that the lawyer, Plantey, abused his authority; he had "a petulant character, a vindictive soul" and was "governed entirely by passion and bad faith."[89] His petition was returned with an explanation that, despite his large family, his request would not be granted. Likewise, royal officials hesitated to grant money to the nobleman Gérard Dupleix when investigation revealed that despite his claims of poverty, several of his sons were frequently seen in town dressed in expensive finery and gambling.[90] Although it was an isolated case, royal officials even intervened in the family affairs of a Norman nobleman who was reputed to beat his wife and flagrantly carry on adulterous liaisons. They refused any grant to help him provide for his family, and even gave his wife money to rent an apartment in Bayeux away from her violent husband.[91] In these cases, the royal government wielded its new-found power to evaluate and reject the claims of prolific fathers as a disciplinary tool. In addition to fathering large families, those hoping for royal recognition needed to meet standards of virtue, industry, and prudence appropriate to their social station. The *père de famille nombreuse* was to be a model member of his community, not just a successful propagator.

The pronatalist program that royal officials revived in the eighteenth century gave them by design increased power to determine who would receive the king's largesse. It also subtly changed the attitudes of prolific fathers' neighbors to the pronatalist program. In the seventeenth century, the award of tax privileges to large families had inspired considerable resentment. Taxpayers saw clearly that they themselves were paying more to make up for prolific fathers' privileged status, a status these men gained purely by the number of children they had and without regard to their wealth. The new program addressed these complaints in several ways. First, as we have seen, royal administrators sought to allocate pronatalist funds preferentially to those who were actually "in need" because of their large families. Just as important, the new program doled out aid rather than out-right legal privilege; in other words, the money a prolific father received did not obviously increase his neighbor's tax burden. As a result of these changes, communities evinced much less hostility to the revived pronatalist program. In fact, many embraced it, concluding that pronatalist rewards were charitable resources they might tap into on their poor neighbors' behalf.[92] The curé and community of the parish of Landelles in the Norman *élection* of Vire, for example, addressed a note to the subdelegate on the form that accompanied Thomas Rohée's request for pronatalist aid in 1784. Although Rohée had only nine children still living of the eleven born and listed on the form, they argued that he nevertheless merited the king's aid, due to "his miserable poverty, his probity, and his scrupulousness (*délicatesse*) in never sending his own poor children to [other people's] doors"—that is, to beg.[93] Rohée and his wife had provided as well as they could for their children through their labor and through the "help offered by charitable souls"; now, the neighbors hoped, the king would do his part. When fathers were not perceived as poor, on the other hand, local responses might be tepid. The communal assembly of Rozoy, for example, wrote to express a lack of support for the award solicited by Simon Tournant, who kept the local cabaret, noting that he was among the community's most comfortable members and hardly in need of royal aid.[94] In the old system, Tournant would have been legally entitled to tax exemption and his neighbors' opinions would have counted for little. The new system gave them a voice and encouraged their complicity with royal efforts to identify qualified *pères de familles nombreuses*.

The quest to channel aid toward poverty-stricken households like Thomas Rohée's raises the question of how pronatalist awards were related to broader problems of indigence. Children, as both contemporaries and historians have recognized, often bore the brunt of the economic distress faced by their parents.[95] One illustration of this distress was the growing phenomenon of child abandonment in the middle part of the eighteenth century: from 3,150 children abandoned in Paris in 1740, the number rose to 7,676 by 1772.[96] While the increase in numbers stemmed, in part, from a rising tide of illegitimate births, significant numbers were abandoned by married parents too poor to provide for them; in Nantes, 38 percent of infants abandoned between 1766 and 1786 were the offspring of married parents. When times were hard, men and women might abandon newborns in public places, send older children to beg (which caused them to be arrested), or even send children directly to hospitals for temporary incarceration. This use of the charity hospital system as a kind of emergency child care created a huge fiscal burden for such institutions; children under the age of 13 accounted for 38.2 percent of those incarcerated in Grenoble's hospital in the eighteenth century.[97]

Child abandonment—whether at infancy or later—represented a transfer of the economic burden of parenthood from parents to the royal government and the local communities who financed poor relief and foundling hospitals. It is reasonable to suspect that pronatalist aid was, in some cases, being used by both royal and community officials as a prophylactic measure intended to prevent parents in distress from being reduced to this extremity. There is some evidence of direct connection; fathers of many children, or those writing on their behalf, sometimes mention that the family had been forced to send children out to beg. The printed form for pronatalist applications produced in the *généralité* of Caen even requested information on this score. The form included a line asking local officials to note how many of a prolific father's children were currently residing in local hospitals. Unfortunately, overburdened subdelegates rarely filled out the form completely, making it difficult to quantify the relationship between the households receiving pronatalist aid and those reliant upon charitable institutions.

What was the royal government hoping to achieve by providing aid to fathers of large families, and did officials consider the program successful? By the late eighteenth century, it is clear that royal officials had, like most population theorists, ceased to believe that rewards to fathers of large families actually encouraged population growth. Rather than an effective response to the problem of depopulation, the relatively small grants to men with large families were intended, as the intendant Fargès explained it, to "encourage the industry" of beleaguered parents trying to provide for their large families. By giving them even small sums, the king illustrated his paternal beneficence toward his subjects and recognition of prolific fathers' reproductive contribution to the state.

In its changed form, the pronatalist tradition dating from the reign of Louis XIV provided less lucrative rewards for men with large families, but proved far more popular with the rest of the king's subjects. Few doubted the "justice" of providing tax relief to men with large families, especially when these fathers enjoyed the respect of their communities. As intendants recognized, the grants secured the gratitude of fathers who received them and, in certain cases, relieved pressing need. Just as important, the resurrected pronatalist program provided some indication of the king's abiding concern about his subjects' fertility to a public increasingly informed about population matters, and prepared to hold the royal government accountable for population decline.[98]

Royal pronatalist aid, of course, had little apparent effect on the birthrate or prevalence of large families. Historical demographers have documented measurable declines in the average size of households, even in rural villages, beginning in the third quarter of the eighteenth century; smaller households had become the norm among nobles and urban elites even before then.[99] Contemporaries appear to have sensed the trend, and did not expect the small pronatalist awards to reverse it. Nevertheless, the aid the royal government distributed to thousands of fathers with many children was important as a symbolic reaffirmation of the central place of the conjugal family in the social and political order of the monarchical state. As the writer Restif de la Bretonne explained in his didactic *L'École des pères* (1776), "the state is a large family, composed of all individual families, and the prince is the father of [all the] fathers."[100] By becoming in a visible way the patron and protector of prolific fathers, the royal government invested its fiscal and administrative resources to sustain a vision of a harmonious, traditional social order where fathers (and by extension kings) ruled beneficently over burgeoning, fecund households. In an era marked by anxiety both about depopulation and the changes in the gender and reproductive order that had caused it, fathers with many children had become favored symbols of the stable social and political order of the Old Regime.

Conclusion

Ideas about the significance of the *famille nombreuse,* enshrined in French law and administrative practice since the seventeenth century, proved durable in French political life. In October of 1788, the *élection* assembly in the city of Aurillac seized upon fatherhood as a means to express their hopes for political regeneration. Inventing a civic ritual to accompany the traditional religious baptism that claimed newborns as members of the community of the faithful, the assembly proclaimed itself the "adoptive" father of the twelfth child of one of its members. They designated a godfather for the child, naming a local nobleman, and pledged a vow that all fecund fathers of twelve would henceforth be exempt from taxation in their *élection.*[1] In the fall before the Old Regime's last Estates General convened, this provincial community seized for itself the right to renew the terms of the 1666 Edict of Marriage, granting privilege to fathers of large families. By doing so, they celebrated fatherhood as a political identity that had the capacity to bind men together. The act of these provincial citizens allowed them to reclaim pronatalist ideology and translate it for use in a new political era.

Providing benefits to fathers of large families had been routine administrative practice for decades, of course. Ignoring Enlightened critiques that charged that depopulation could never be halted merely with rewards to those "prodigies" who produced large families, the royal government's pronatalist policy had taken a deeply traditional form. The king and his officials had continued to offer tax reductions and token payments to men who had fathered many children. Royal administrators, whose workload increased throughout the century, dutifully referred to the program in terms of "population," but most had little time or inclination to ponder whether or not this policy actually encouraged the king's subjects to produce more babies. When they did think about this question, they assumed that it did not. Rather than a demographically effective pronatalist policy (that is, one that would actually increase the birthrate, as seventeenth-century policymakers had intended) the rewards to fathers with large families came to serve other purposes that testify to the evolution of relations between families and the state.

At one level, fathers of large families became targets of charity. Over the course of the late seventeenth and eighteenth centuries, pronatalist intervention in French households had gradually been transformed from an expression of wise princely leadership into a early social welfare policy. Royal officials specified by the mid-eighteenth century that pronatalist awards were for *needy* men with many children. Even if neediness was often defined in relation to social status, this small change in the administration of the program reflected broader transformations in the governing practices of the Old Regime. A utilitarian intention to support the integrity of conjugal households with many mouths to feed vied with, and ultimately displaced, the practice of awarding privileges to men merely on the basis of their procreative output. In pronatalism, as in other spheres of state fiscality, the royal government was moving away from governing practices that created distinctions between taxpayers without regard to their ability to pay. Pronatalism had become justifiable in bureaucrats' eyes primarily as a means to provide for vulnerable young children incapable of earning their own sustenance.

In fact, rather than esteeming fathers of many children as men who had served the king in ways that merited privilege, eighteenth-century royal officials seemed, on the whole, to pity them. Their attitudes toward the *famille très nombreuse* reflected broader changes in French demographic behavior. By the late eighteenth century, family sizes were declining precipitously among all social groups. The typical citizen of Rouen, married around 1670, sent eight infants to baptism. By the end of the Old Regime, his descendant sent just four. In the last third of the seventeenth century, when Louis XIV's pronatalist policy had been created, frequent births and large families were relatively common in urban environments: 11 percent of Rouennais couples married in the last three decades of the seventeenth century baptized twelve or more infants over the course of their marriage. But among couples married a century later, only 3 percent reached this acme of fecundity, and they were decidely less likely to be members of the aristocracy or civic elites.[2] At the moment these new behaviors were taking hold, "political arithmetic" and demographic questions became familiar topics of French political discussion, and contemporaries increasingly took note of shifting familial norms and pondered the reasons for them. It is little wonder that few of Louis XVI's provincial intendants imagined that the king's subjects would rush to produce a *famille très nombreuse* in order to secure a pronatalist reward. They conceded that the meager sums at their disposal could do little to change procreative behavior.[3] Indeed, when intendants printed forms that asked their subordinates to specify how many of a given *père de famille nombreuse*'s children were inmates at charity hospitals, we see royal officials stumbling toward a Malthusian understanding of the connections between high fertility and poverty.

Even if they did not produce population growth, rewards to fathers of large families continued to be appealing to royal officials because they stood for an ideology that linked kings and fathers. As royal officials noted, the awards were a symbolic recognition of the king's paternal concern for his subjects. And the idea that fathers were critical to social order had never ceased to stir French hearts. If anything, the influence of the raging depopulation controversy and the familial rhetoric of Enlightenment philosophy and sentimental literature had intensified awareness of the political significance of family life and disseminated these ideas even more widely throughout French society. Out of this crucible, historians and scholars of literature have argued, came a transformed image of fathers.[4] Gone was the stern, forbidding, disciplinarian father that acted legitimately as "king" in his household, securing a stable, traditional social order that stretched from households to state to God, the father of all mankind. By the mid-eighteenth century, the divinely sanctioned father whose image had inspired pronatalism in the seventeenth century seemed too stern and forbidding. Fathers continued to be seen as crucial for social and political order, but their role as caregivers responsible for raising the next generation took pride of place over the stress on discipline that had marked writings about the family a century earlier. Under the influence, in particular, of writers like Diderot and the fictional writings of Rousseau, concerned and loving fathers became linchpins of a renewed and sentimentalized social order that emanated from nature. Fathers of large families became heroic examples of this organic vision of social harmony, all the more reason for the king to give them his "particular protection."

It was this harmonious vision of fatherhood that royal subjects invoked when, in the late 1780s, they used the small openings the royal government afforded them for increased participation in politics to request that pronatalist policy be extended further. In 1787, for example, the Agricultural Society in Laon devoted itself to developing a new, improved legal text based on Louis XIV's 1666 pronatalist edict. The gentlemen of the association believed that the progress of agriculture in France depended upon a numerous, active, and industrious labor force, and they hoped that reviving the terms of the 1666 law—albeit with a few minor improvements—would help ensure it.[5] By 1788, the Commission Intermediaire de Soissons had petitioned the royal government to revive the terms of the 1666 law according to the Agricultural Society's plan. The assembly in Aurillac made similar requests: no one, these groups argued, could be a more exemplary citizen than the father of a large family.

When the Old Regime collapsed, the king's former subjects found themselves empowered to reconstruct the political realm according to new principles. Yet pronatalist ideology—stripped of its formerly royalist, patriarchalist garb—survived the transition to color debates about how humans' natural duty to reproduce might be enlisted to serve the new nation. Perhaps the most dramatic example of this came in the revolutionary movement to abolish religious celibacy, already underway by 1789. Pronatalist convictions were only one reason for Revolutionary legislators' hostility to clerical celibacy, of course; the privileged status of the celibate clergy, the church's role in the persistence of

feudal inequality, and the wealth of church were, arguably, more important reasons to attack the institutions of the church and the celibacy that defined mem-
bership in the first estate. Nevertheless, writers and citizens voiced pronatalist
arguments to justify this radical break with French tradition. If France's forty
thousand parish priests were to marry, one pamphlet argued, the new nation
would gain five thousand additional births every year.[6] Moreover, vows of celibacy—so often broken, as common wisdom had it—did not promote sexual
morality, but instead corrupted it. As Roderick Phillips notes, the Popular
Society of Calais used this argument to urge lawmakers to eliminate celibacy as
"the most certain way of regenerating the morals without which there can be no
enduring government."[7] Only the natural bonds of marriage and parenthood
could seal men and women into stable and enduring political relationships.

The persistence and evolution of pronatalist thinking through the seventeenth
Historians have noted that in the course of these arguments, revolutionary
pamphleteers and lawmakers made strong claims about the state's right to the
procreative capacities of its subjects: "there is a hint here that the very bodies of
the clergy were, like the lands of the church, to be put at the disposal of the
Nation," Roderick Phillips has written. Monks and nuns were treated, respectively, as "lazy, good-for-nothing[s]" and "virgins condemned to a futile way of
life."[8] The refusal to marry made people parasites on the body politic, "useless
members" that must be cut off for its health.[9] As "dechristianized" as this rhetoric
was, the arguments about the state's interest in the reproductive services of its
citizens had precedents stretching back at least to the Reformation era. The revolutionary variants differed mainly in their vehemence from those espoused in
the midst of the seventeenth-century debate about royal authority to regulate
monastic vows. As Roland le Vayer de Boutigny had written in 1669, God ruled
the empire of souls, but He had left to secular governments "sovereignty over
bodies and over everything that concerns property and the civil and temporal
rights of their subjects."[10] It was vital to restrain French men and women's flight
to the cloister, which had fomented a variety of "abominations so shameful that
it is much more advantageous to religious sentiment to hide them."[11]

The persistence and evolution of pronatalist thinking through the seventeenth
and eighteenth centuries is a reminder of two key arguments laid out in this
book. It suggests that the belief that reproduction is a fundamental concern of
civil government, and a legitimate target for secular lawmaking, has a longer history than some have recognized. The recognition that marrying and forming a
family is a matter of political, economic, and moral significance for the commonwealth accompanied the process of state formation in Europe. It propelled leaders of
centralizing states to assert their powers to regulate marriage, family, and procreation and to develop new institutions to govern the domestic and conjugal realm.
When revolutionary lawmakers denounced the costs of celibacy to the French
nation, they were building on this tradition, recognizing as had policymakers

before them that the conjugal and procreative lives of individuals shaped the political community in crucial ways.

Secondly, the fact that these arguments had not resulted in more thorough-going reforms under the Old Regime points to limitations on the nascent state power that the secularizing Revolution helped to sweep aside. Royal pronatalist law had referred to marriages as "sacred *and* politic unions," hoping to strike a balance between temporal and spiritual jurisdictions. Asserting the interest of the king in marriage did not imply a denial that marriage was a sacred bond as well. Where precisely to fix the boundary between the respective jurisdiction of church and state was a vexed question under the Old Regime, one that divided the social elites on whom the royal government depended. Louis XIV's advisors realized that the perception that the king's law had overstepped its temporal jurisdiction was likely to provoke concerted resistance. Sometimes they under-estimated the strength of such resistance; in the 1660s, even Jean-Baptiste Colbert's studied, moderate plan to raise the age of majority for pronouncing religious vows foundered against the outcry of clergy, papacy, and pious sub-jects. It was only a century later, in the face of monastic institutions' declining fortunes and of waning monastic professions, that the royal government suc-ceeded in making such moderate reforms.[12]

When revolutionaries embarked on the construction of a secular, egalitarian state, they set in motion far more radical reconceptualizations of the way that procreation structured the relationship between individuals, state, and God. In fact, the results of their attempt illustrated the paradox that the new republican nation could, in some arenas, act with fewer limits than the supposedly "abso-lutist" monarchical system that preceded it. Even the Revolutionary regime's broad powers depended in some ways on the consent and collaboration of the governed; the attack on vows of celibacy appears to have had broad support in many areas. Revolutionary legislators' decision to subordinate the sacred to the political bitterly divided the new citizens, engendering resistance and violence.

It was not just in the matter of religious celibacy that pronatalist ideology found new expression. Revolutionary legislators also turned their attention to marriage, the institution that the Old Regime's pronatalist policymakers had called "the most important act of civil life" because it was "the seminary of sub-jects." In harmony with their quest to found a nation devoted to liberty and equality among citizens, revolutionary legislators took up the charge to rewrite marriage laws to guarantee liberty and equality; in other words, they set out to dismantle the marital legislation that had made conjugal households sites for the reproduction of the hierarchical, patriarchal, monarchical society of the Old Regime. Key steps in this fraught, conflict-ridden process included reducing parental power that kept men and women from marrying according to individual will, rejecting the indissolubility that distinguished Catholic, sacramental marriage from its practice elsewhere, eliminating distinctions between legitimate and illegitimate children, and eventually, guaranteeing greater legal and economic freedom to wives. These changes, as Suzanne Desan argues, responded in large measure to the demands of the newly empowered citizenry, in particular women. They reached into the most intimate personal relationships, promising to reform and regenerate them. Familiar pronatalist arguments emerged when writers and legislators claimed that a higher birthrate would surely result when marital tyranny ended, liberating men and women to couple out of inclination, and thereby to fulfill more efficiently the reproductive purpose nature intended; or when they spoke of marriage (much as Old Regime jurists had) as a "contract" which bound the individual to the nation with an implicit promise to reproduce himself.[13]

The Revolution empowered French lawmakers to experiment with fundamental changes to France's marital and domestic order, and to pursue social regeneration on a deeper level than through mere encouragement of traditional conjugal life and procreation. In the midst of revolutionary tumult, some French writers and lawmakers nevertheless continued to pursue a populationist agenda with familiar tools from the Old Regime's pronatalist toolbox. Revolutionary legislation, for example, offered a number of fiscal benefits to men with large families. By 1791, the National Assembly had set tax rates to benefit prolific fathers, offering its first breaks for families with three children, and better rates for families with six or more offspring.[14] These numbers were probably more realistic incentives for people in the late eighteenth century than were the heroic procreative feats demanded (at least theoretically) to qualify for tax benefits under the Old Regime. Even so, in 1801, the author Poncet de la Grave recommended a new set of measures to promote reproduction, optimistically based on the prodigious fecundity that had been rewarded in the past. He proposed dividing the population into classes: the first class of "*premier citoyens*" would include fathers of ten or more children, who were to be exempt from taxation, allowed to wear distinguishing honorific insignia, and whose names were to be inscribed in gold on a public monument and published in every newspaper. Citizens with six to nine children would qualify only for the second class.[15]

Alongside rewards for fathers of many children, Revolutionary lawmakers decreed fiscal penalties for celibates. This was terrain where the authority guaranteed to parents impeded pronatalist action under the Old Regime; even when the king proposed taxing unmarried men in 1666, royal courts had effectively prevented it on the grounds that as legal minors such men were free neither to dispose of themselves nor of property. Once the Revolution reduced this barrier with laws setting the age of majority for both men and women at the lower age of twenty-one, the nation's lawmakers penalized the unmarried with higher tax rates and contributions to forced loans. After some debate, legislators determined not to exclude women from the fiscal exactions that burdened unmarried citizens, a manifestation of men and women's equality. In these ways, an arsenal of fiscal measures drawn from classical antiquity and intended to channel marital and sexual behavior toward politically useful ends were dusted off once again and placed in the service of the new political order.[16]

The Revolution's radical attempt to transform the household order did not endure beyond the composition of the Napoleonic Civil Code of 1804. Historians situate the Civil Code as an attempt to reconstitute a stable social order after more than a decade of sometimes chaotic shifts in the laws that regulated family life. Based on ostensibly "natural" truths about human nature, the Code reinforced paternal power, closed off the possibility of divorce, and deprived married women of the legal and economic freedoms they had gained during the Revolution.[17] Carol Blum describes the household idealized in the Civil Code as a triumph of the vision of Jean-Jacques Rousseau, a domestic unit "animated with populationist sentiment, dominated by the protective father, dependent on the submissive, fertile mother, and underwritten by the providential state."[18] Yet from the early nineteenth century until France's defeat in the Franco-Prussian war, governing elites ceased making populationist pronatalism a governing priority. They remained intensely interested in the household as a site where the morality of the nation's next generation would be formed. But the gradual spread of Malthusian ideas offered the disturbing possibility that laws encouraging marriage and reproduction would serve only to multiply society's miserable, dangerous elements. This, too, marked an important transformation in ideas about the relation of individuals to the social whole. Louis XIV's advisors had believed that by encouraging men to marry young and become fathers, sinful, potentially criminal passions were channeled toward politically useful ends. Malthus drew on the population science of the eighteenth century to turn this age-old moral equation on its head. Readers interpreted his theories to mean that the institution of marriage and the reproduction that it naturally entailed could become a dangerous source of moral and economic disorder.[19]

Assessing the consequences of all these changes for men and women as gendered individuals constitutes a lively arena for debate among historians and feminists. Throughout the Revolutionary era and into the nineteenth century, a dominant, Rousseauian model of domesticity focused on the household as a critical site of moral training, and identified mothers as keys to raising a numerous and virtuous citizenry. This attention arguably afforded women greater cultural authority and political significance than they had enjoyed in the past. It might, as some feminists argued it should, have led to women's empowerment as citizens, on the basis of their status as mothers. Nevertheless, the authority women exercised as mothers did not legitimize them as political actors in the way fatherhood had empowered men as fathers. Despite the reformulation of politics as a contract that bound individuals free and equal by birth, women were excluded from citizenship. Among the explanations historians offer for this exclusion, women's reproductive role frequently plays a large part. Somehow, the necessity that human beings procreate and thus perpetuate the human and political communities—the natural purpose of their sexual difference, as contemporaries understood it—eroded men and women's fundamental equality as individuals.

Since procreation was central to explaining the relationship of individuals to the political whole, it surely mattered that these issues were debated against a backdrop of rapidly changing procreative behavior. At the basis of traditional Old Regime political theory lay the notion that political relationships were based in procreation, and set in place by God. Over the course of the seventeenth and eighteenth centuries, it became increasingly clear that the procreative order was, in large measure, governed by human customs and susceptible, for good or ill, to human intervention. The notion that elemental human relationships could be transformed inspired both political experiments and anxieties about where those changes might lead.

Appendix
Provisions and Implementation
of the 1666 Pronatalist Edict

Provision	Result
Taxable subjects married before age twenty exempted from taxation (*the taille and other charges publiques*) until the age of twenty-five	Technically in force until the Revolution, but amended so that young married men would pay taxes on profits from land in lease (*à ferme*)
Taxable subjects married before age twenty-one exempted from taxation (*taille* and other *charges publiques*) until the age of twenty-four	Technically in force until the Revolution, but amended so that young married men would pay taxes on profits from land in lease (*à ferme*)
Taxable subjects **not** married by age twenty-one heretofore subject to taxation	The Paris *Cour des Aides* amended this provision at registration because unmarried men of this age not earning an independent living were minors not considered to own property subject to taxation.
Taxable householders (*pères de famille*) with ten living, legitimate children who have not taken religious vows exempted from acting as tax collector, from *tutelle* and *curatelle*, from billeting soldiers, and from civic guard duty or fees paid toward same. Sons who have died in royal service to be counted as living	In force throughout 1667–83. Revoked by Royal Declaration of 13 January 1683. Revocation generally enforced by eighteenth century
Taxable householders with twelve living, legitimate children none of whom have taken religious vows exempted from all things listed above, and also from taxation (*taille, taillon, subsides et impositions*)	In force throughout 1667–83. Revoked by Royal Declaration of 13 January 1683. Revocation enforced by eighteenth century
Noblemen "and their wives" with ten living, legitimate children none of whom have taken religious vows to receive one thousand *livres* pensions. Sons who have died in royal service to be counted as living	Awarded at royal discretion through early 1670s. Never formally revoked; "fallen into desuetude" according to eighteenth-century royal officials

(continued)

Provision	Result
Noblemen with twelve living, legitimate children none of whom have taken religious vows, as above, will receive two thousand *livres* pensions.	Awarded at royal discretion through early 1670s. Never formally revoked; "fallen into desuetude" according to eighteenth-century royal officials
Inhabitants of tax-exempt cities, *bourgeois* neither subject to tax nor noble, with ten or twelve living children, none of whom have taken religious vows, to receive pension amount half of those awarded to nobles. Also exempt from civic guard duty and other *charges de ville*	Minimal evidence of payment of pensions in late 1660s. Exemptions dependent on local interpretation.

Sources: François Isambert et al., *Recueil générale des anciennes lois françaises, depuis l'an 420, jusqu'à la Révolution de 1789*, vol. 17:90–93 and 19:43; "Extrait des registres de la Cour des Aydes de 9. Decembre 1666," in *Nouveau Code des Tailles* (Paris, 1740), Vol. I: 255.

Introduction

1. "Dieu avoit beny son mariage du nombre du douze enfans nez de luy et de Marie Anne Pichery son Epouse," AC Auxerre GG. 139 (8 August 1735).

2. On the medical and ritual practices surrounding birth, see Jacques Gélis, *History of Childbirth: Fertility, Pregnancy and Birth in Early Modern Europe* (Cambridge, England: Polity Press, 1991), 188–212.

3. The text of the edict is available in François Isambert et. al., *Recueil général des anciennes lois françaises depuis l'an 420 jusqu'à la révolution de 1789*. 29 volumes (Paris: 1821–33), 18: 90–93. For a chart summarizing its provisions, see appendix 1.

4. For a review of some of these policies, see C. Alison McIntosh, "Recent Pronatalist Policies in Western Europe," *Population and Development Review* 12, Supplement: "Below-Replacement Fertility in Industrial Societies: Causes, Consequences, Policies" (1986): 318–34. For a discussion of how such modern policies relate to nationalist ideologies throughout the world, see Leslie King, "Demographic Trends, Pronatalism, and Nationalist Ideologies in the Late Twentieth Century," *Ethnic and Racial Studies* 25:3 (May 2002): 367–89.

5. Marilyn Strathern, *Reproducing the Future: Essays on Anthropology, Kinship and the New Reproductive Technologies* (New York: Routledge, 1992), 10.

6. Historical work on the political and ideological significance of pronatalist policies is vast, even when limited to France. For works that focus on the gender ideologies implicit in French pronatalism, see Karen Offen, "Depopulation, Nationalism, and Feminism in Fin-de-siècle France," *American Historical Review* 89 (1984): 648–76; Joshua Cole, *The Power of Large Numbers: Population, Politics and Gender in Nineteenth-Century France* (Ithaca, NY: Cornell University Press, 2000); Mary Louise Roberts, *Civilization Without Sexes: Reconstructing Gender in Postwar France, 1917–27* (Chicago: University of Chicago Press, 1994); Carol Blum, *Strength in Numbers: Population, Reproduction and Power in Eighteenth-Century France* (Baltimore, MD: Johns Hopkins University Press, 2002); Kristin Stromberg Childers, *Fathers, Families and the State in France* (Ithaca, NY: Cornell University Press, 2003); and the introduction by Rachel Fuchs and articles by Joshua Cole, Cheryl Koos, Jean Elisabeth Pedersen, and Andrés Horace Reggiani in the forum, "Population and State in the Third Republic," in *French Historical Studies* 19:3 (Spring 1996): 633–754. For work that focuses more on the racial ideologies implicit in pronatalist policies, see Elisa Camiscioli, "Producing Citizens, Reproducing the French 'Race': Immigration, Demography and Pronatalism in Early Twentieth-Century France," *Gender and History* 13:3 (November 2001): 594–621.

7. Jean Bodin, *Six livres de la république* 5:7. Quoted in Perrot, 547. On the evolution of population thought during the seventeenth and eighteenth centuries, see Jean-Claude Perrot, "Les Economistes, les philosophes et la population," in Jacques Dupâquier et al., *Histoire de la population française*, vol. 2; Joseph. J. Spengler, *French*

Predecessors of Malthus (Durham, NC: Duke University Press, 1942); James C. Riley, *Population Thought in the Age of the Demographic Revolution* (Durham, NC: Duke University Press, 1985); Carol Blum, *Strength in Numbers: Population, Reproduction and Power in Eighteenth-Century France* (Baltimore: Johns Hopkins University Press, 2002); Joshua Cole, *The Power of Large Numbers: Population, Politics and Gender in Nineteenth-Century France* (Ithaca, NY: Cornell University Press, 2000).

8. Gomont and Auzanet, "Des privilèges de ceux qui ont eu nombre d'enfans," BN Mélanges de Colbert Volume 33:743.

9. Bossuet, *Politics Drawn from the Very Words of Holy Scripture*, Patrick Riley, ed. (Cambridge: Cambridge University Press, 1999), 62.

10. Bodin, *Six Books of the Commonwealth* I:4.

11. For a brief sketch of these results, see Angus McLaren, *A History of Contraception* (Oxford, UK: Blackwell, 1990), 146–47. For a fuller introduction to the problem of identifying the advent of birth control, and for bibliographical guidance on this question, see Alain Bideau and Jean-Pierre Bardet, "Fluctuations chronologiques ou début de la revolution contraceptive?" in Jacques Dupâquier et al. *Histoire de la population française*, vol. 2: de la Renaissance à 1789 (Paris: Quadrige/PUF, 1995), 373–98.

12. Etienne Van de Walle, "Fertility Transition, Conscious Choice, and Numeracy," *Demography* 29:4 (November 1992): 487–502. The quotation appears on 489.

13. For a review of these theories, tied to the political context in which birth control appeared, see Philip Kreager, "Early Modern Population Theory: A Reassessment," in *Population and Development Review* 17:2 (June 1991): 207–27.

14. Work on the "fertility transition" is voluminous and crosses several disciplinary boundaries. For introduction, reviews of the theories that have been offered to explain the motivations for birth control, and additional bibliographic references, see Bideau and Bardet, "Fluctuations chronologiques ou début de la revolution contraceptive?"; Michael W. Flinn, *The European Demographic System, 1500–1820* (New York: Harvester Wheatsheaf, 1981), 25–46; Jacqueline Hecht, "From 'Be Fruitful and Multiply' to Family Planning: The Enlightenment Transition," *Eighteenth-Century Studies* 32:4 (1999): 536–51; Angus McLaren, *A History of Contraception* (Oxford: Blackwell, 1990), 141–77; idem, *Sexuality and Social Control* (New York: Holmes & Meier, 1983), 14–17; Etienne Van de Walle, "Motivations and Technology in the Decline of French Fertility," in Robert Wheaton and Tamara K. Hareven, eds., *Family and Sexuality in French History* (Philadelphia: University of Pennsylvania Press, 1980), 135–78.

15. Quoted in Van de Walle, "Fertility Transition," 491.

16. Ibid., 493.

17. Van de Walle, "Fertility Transition," 496–501. For a consideration of numerical thinking in the early modern period, see Keith Thomas, "Numeracy in Early Modern England," the Prothero Lecture, given 2 July 1986, published in *Transactions of the Royal Historical Society*, 5th series 37 (1987): 103–32.

18. "Fertility Transition," 501.

19. The term "natural fertility" has generated controversy. Used by demographers, it has a measurable, technical meaning denoting a fertility regime without evidence of "parity specific" changes in behavior—in laymen's terms, the absence of evidence that couples seek to limit births in order to achieve a specific family size. Critics

charge that its neat division between planned and "uncontrolled" fertility is misleading and worry about the bias inherent in the model's assumption that fertility control strategies always aim to limit the number of births. Because of the confusion possible with this term, I have chosen not to use it. For more information on the limitations of the "natural fertility" model, see Chris Wilson, Jim Oeppen, and Mike Pardoe, "What is Natural Fertility? The modeling of a concept," *Population Index* 54:1 (1988): 4–20. For a fascinating critique of the assumption that "fertility control" will aim to reduce the number of births, see Caroline H. Bledsoe, *Contingent Lives: Fertility, Time, and Aging in West Africa* (Chicago: University of Chicago Press, 2002).

20. The averages are derived from data from the Norman village of Crulai in the period 1674–1742, presented in Alain Bideau and Jean-Pierre Bardet, "Mesure de la fécondité," in Dupâquier et al. *Histoire de la population française*, 353–57. As the authors note, averages must be used cautiously due to significant regional variation. For explanation of the fertility consequences of the European marriage pattern, see Flinn, 27–34.

21. Marcel Lachiver, *La Population de Meulan du XVIIe au XIXe siècle* (Paris: SEVPEN, 1969), 170–72.

22. Ibid.

23. Jacqueline Hecht, "From 'Be Fruitful and Multiply' to Family Planning: The Enlightenment Transition," *Eighteenth-Century Studies* 32:4 (1999): 536–51.

24. For a classic discussion of the significance of family strategies as factors in modernization, see Natalie Zemon Davis, "Ghosts, Kin and Progeny: Some Features of Family Life in Early Modern France," *Daedalus* 106:2 (Spring 1977): 87–114.

25. The power of the revisionist critique has been such that, while much of this narrative still orients textbook treatments of seventeenth-century France, it is difficult to name a recent historian who exemplifies these views. For discussions of the theory of "absolutism" and what is at stake in its definition, see Fanny Cosandey and Robert Descimon, *L'absolutisme en France: Histoire et historiographie* (Paris: Éditions du Seuil, 2002); in English, see Richard Bonney, "Absolutism: What's in a Name?" *French History* 1:1 (1987): 93–117; and the compelling and astute review in Michael Breen, *Law, City and King: Legal Culture, Municipal Politics, and State Formation in Early Modern Dijon* (Rochester, NY: University of Rochester Press, 2007), esp. 17–21.

26. William Beik offers a synthesis of this viewpoint in "Louis XIV's Absolutism as Social Collaboration," *Past and Present* 188 (August 2005): 195–224.

27. Important exceptions include Carolyn Lougee's *Le Paradis des Femmes: Women, Salons and Social Stratification in Seventeenth-Century France* (Princeton, NJ: Princeton University Press, 1976); Joan DeJean, *Tender Geographies: Women and the Origins of the Novel in France* (New York: Columbia University Press, 1991); and Abby E. Zanger, *Scenes from the Marriage of Louis XIV: Nuptial Fictions and the Making of Absolutist Power* (Stanford: Stanford University Press, 1997).

28. This quotation is drawn from "De la puissance des empêchemens du mariage, par Monsieur de Launoy," in *J. Launoii Opera* Volume I part 2, 1003; similar sentiments are expressed in many seventeenth-century legal sources dealing with marriage.

29. For Germany, see Joel F. Harrington, *Reordering Marriage and Society in Reformation Germany* (Cambridge: Cambridge University Press, 1995); Isabel Hull, *Sexuality, State, and Civil Society in Germany 1700–1815* (Ithaca, NY: Cornell University Press, 1996); Lyndal Roper, *The Holy Household: Women and Morals in Reformation Augsburg* (New York: Oxford, 1989); Ulrike Strasser, *State of Virginity: Gender, Religion and*

Politics in an Early Modern Catholic State (Ann Arbor: University of Michigan Press, 2004). For a historical sociologist's assessment of this dynamic, see Julia Adams, *The Familial State: Ruling Families and Merchant Capitalism in Early Modern Europe* (Ithaca, NY: Cornell University Press, 2005). For connections between conjugal life and state formation in the United States, see Nancy Cott, *Public Vows: A History of Marriage and the Nation* (Cambridge, Mass.: Harvard University Press, 2000).

30. Sarah Hanley, "Engendering the State: Family Formation and State Building in Early Modern France," *French Historical Studies* 16:1 (Spring 1989): 4–27. See also, idem, "Family and State in Early Modern France: The Marital Law Compact," in Marilyn J. Boxer and Jean H. Quataert, *Connecting Spheres: European Women in a Globalizing World, 1500 to the Present* (New York: Oxford University Press, 2000), 61–71; "The Monarchic State in Early Modern France: Marital Regime Government and Male Right," in Adrianna Bakos, ed., *Politics, Ideology and Law in Early Modern Europe: Essays in Honor of J.H.M. Salmon* (Rochester, NY: University of Rochester Press, 1994), 107–26; " 'The Jurisprudence of the Arrêts': Marital Union, Civil Society and State Formation in France, 1550–1650," *Law and History Review* 21:1 (Spring 2003): 1–40; "Social Sites of Political Practice in France: Lawsuits, Civil Rights and the Separation of Powers in Domestic and State Government, 1500–1800," *American Historical Review* (1997): 27–52.

31. Hanley, "Engendering the State," 6–9.

Chapter 1

1. *Lettres de Gui Patin* III: 225–26 (22 June 1660). On abortion in early modern Europe, see Angus McLaren, *A History of Contraception* (Oxford: Blackwell, 1990), 159–62. For details on the treatment of abortion in French law, see James R. Farr, *Authority and Sexuality in Early Modern Burgundy 1550–1730* (New York: Oxford University Press, 1995), 125–32.

2. "On dit que sa maison étoit un bordel public, et que quantité de garces alloient accoucher dedans, *vel abortum passurae*," *Lettres de Gui Patin* III: 236 (15 July 1660).

3. *Lettres de Gui Patin* III: 236 (15 July 1660).

4. *Lettres de Gui Patin* III: 249 (26 August 1660). On royal rigor regarding pardons for infanticide, see Natalie Zemon Davis, *Fiction in the Archives: Pardon Tales and the Tellers in Sixteenth-Century France* (Stanford: Stanford University Press, 1990), 85–87.

5. See Bodin, *Six Books of the Commonwealth*, book 6, chapters 4 and 5.

6. Late medieval jurists claimed that Salic Law was *the* primordial, fundamental law of the French royal succession dating back to the Salian Franks. But Salic Law was actually an "invented tradition" that served to exclude English heirs of Isabelle, daughter of Philip IV, from the French throne. In addition, Sarah Hanley has argued that the "discovery" of the Salic Law provided a context for early humanistic writers to defame women. For the uses of the Salic Law in the late medieval context, see Ralph Giesey, "The Juristic Basis of Dynastic Right to the French Throne," *Transactions of the American Philosophical Society* 51:5 (1961); see also Hanley, "La loi salique," in *Encyclopédie politique et historique des femmes*, ed. Christine Fauré (Paris: PUF, 1997): 11–30.

7. For an account of the Fronde, see Orest Ranum, *The Fronde: A French Revolution, 1648–52* (New York: W.W. Norton, 1993). For a recent examination of the Regency of Anne of Austria, with a focus on the gendered nature of the Regent's difficulties,

see Katherine Crawford, *Perilous Performances: Gender and Regency in Early Modern France* (Cambridge, Mass.: Harvard University Press, 2004), 98–136.

8. *Lettres de Gui Patin* III: 280–81 (19 October 1660). "Foreigner" was Patin's own embellishment on the biblical warning. For the same verse echoed in Bodin, see *Six Books of the Commonwealth* 6:4.

9. *Lettres de Gui Patin* III: 337 (7 March 1661).

10. Abby E. Zanger has recently traced the importance of the royal marriage to the creation of Louis XIV's authority. This chapter is in part an attempt to heed her call to "extend and modify the important inquiries of [historians focusing on the ritual constructions of royal power] by endeavoring to recover...rituals (marriage, childbirth)...not formally associated with generating significant fictions of sovereignty." *Scenes from the Marriage of Louis XIV: Nuptial Fictions and the Making of Absolutist Power* (Stanford: Stanford University Press, 1997), quotation from page 163.

11. "Enfin...la paix générale, mon mariage, mon autorité plus affermie et la mort du Cardinal Mazarin m'obligèrent à ne pas différer davantage ce que je souhaitais et que je craignais tout ensemble depuis si longtemps." Louis XIV, *Mémoires et réflexions, 1661–1715* (Paris: Communication et Tradition, 1997), 14.

12. *Lettres de Gui Patin* III: 337 (7 March 1661) and 344 (18 March 1661).

13. Joseph de Champeaux, *Devises: cris de guerre, légendes dictons* (Dijon, 1890), 168.

14. For the symbolism of the sun, see Blum, *Strength in Numbers*, 5–6; on the monarch's depiction as Mars, see Collins, *The State in Early Modern France* (Cambridge: Cambridge University Press, 1995), 83.

15. Zanger, 8–12.

16. On the symbolism of the king's leg, see Zanger, 19–26.

17. I thank Lisa Perella for first bringing this image to my attention. For an analysis of the way ephemera negotiated the problem of the queen's role in royal reproduction, see Jennifer Germann, "Fecund Fathers and Missing Mothers: Louis XV, Marie Leszcsinska, and the Politics of Royal Parentage in the 1720s," *Studies in Eighteenth-Century Culture* 36:1 (2007): 105–26.

18. An implicit subject of this image may be France's imperial rival England. The accession of James II in 1685, who had not yet produced a son by his wife Mary of Modena, raised awareness of dynastic continuity and its political consequences.

19. For a recent account of clash over the status of the king's illegitimate children, see Matthew Dean Gerber, *The End of Bastardy: Illegitimacy in France from the Reformation through the Revolution* (Unpublished PhD diss., University of California, Berkeley, 2004).

20. Once again, a point made by Zanger, esp. 163.

21. Seventeenth-century population figures for France are still matters for debate, due primarily to unreliable registration of deaths. See Jacques Dupâquier et al., *Histoire de la population française* 2:65–68.

22. Antoine de Montchrestien, *Traité de l'oeconomie politique*. Théophile Funck-Brentano, ed. (Paris: Rivière, 1920), 275. The spelling is often modernized to Montchrétien; I have chosen Montchrestien because it is used in the Library of Congress catalogue.

23. Montchrestien, 24, 25, 68.

24. For different views on Montchrestien, see Joseph J. Spengler, *French Predecessors of Malthus* (Durham, NC: Duke University Press, 1942), 16–18 and Nannerl O. Keohane, *Philosophy and the State in France* (Princeton, NJ: Princeton University Press, 1980), esp. 163–68.

25. Evelyn, *Diary*, and Veryard, *An account of diverse Choice Remarks . . . Taken in a Journey through the Low Countries, France, Italy and part of Spain, with the Isles of Sicily and Malta, as also a Voyage to the Levant*, quoted in John Lough, *France Observed in the Seventeenth Century by British Travellers* (Boston: Oriel Press Stocksfield, 1985), 32. Lough notes that John Locke, who toured France extensively in the 1670s, saw many ruined farmhouses and wondered whether they signaled a decline in the rural population. Lough, 39–40.

26. Paul Hay, Marquis du Chastelet, *Traitté de la politique de France* (Cologne: 1672), 33 [originally published Paris, 1669].

27. Several sources mention attempts to count the population during the sixteenth century, and other surveys under Louis XIII suggest concerted efforts to track population movements. See Guy Cabourdin and Jacques Dupâquier, "Les Sources et les institutions," in Dupâquier et al., *Histoire de la population française* 2:27–30.

28. On Colbert's interest in population matters, see Jacques Dupâquier, "Le pouvoir royal et la statistique démographique," in François Bédarida, ed., *Pour une histoire de la statistique* (Paris: Institut national de la statistique et des études economiques, 1977). Also, see Robert Bradley Scafe, *The Measure of Greatness: Population and the Census under Louis XIV* (Unpublished PhD diss., Stanford University, 2005). On the seventeenth-century beginnings of efforts to enumerate the population, see Eric Brian, *La mesure de l'Etat: Administrateurs et géometres au XVIIIe siècle* (Paris: Albin Michel, 1994), 153–78.

29. This argument derives from the work of Michel Foucault and his notion of biopower. See, in particular, *The History of Sexuality Volume 1: An Introduction* (New York: Vintage, 1990). For a helpful synopsis of Foucault's thinking on biopower, see Hubert L. Dreyfus and Paul Rabinow, *Michel Foucault: Beyond Structuralism and Hermeneutics* (Chicago: University of Chicago Press, 1983), 126–83. Jay Smith offers an innovative, somewhat different Foucauldian interpretation of Louis XIV's quest for information in *The Culture of Merit: Nobility, Royal Service and the Making of Absolute Monarchy in France* (Ann Arbor: University of Michigan Press, 1996), 125–90.

30. Jacques-Bénigne Bossuet, *Politics drawn from the Very Words of Holy Scripture*. Translated and edited by Patrick Riley (Cambridge: Cambridge University Press, 1990). As Riley explains, Bossuet began the treatise in the 1670s, but did not write the last books until around 1700, shortly before his death. The sections on population were completed at this later time. However, they show little evidence of being influenced by developments in population thought at the end of the seventeenth century.

31. Bossuet, *Politics*, 355.

32. Ibid.

33. If this is what Bossuet had in mind, his position would be closer to that of royal critics.

34. Bossuet, *Politics*, 356.

35. Gomont and Auzanet, "Des privilèges de ceux qui ont eu nombre d'enfans," BN Mélanges de Colbert 33:742 verso.

36. D'Orgeval, "Traicté du commerce et reforme de la justice et de l'estat ecclesiastique," BN Mélanges de Colbert 33:364–73, quotation 364 verso.

37. Montchrestien, *Traité*, 315.

38. Evelyn, *Diary*, quoted in Lough, 32.

39. The quotation is from Robert Schwartz, *Policing the Poor in Eighteenth-Century France* (Chapel Hill, NC: University of North Carolina Press, 1988). See also Cissie Fairchilds, *Poverty and Charity in Aix* (Baltimore: Johns Hopkins University Press, 1976); Jean-Pierre Gutton, *La societé et les pauvres en Europe, XVI–XVIIIe siècles* (Paris: PUF, 1974); Olwen Hufton, *The Poor in Eighteenth-Century France* (Oxford: Oxford University Press, 1976); Howard Solomon, *Public Welfare, Science and Propaganda in Seventeenth-Century France* (Princeton, NJ: Princeton University Press, 1972).

40. Schwartz, 21–26.

41. Ibid., 13–34. See also Tim McHugh, *Hospital Politics in Seventeenth-Century France: The Crown, Urban Elites, and the Poor* (Aldershot, Hampshire, and Burlington, Vt.: Ashgate, 2007).

42. Tim McHugh, *Hospital Politics*, 86.

43. Kathryn Norberg, *Rich and Poor in Grenoble, 1600–1814* (Berkeley: University of California Press, 1985), esp. 20–60.

44. See, for example, Jean-Pierre Gutton, *Société et les pauvres: L'exemple de la généralité de Lyon 1534–1789* (Paris: Sociéte d'édition "les belles letters", 1971), 101–6, 389–93; Kathryn Norberg, "Prostitution," in Natalie Zemon Davis and Arlette Frage, eds., *A History of Women: Renaissance and Enlightenment Paradoxes* (Cambridge, Mass.: Belknap Press, 1993), 458–74.

45. Angus McLaren, *Reproductive Rituals: The Perception of Fertility in England from the Sixteenth Century to the Nineteenth Century* (London: Methuen, 1984), 45; Katherine Crawford, *European Sexualities 1400–1800* (New York: Cambridge University Press, 2007), 120–23.

46. Norberg, *Rich and Poor*, 27–64.

47. For a wide-ranging consideration of changing attitudes toward illegitimacy, see Gerber, *The End of Bastardy*. For the nineteenth century, see Rachel G. Fuchs, *Poor & Pregnant in Paris: Strategies for Survival in the Nineteenth Century* (New Brunswick, NJ: Rutgers University Press, 1992), 35–55 and Angus McLaren, *Sexuality and Social Order: The Debate over the Fertility of Women and Workers in France, 1770–1920* (New York: Holmes & Meier, 1983), 138–39.

48. On the edict of 1556, see Hanley, "Engendering the State: Family Formation and State Building in Early Modern France," *French Historical Studies* 16:1 (Spring 1989): 4–27; on enforcement of the edict, see Farr, 124–33.

49. This is James Farr's conclusion from his work in Burgundian sources. He found that the Parlement of Dijon confirmed forty-seven of the fifty-eight death sentences for infanticide handed down by lower courts between 1582 and 1730, and augmented lesser sentences to death in three cases. But he also noted a change in jurisprudence in the latter half of the seventeenth century. Of the eleven death sentences the Parlement overturned, eight came after 1668. Farr does not offer a specific reason for the change, but he implies that changing evidentiary standards were the likely cause. Of the eight post-1668 overturned death sentences, only one of the women was acquitted; five were threatened with rearrest if additional evidence emerged. Farr, *Authority and Sexuality*, 132.

50. Bineteau to Colbert, 11 December 1666. BN Mélanges de Colbert 142 bis fol. 617–19.

51. Ulrike Strasser, *State of Virginity: Gender, Religion and Politics in an Early Modern Catholic State* (Ann Arbor: University of Michigan Press, 2004), 53–55; see also Lyndal

Roper, *Witch Craze: Terror and Fantasy in Baroque Germany* (New Haven, Conn.: Yale University Press, 2004), 127–35.

52. Schwartz, *Policing the Poor*, 114; Olwen Hufton, *The Prospect Before Her: A History of Women in Western Europe* Vol I, 1500–1800 (New York: Alfred A. Knopf, 1996), 69–101.

53. Norberg, *Rich and Poor*, 37–38.

54. Montaigne, "Apology for Raymond Sebond," in *The Complete Works of Montaigne*, translated by Donald Frame. (London: Hamish Hamilton, 1957), 437.

55. Ibid.

56. Montaigne, "Of the affection of fathers for their children," in *Complete Works*, 279–80.

57. Ibid., 440–41.

58. See Montaigne, "Apology for Raymond Sebond," 440 and Gaya, *Ceremonies nuptiales de toutes les nations* (Paris, 1680) (unpaginated).

59. See Hélène Bergues, "La population vue par les utopistes," *Population* 6:2 (April–June 1951): 265–67.

60. Solomon, *Public Welfare, Science and Propaganda*, 60–99; Kathleen Wellman, *Making Science Social: The Conferences of Théophraste Renaudot, 1633–1642* (Norman: University of Oklahoma Press, 2003).

61. *A General Collection of Discourses of the Virtuosi of France, Upon Questions of all Sorts of Philosophy and Other Natural Knowledg. Made in the Assembly of the Beaux Esprits at Paris, by the Most Ingenious Persons of that Nation*, (London: Thomas Drink and John Starkey, 1664), I:451–53, II:135–38. During the 1630s, accounts of the meetings were published weekly on cheap paper. They were later collected and published in more expensive editions.

62. For a typical explanation, see Marie de l'Incarnation, *L'Ecole Sainte, ou explication familiere des mysteres de la foy* (Paris, 1684), 553.

63. Modern interpretations of the Münster experiment tend to explain polygamy as a social control effort rather than theological innovation; the faction seeking to control the city was faced with an inordinate imbalance in the gender ratio. On the Münster polygamists and Protestant experiments with alternative marital systems, see Lyndal Roper, "Sexual utopianism in the German Reformation," in *Oedipus and the Devil* (London: Routledge, 1994), 79–103; also, Ronald Po-Chia Hsia, "The Münster Anabaptists," in idem, ed. *The German People and the Reformation* (Ithaca, NY: Cornell University Press, 1988).

64. J. Waterworth, translator. *Canons and Decrees of the Sacred and Oecumenical Council of Trent* (London: C. Dolman, 1848), 193–94.

65. Blum, *Strength in Numbers*, 79–81.

66. *Another Collection of Philosophical Conferences of the French Virtuousi Upon Questions of all Sorts; For the Improving of Natural Knowledge. Made in the Assembly of Beaux Esprits at Paris, by the most Ingenious Persons of that Nation.* (London: Dring and Starkey, 1665), 135–36.

67. Jacques Chaussée, *Traité de l'excelence du mariage: de sa necessité, et des moyens d'y vivre heureux* (Paris, 1685), 136.

68. Blum, 77 and 81.

69. Blum, *Strength in Numbers*, 77–81.

70. [Philippe de Béthune], *Le Conseiller d'etat, ou recueil des plus generales considerations servant au maniment des Affaires politiques.* (Paris, 1641), 486–87.

71. Jacques Chaussée, *Traité de l'excelence du mariage: de sa necessité, et des moyens d'y vivre heureux* (Paris, 1685), 137–38.

72. Gerber, 47–87.

73. Gerber, 159; Eve Castro, *Les bâtards du soleil* (Paris: Olivier Orban, 1987).

Chapter 2

1. Olivier Lefèvre d'Ormesson *Journal*, M. Chéruel, ed., 2 vol. (Paris: 1861), 2:524–25. Chéruel transcribed the family name as "Janvoy" but my research leads me to believe that the family name was Janvry. The prospective bride was probably Hélène Ferrand, daughter of Michel Ferrand, seigneur de Janvry (d. 1666) and Hélène Gillot. See the genealogical information in *Lettres de la présidente Ferrand au Baron de Breteuil* (Paris, 1880), 185. We do know that J. B. Colbert worked on behalf of Charon de Ménars to secure him a position in the Parlement of Paris and the *dispense d'âge* he would need to exercise it. See Pierre Clément, *Lettres, instructions et mémoires de Colbert*. 7 vols. (Paris, 1861–73), 6:4 note 2.

2. D'Ormesson, *Journal* 2:525.

3. Ibid.

4. The Louisquatorzian legal reform is discussed in François Olivier-Martin, *Les lois du Roi* (Paris: Editions Loysel, 1988); William F. Church, "The Decline of French Jurists as Political Theorists, 1660–1789," *French Historical Studies* 5:1 (Spring 1967): 1–40, esp. 3–6; Francis Monnier, *Guillaume de Lamoignon et Colbert: Essai sur la législation française au XVIIe siècle* (Paris, 1862); Marc Boulanger, "Justice et Absolutisme: La grande ordonnance criminelle d'Août 1670," *Revue d'histoire moderne et contemporaine* 47:1 (2000): 1–36; Marguerite Boulet-Sautel, "Colbert et la législation," in Roland Mousnier, ed. *Un Nouveau Colbert: Actes du colloque pour le tricentenaire de la mort de Colbert* (Paris: SEDES, 1983), 119–32.

5. Lefebvre, *Cours de doctorat sur l'histoire de droit matrimonial français* (Paris: 1913), esp. 101–09.

6. Lefebvre, *Cours de doctorat sur l'histoire de droit matrimonial français* (Paris: 1913). See also James Traer, *Marriage and Family in Eighteenth-Century France* (Ithaca, NY: Cornell University Press, 1980), 31–39.

7. For the best example, see C. W. Cole, *Colbert and a Century of French Mercantilism* (New York: Columbia University Press, 1939).

8. The most important work on this theme is J. L. Bourgeon, *Les Colbert avant Colbert: Destin d'une famille marchande* (Paris: PUF, 1986). See also Jean Meyer, *Colbert* (Paris: Hachette, 1981), 37–89. For an insightful analysis of elite families, patronage, and the connection of family networks to the development of royal government, see Sara Chapman, *Private Ambition and Political Alliances in Louis XIV's Government: The Phelypeaux de Pontchartrain Family, 1650–1715* (Rochester, NY: University of Rochester Press, 2004).

9. Bourgeon, 147, 255–57. For the effects of wet-nursing on fertility, see below, 132–34.

10. Ibid., 222–24. After a review of Colbert's private correspondence, Jean Vilain suggests Charon was pregnant fifteen times, the last time in 1672, when she was forty-two years old. Vilain, *La Fortune de Colbert* (Paris: Imprimerie Nationale, 1994).

11. "Mémoire sur la réformation de la justice," in Clément 6:5.

12. Ibid., in Clément 6:10.
13. The mémoires are collected in BN Collection Clairambault Vol. 613. For those complaining about the number and quality of judges, see, in particular, Barillon (fol. 21) and Pussort (fol. 395). See also Peter Arend Jen Van der Burg, *The Politics of European Codification* (Groningen: Europa Law Publishing, 2007), esp. 132–37.
14. BN Clairambault 613:389.
15. D'Ormesson, *Journal*, 2:480.
16. See, for example, the comments of Gobelin, BN Clairambault 613:154–54 verso.
17. Colbert, "Mémoire sur la réformation de la Justice," 6:10.
18. Ibid., 6:11.
19. Jean de Gomont "Traité du mariage" (dated April 1670) in Bibliothèque Municipale de Sens MS 208, 729–98.
20. Jean de Gomont, "Pour faciliter les Mariages et rendre plus difficiles les voeux de Religion," BN Clairambault 613:179–200.
21. On Auzanet, see Clément 6:12 note 3.
22. Nicolas Le Camus, "Mémoire sur l'édit des mariages," (n.d.) in Bibliothèque de l'Arsenal, Recueil Le Camus Vol. 674, 380–84. For a different legal project demonstrating a similar process of consultation, proposal, etc., see Achille II de Harlay, "Projet que j'ai dressé," [regarding nuns' dowries] (1667) BN MF 15765, 10–21, and the accompanying memorandum, 24–29.
23. On these measures, see Pál Csillag, *The Augustan Laws on Family Relations* (Budapest: Akademiai Kiado, 1976); P. A. Brunt, *Italian Manpower* (Oxford: Oxford University Press, 1987); Richard Frank, "Augustus' Legislation on Marriage and Children," *California Studies in Classical Antiquity* 8 (1975): 41–52.
24. Michael Breen discusses the values and political thought characteristic of seventeenth-century legal training and practice in *Law, City, and King: Legal Culture, Municipal Politics, and State Formation in Early Modern Dijon* (Rochester, NY: University of Rochester Press, 2007), esp. 39–47, 151–79.
25. Gomont, "Traité du mariage," 763.
26. Ibid., 732.
27. Ibid., 739.
28. Gomont, "Pour faciliter," 184.
29. Gomont, "Traité du mariage," 735.
30. Ibid., 763.
31. Auzanet and Gomont, "Des privilèges de ceux qui ont eu nombre d'enfans," BN Mélanges de Colbert 33:741–45, quotation from 743.
32. Auzanet and Gomont, 743.
33. On patriarchalist themes in seventeenth-century political theory, see Gordon Schochet, *Patriarchalism in Political Thought* (Oxford: Blackwell, 1975).
34. Auzanet and Gomont, 743.
35. Gomont, "Traité du mariage," 762.
36. Auzanet and Gomont, 742 verso.
37. See, in particular, Hanley, "Engendering the State: Family Formation and State Building in Early Modern France," *French Historical Studies* 16:1 (Spring 1989): esp. 4–15.
38. Le Camus, "Mémoire sur l'édit des Mariages," quotation from 384.
39. Auzanet and Gomont, 742.
40. Le Camus, "Mémoire sur l'édit des Mariages," 382.

41. Gomont, "Pour faciliter," 185.

42. Le Camus, "Mémoire," 383.

43. Colbert, "Notes pour M. de Gomont," Clément 6:13.

44. Gomont, "Pour faciliter," 196.

45. Colbert, "Notes pour M. de Gomont," Clément 6:13.

46. Le Camus, "Mémoire," 383 verso.

47. Ibid.

48. Etienne Van de Walle, "Fertility, Conscious Choice, and Numeracy," *Demography* 29:4 (November 1992): 487–502. Also see the introduction.

49. Isambert et al., eds. *Recueil général des anciennes lois françaises*. 29 vols. (Paris: 1821–33): 18:90.

50. Isambert 19:91.

51. See Marcel Marion, *Dictionnaire des institutions de la France* (Paris: Editions Picard, 1969), s.v. "tutelle" and "curatelle." Fathers of five children were already exempted from the tutelle throughout much of France, so it is not clear what the significance of this provision was, except to raise the profile of prolific fatherhood by endowing it with privileges.

52. Isambert 18:91.

53. Ibid.

54. Isambert 18:91–92.

55. This caveat was appended to printed versions of the edict of 1666 in circulation during the seventeenth and eighteenth centuries, but is not included in published version of the edict in Isambert. See, for example, the "Edit du Roy du mois de Novembre 1666 en faveur des mariages, verifié en la Cour des Aydes, le neufième Decembre audit an," preserved in AD Marne C. 938.

56. See d'Aguesseau to Colbert (26 November 1666) BN Clairambault 791:100 and also Clairambault 791:103 and 112.

57. *The canons and decrees of the sacred and oecumenical Council of Trent*, ed. and trans. J. Waterworth (London: Dolman, 1848), 195.

58. See Elizabeth Rapley, *The Dévotes: Women and Church in Seventeenth-Century France* (Montreal: 1990) and Barbara Diefendorf, *From Penitence to Charity: Pious Women and the Catholic Reformation in Paris* (New York: Oxford University Press, 2004).

59. *Le nombre des Ecclesiastiques en France, celuy des religieux et religieuses, le temps de leur établissement, ce dont ils subsistent, & à quoy ils servent* (n.p., n.d.). Internal clues date the pamphlet in the 1670s.

60. Gomont, "Pour faciliter les mariages," BN Clairambault 613:181.

61. Gomont, "Pour faciliter," 181.

62. "Traité du commerce et reforme de la justice et de l'estat ecclesiastique," BN Mélanges de Colbert 33:366.

63. D'Orgeval, "Traicté du commerce et réforme de la justice et de l'estat ecclesiastique," BN Mélanges de Colbert 33:364–73; Gomont, "Pour faciliter"; [Etienne Baluze] "Projet de déclaration concernant la profession des filles," n.d., BN Collection Baluze 179:282–89.

64. Clément 6:13.

65. Elizabeth Rapley, *A Social History of the Cloister: Daily Life in the Teaching Monasteries of the Old Regime* (Montreal: McGill-Queen's University Press, 2001).

66. Bibliothèque Nationale Collection Baluze 179, "Mémoires sur diverse matières ecclesiastiques et autres, minutes, et mises au net, pour la plupart de la main de Baluze et composés pour Colbert," 284–89. The pages in question appear to be minutes of meetings on January 14, 15, 23, 27, and 28, 1667. Speakers of various opinions are only occasionally identified by name, but include (Daniel) Voisin, (Joseph) Foucault, (Louis-Philippe) Ragueneau, (?) Hotman, (Antoine) Bilain, and Jean de Gomont, all members of the Council of Justice. For a list of the Council's Members, see Boulanger, "Justice et Absolutisme," 27.
67. BN Baluze 179, 284–89.
68. Ibid.
69. Ibid.
70. Ibid.
71. Barbara Diefendorf, *From Penitence to Charity: Pious Women and the Catholic Reformation in Paris* (New York: Oxford University Press, 2004), esp. 173–201.
72. Isambert 15:69.
73. Ibid., 388–89.
74. Here I am relying in part on explanations of this complicated legal history provided for Colbert by his legal advisor Jean de Gomont in the memorandum entitled "Pour faciliter les mariages et rendre plus difficiles les voeux de religion," BN Clairambault 613:190–93. See also Diefendorf, "Give us Back our Children: Patriarchal Authority and Parental Consent to Religious Vocations in Early Counter-Reformation France," *Journal of Modern History* 68:2 (June 1996): 1–43.
75. Baluze 179:284.
76. Gomont, "Pour faciliter," 194.
77. Malov, "Le project Colbertiste de la réforme monastique," in *Un Nouveau Colbert*, 167–76.
78. Malov, 169–72.
79. D'Ormesson, *Journal*, 2:480, 498–99.
80. Ibid., 500.
81. Isambert 18:94–99.
82. Louis XIV, *Mémoires et réflexions*, 113.

Chapter 3

1. Jean Ribou, ed. *Les Delices de la poésie galante.* Troisieme Partie (Paris, 1667), 1–12. The poem has been attributed to Régnier-Desmarais. See Jean Michel Pelous, *Amour précieux, amour galante: 1654–1675* (Paris: Klincksieck, 1980), 184.
2. Joan DeJean, *Tender Geographies: Women and the Origins of the Novel in France* (New York: Columbia University Press, 1991), 57.
3. Works that discuss the political, literary, and social role of salons and the elite women who presided over them include Roger Lathuillère, *La Préciosité: Etude Historique et Linguistique* 2 vols. (Geneva: Droz, 1966); Carolyn Lougee, *Le Paradis des Femmes: Women, Salons and Social Stratification in Seventeenth-Century France* (Princeton, NJ: Princeton University Press, 1976); Erica Harth, *Ideology and Culture in Early Modern France* (Ithaca, NY: Cornell University Press, 1983); idem, *CartesianWomen* (Ithaca, NY: Cornell University Press, 1992); Joan DeJean, *Tender Geographies: Women and the Origins of the Novel in France* (New York: Columbia University Press, 1991); Dena

Goodman, *The Republic of Letters: A Cultural History of the French Enlightenment* (Ithaca, NY: Cornell University Press, 1994); Daniel Gordon, *Citizens Without Sovereignty: Equality and Sociability in French Thought, 1670–1789* (Princeton, NJ: Princeton University Press, 1994); Myriam Maître, *Les Précieuses: Naissance des femmes de lettres en France au XVIIe siècle* (Paris: Honoré Champion, 1999); Steven Kale, *French Salons: High Society and Political Sociability from the Old Regime to the Revolution of 1848* (Baltimore: Johns Hopkins University Press, 2004); Antoine Lilti, *Le monde des salons: sociabilité et mondanité à Paris au XVIIIe siècle* (Paris: Fayard, 2005); Faith E. Beasley, *Salons, History, and the Creation of Seventeenth-Century France* (Aldershot, Hampshire: Ashgate, 2006). A scholarly dispute has arisen since the publication of Antoine Lilti's *Le monde de salons* over whether eighteenth-century salons, in particular, can be construed as part of an evolving "bourgeois public sphere" that challenged the *locus classicus* of monarchical politics. Despite their differences on the nature of the salons, none of these scholars questions my premise that elite sociability in the seventeenth century called upon women to pursue goals outside the framework of conjugal domesticity and motherhood.

4. Dejean, *Tender Geographies*, 21–22.
5. Ibid.
6. Hanley, "Engendering the State," 12 n.14.
7. For the classic discussion of this point, see Carole Pateman, *The Sexual Contract* (Stanford: Stanford University Press, 1988), esp. 19–38, 92–103.
8. For seminal works on this theme, see Lawrence Stone, *The Family, Sex and Marriage in England 1500–1800* (New York: Harper and Row, 1979); Steven Ozment, *When Fathers Ruled: Family Life in Reformation Europe* (Cambridge, Mass.: Harvard University Press, 1983); Jean-Louis Flandrin, *Families in Former Times: Kinship, Household and Sexuality* (Cambridge and New York: Cambridge University Press, 1979); Jean Delumeau and Daniel Roche, eds., *Histoire des pères et de la paternité* (Paris: Larousse, 1990).
9. *Dictionnaire de l'Académie française* (Paris, 1694), s.v. "pere," 218.
10. Jacques-Joseph Duguet, *Conduite d'une dame chrétienne pour vivre saintement dans le monde* 3rd ed. (1730), quoted in Lougee, *Le Paradis des Femmes*, 87–88.
11. Ursuline spirituality even emphasized the "maternal" role of nuns who gave birth to "spiritual children" through their teaching. See Linda Lierheimer, "Female Eloquence and Maternal Ministry: the Apostolate of Ursuline Nuns in Seventeenth-Century France" (PhD diss., Princeton University, 1994).
12. Isabelle Brouard-Arends, *Vies et images maternelles dans la littérature française du dix-huitième siècle* (Oxford: Voltaire Foundation, 1991), 77–81. There is as much disagreement about the timing of the advent of sentimental motherhood as about the so-called "discovery of childhood." For a review of the Ariès thesis and the view that parental love and concern is continuous rather than new, see Linda Pollock, *Forgotten Children: Parent-Child Relations from 1500–1900* (Cambridge and New York: Cambridge University Press, 1983). For considerations of maternal roles, see Yvonne Knibiehler and Catherine Fouquet, eds., *L'Histoire des mères du Moyen-Age à nos jours* (Paris: Montalba, 1980).
13. *Six Books of the Commonwealth*, I:2.
14. For information on these attacks, see Jeffrey Merrick, "The Cardinal and the Queen: Sexual and Political Disorders in the Mazarinades," *French Historical Studies* 18 (1994):

667–99 and Lewis Seifert, "Eroticizing the Fronde: Sexual Deviance and Political Disorder in the Mazarinades," *L'Esprit Créateur* 35 (1995): 22–36. For a broader view of the difficulties of regency government, see Katherine Crawford, *Perilous Performances: Gender and Regency in Early Modern France* (Cambridge, Mass.: Harvard University Press, 2004).

15. Claudia Opitz, "Female Sovereignty and the Subordination of Women in the Works of Martin Luther, Jean Calvin, and Jean Bodin," in Christine Fauré, *Political and Historical Encyclopedia of Women* (New York: Routledge, 2003), 13–22.

16. On these theories, see Maryanne Cline Horowitz, "The 'Science' of Embryology Before the Discovery of the Ovum," in Marilyn J. Boxer and Jean H. Quataert, eds., *Connecting Spheres: European Women in a Globalizing World, 1500 to the Present*, 2nd edition (New York: Oxford University Press, 2000); Pierre Darmon, *Le Mythe de la procréation à l'âge baroque* (Paris: J. J. Pauvert, 1977); Thomas Laqueur, *Making Sex: Body and Gender from the Greeks to Freud* (Cambridge, Mass.: Harvard University Press, 1990); Jacques Roger, *The Life Sciences in Eighteenth Century French Thought* trans. Robert Ellrich (Stanford: Stanford University Press, 1997).

17. Evelyne Berriot-Salvadore, "The Discourse of Medicine and Science," in Natalie Davis and Arlette Farge, eds., *A History of Women in the West III: Renaissance and Enlightenment Paradoxes* (Cambridge, Mass.: Belknap Press,1993), 348–88.

18. Cline Horowitz, 87–88; Laqueur, 40–43.

19. Laqueur, 142–48.

20. What was identified turned out to be a Graafian follicle, and not the ovum. See Cline-Horowitz, 90–91.

21. See Holly Tucker, *Pregnant Fictions: Childbirth and the Fairy Tale in Early-Modern France* (Detroit: Wayne State University Press, 2003).

22. Carol Pateman discusses how the classic patriarchal ideology of the seventeenth century obscures the related necessity for male control over women in *The Sexual Contract* (Stanford: Stanford University Press, 1988). For a summary of the legal changes affecting both paternal and conjugal power, see Sarah Hanley, "Engendering the State." For an analysis of legal changes touching mother's rights, see Christopher Corley, "Gender, Kin and Guardianship in Early Modern Burgundy," in Suzanne Desan and Jeffrey Merrick, ed., *Family, Gender and Law in Early Modern France* (University Park: Pennsylvania State University Press, 2009), 183–222, esp.186–93.

23. See Bodin, *Six livres* I:4.

24. "...qui sont tous arguments indubitables, pour monstrer l'auctorité, puissance, et commandement, que le mari a sur la femme de droit divin et humain..." *Six livres* I:3 (p. 62). Bodin did note that a wife's duty did not oblige her to follow commands of her husband to perform illicit or dishonorable acts.

25. Opitz, "Female Sovereignty," 19.

26. John Locke, *The Second Treatise of Government* (London, 1690). On Locke's views of marriage, see Rachel Weil, *Political Passions: Gender, the Family and Political Argument in England, 1680–1714* (Manchester: Manchester University Press, 1999).

27. François Poulain de la Barre, *De l'égalité des sexes* (Paris, 1673) in *Three Cartesian Feminist Treatises*, trans. Vivien Bosley (Chicago: University of Chicago Press, 2002), quotations from 77–78.

28. Siep Stuurman, *François Poulain de la Barre and the Invention of Modern Equality* (Cambridge, Mass.: Harvard University Press, 2004), esp. 162–71.

29. See Pateman, *The Sexual Contract*.

30. Some families, especially in the working classes, found ways around these rules. See Kristen Gager, *Blood Ties and Fictive Ties: Adoption and Family Life in Early Modern France* (Princeton, NJ: Princeton University Press, 1996).

31. The system did not work this way in practice. Illegitimate children were frequently baptized fraudulently, under false names, to conceal their origins and illegitimacy. See Matthew Dean Gerber, *The End of Bastardy: Illegitimacy in France from the Reformation through the Revolution*, (unpublished PhD diss., University of California, Berkeley, 2004).

32. Robert Joseph Pothier, *Traité du contrat du mariage* 5:293, quoted in DeJean *Tender Geographies*, 152.

33. Isambert, 12:160.

34. Gérard Chianea, "La Mère et l'Enfant dans le Droit Dauphinois de la fin de l'Ancien Régime," *Cahiers d'Histoire* 25 (1980): 259–64. Chianea interprets the *déclarations* as signs of female power within the domestic sphere. Zoë Schneider has suggested that in Normandy, obtaining support from the named father was a major reason that women made the declarations. "Women Before the Bench: Female Litigants in Early Modern Normandy," *French Historical Studies* 23:1 (Winter 2000), 17.

35. Isambert, 12:160.

36. On this point, see Montesquieu, *Spirit of the Laws*, 23:2.

37. Gabriel Guéret and Claude Blondeau, eds., *Journal du palais ou recueil des principales décisions de tous les parlemens et cours souveraines de France.* 2 volumes (Paris, 1701) I: 712–20.

38. "seuls [les registres] ont droit de regler la naissance & la qualité des personnes . . . . [le Seigneur Beaulieu] n'est point présumé leur pere, selon la loy, ny selon la nature mesme, qui ne se fait connoistre que par les precautions de la loy." *Journal du Palais*, 717.

39. "Autrement, il ne dependroit que d'un homme de reconnoistre tels enfans qu'il voudroit, bien qu'il ne fust pas leur père, & d'introduire parmy nous la liberté de l'adoption, que nostre jurisprudence François ne peut souffrit." *Journal du Palais*, 717.

40. On the legal situation of widowed mothers, see Corley, "Gender, Kin, and Guardianship"; "Diefendorf, *Paris City Councillors*, 279–97; Jacques Poumarède, "Le droit des veuves sous l'Ancien Régime (XVIIe–XVIIIe siècles) ou comment gagner son douaire," in Danielle Haase-Dubosc et Eliane Viennot, eds., *Femmes et pouvoirs sous l'ancien régime*, (Paris: Rivages, 1991), 64–76.

41. Isambert 18:93. Emphasis mine.

42. Noble widows accounted for one out of thirty-one known families (3 percent) that applied for pronatalist benefits in 1667 and 1671. Among roturier families applying for pronatalist tax exemptions in the *élection* of Romans (Dauphiné) and the city of Auxerre between 1660 and 1760, only one (one out of thirty-one known cases, or 3 percent) is clearly headed by a widow, though missing records make for significant uncertainty. In the late eighteenth century, women appear to have fared somewhat better. Of 136 families receiving *capitation* reductions in the generality of Bordeaux in 1768, eleven (9 percent) were headed by women. James Collins has suggested that the percentage of female-headed households after 1620 was significant. He found that some 12 to 20 percent of households in customary-law regions were headed by

women, while female-headed households accounted for a somewhat lower proportion (5 to 10 percent) in Roman-law areas. ("The Economic Role of Women in Seventeenth-Century France," *French Historical Studies* 16 [1989] 437–70.) Only in the late eighteenth century did the proportion of widows among pronatalist benefi- ciaries reach these levels. Still, because families with ten or more children are something of a demographic anomaly, it is difficult to know how many families headed by women should be expected among this group, and impossible, therefore, to determine whether widows were statistically underrepresented.

43. BN MdC 286 fo. 47–67.

44. The patrilineal definition of nobility was being more firmly defined during this era. During the investigations of noble titles carried out during the 1660s and 1670s, sur- viving traces of the so-called "uterine nobility" passed down through females, espe- cially in Champagne (which had long ceased to confer privileged tax status) were eliminated by royal intendants. On uterine nobility, see Pierre Biston, *De la noblesse maternelle en Champagne* (Paris: A. Labitte, 1878).

45. Ten out of eighty-three pension recipients in 1670, or 12 percent (BN MdC 286, fo. 47–67). See also below, chapter five.

46. AN H1 1688 fo. 201 (April 20, 1668).

47. Ibid.

48. BN MdC 286, fo. 58.

49. "...de grace, éclaircissez-moy/D'un bruit à croire difficile./On dit que tous les Habitans,/Tant Roturiers que Gentils-hommes/ Chargez de dix ou douze enfans/ Auront par an certaines sommes/ Si le GRAND ROY qui nous est cher/ A resolu cette enterprise/ C'est le vray moyen d'empescher/Que les femmes, la nuit, ne cousent leur chemise." *La Muse de la Cour*, Friday, December 17, 1666, reprinted in Adrien-Thomas Perdoux, le Sieur de Subligny [attributed], *La Muse Dauphine* (Paris, 1668), 280. The *Muse de la Cour* was retitled *la Muse Dauphine* early in 1667. Perdoux de Subligny, its author, is also credited with several literary works that suggest an interest in the debates about the *précieuses*: *La folle querelle, ou la critique d'Andromaque* (1668) and *La fausse Clélie, historie française galante et comique* (1671); other than this, little is known about Subligny. According to the Académie Française dictionary, a "chemise" was the article of clothing worn next to the skin. It can mean, specifically, a nighshirt (*chemise de nuit*).

50. Among late nineteenth- and early twentieth-century working-class women, absti- nence was one of the most important modes of birth control. Women reported "staying up mending" to avoid sex among the practical steps they took to avoid preg- nancy. Wally Secombe, "Starting to Stop: Working-Class Fertility Decline in Britain," *Past and Present* 126 (February 1990): 151–188.

51. Louis Henry, *Anciennes familles genèvoises* (Paris: PUF, 1956), 71–110.

52. Jean-Pierre Bardet, *Rouen aux XVIIe et XVIIIe siècles: Mutations d'une espace sociale.*

53. Louis Henry and Claude Lévy, "Ducs et pairs sous l'ancien régime: caractéristiques démographiques d'une caste," *Population* 15:5 (1960): 820. See also Jacques Houdaille, "La noblesse française, 1600–1900," *Population* 44:3 (1989): 501–14.

54. *Mme de Sévigné: Lettres* ed. M. Gerard-Gailly (Paris: Gallimard, 1953) 1:437.

55. Ibid.

56. Ibid., letter of 19 February 1672.

57. DeJean, *Tender Geographies*, 21–22.

58. "Personne de la famille, Monsieur, ne veut vous apprendre que Madame de Lavardin est accouchée d'une fille. Je suis la seule qui n'en fais pas de difficulté, sçachant combien vous aimez l'augmentation des sujets du roy et approuvez que les jeunes dames donnent bien des enfants à leurs maris. La nostre s'est si heureusement tirée de sa première affaire qu'elle s'est resolue de recommencer bientost pour nous donner un garçon. Elle veut se rendre digne de vostre adoption, en vous fournissant bon nombre de petits-enfans . . . Je vous rends compte, Monsieur, de toutes ses particularités comme à nostre bon père de famille que nous respectons et aiment chèrement et à qui nous sommes obligés de donner connaissance de tout ce qui se passe dans une maison qui luy appartient." La Douairière de Lavardin to Colbert, (2 September 1668). *Lettres, Instruction et Mémoires de Colbert* 7:356–57.

59. On customs of birth and the birthing room as female space, see Jacques Gélis, *l'Arbre et le fruit* (Paris: Fayard, 1984). Female control of the birthing room started to be challenged by male specialists in this era. See Nina Rattner Gelbart, *The King's Midwife* (Berkeley: University of California Press, 1998); Tucker, *Pregnant Fictions*.

60. See Hardwick, "Women Working the Law," *Journal of Women's History* 9:3 (Autumn 1997), 28–49 and *The Practice of Patriarchy*; Zoë Schneider, "Women Before the Bench," as well as works by Diefendorf and Brunelle, in the bibliography.

61. Schneider, 31.

Chapter 4

1. Philippe Fortin de la Hoguette, *Les elemens de la politique selon les principes de la nature* (Paris: 1663), 120–21. On Fortin, see Guido Canziani, "'Politiques' Pour le Prince: Traités et manuels au début du règne de Louis XIV," in Henry Méchoulan and Joël Cornette, eds., *L'État Classique, 1652–1715* (Paris: Vrin, 1996), 93–112, esp. 100–102.

2. Ann Laura Stoler, *Carnal Knowledge and Imperial Power: Race and the Intimate in Colonial Rule* (Berkeley: University of California Press, 2002); Julia Clancy-Smith and Frances Gouda, eds., *Domesticating the Empire: Race, Gender, and Family Life in French and Dutch Colonialism* (Charlottesville, Va.: University of Virginia Press, 1998); Ann McClintock, *Imperial Leather: Race, Gender and Sexuality in Colonial Conquest* (New York: Routledge, 1995).

3. Jean de Léry, *Histoire d'un voyage fait en la terre du Brésil* (1580) reprint ed. (Geneva: Droz, 1975), 262–71.

4. Baron de Lahontan, *New Voyages to North America* (London, 1703) reprint edition edited by Reuben Gold Thwaites (Chicago: A.C. McClure, 1905), II:451–64.

5. Agnès Walch, *La spiritualité conjugale dans le catholicisme français* (Paris: Editions du Cerf, 2002), 149.

6. Walch, *La spiritualité conjugale*, 21–125, 186–235.

7. For a discussion of these tendencies, see James Farr, *Authority and Sexuality in Early Modern Burgundy 1550–1730* (New York: Oxford University Press, 1995), 33–58.

8. Reuben Gold Thwaites, editor, *The Jesuit Relations and Allied Document* (hereafter, JR) 73 volumes (Cleveland: Burrows Brothers, 1896–1901), 10:315.

9. JR 16:87.

10. Pierre Biard, *Relation of New France* (1616) in JR 3:101–3.

11. JR 15:103–5 (1639) and 13:171 (1637), respectively.

12. Bruce G. Trigger, *The Children of Aataentsic: A History of the Huron People to 1660* (Montreal and London: McGill-Queen's University Press, 1976), I:376–95.

13. Jean de Brébeuf reported that his Huron villagers had adjusted their sexual talk and behavior in order to do nor say nothing contrary to Christian principles in his presence. JR 10:315.

14. JR 21:135.

15. Chrétien LeClerq, *New Relation of Gaspesia, With the Custom and Religion or the Gaspesien Indians* (1691) quoted in Peter Moogk, *La Nouvelle France: The Making of French Canada—A Cultural History* (East Lansing: Michigan State University Press, 2000), 26.

16. Lahontan, *New Voyages*, II:456.

17. See Trigger, *Children of Aataentsic*, and on native women's relative autonomy in marriage customs, Greer, *Mohawk Saint*, 45–46.

18. Peter Moogk argues that the missionaries tended to become more relativistic as time wore on. *La Nouvelle France*, 17–50.

19. JR 10:63.

20. Ibid., 313–17.

21. JR 16:161.

22. Peter Moogk, *La Nouvelle France*, 46. Other authors cite different figures, generally ranging from fifteen to 150 formalized interethnic marriages. The exception to the rule that these marriages were uncommon was Acadia, where interethnic marriages formalized through church weddings contributed significantly to the development of a *métis* population in the French settlement from as early as the 1630s. See John Mack Faragher, *A Great and Noble Scheme: The Tragic Story of the Expulsion of the French Acadians from their American Homeland* (New York: W. W. Norton, 2005), 46–47.

23. Lahontan II:455. On unions between fur traders and native women, see Sylvia Van Kirk, *Many Tender Ties: Women in Fur Trade Society, 1670–1870* (Norman: University of Oklahoma Press, 1980); Jennifer S. H. Brown, *Strangers in Blood: Fur Trade Companies in Indian Country* (Vancouver and London: University of British Columbia Press, 1980); Susan Sleeper-Smith, *Indian Women and French Men: Rethinking Cultural Encounter in the Western Great Lakes* (Amherst: University of Massachusetts Press, 2001); Bruce G. Trigger, *The Children of Aataentsic: A History of the Huron People to 1660* (Montreal and London: McGill-Queen's University Press, 1976), I:365–76.

24. For an excellent treatment of these questions, see Gilles Havard, *Empire et métissages* (Paris: Presses de l'Université de Paris-Sorbonne, 2003), 625–80, esp. 642–44.

25. Marcel Trudel has used parish registers to measure the population of known métis children, coming up with the figure of seventeen for the period from 1632 to 1662, or 1.2 percent of recorded births. *Histoire de la Nouvelle France Vol III: La seigneurie des Cent-Associés* (Montreal: FIDES, 1983) 2:510. Unless métis children were baptized at the behest of their parents, later converted to Catholicism, married, or served as a godparent, they tend to disappear from records. For a discussion of the historical controversy over the question of *métissage* in New France, see Olive Patricia Dickason, "From 'One Nation' in the Northeast to 'New Nation' in the Northwest: a look at the emergence of the métis" in Jacqueline Peterson and Jennifer S. H. Brown, eds., *The New Peoples: Being and Becoming Métis in North America* (Lincoln: University of Nebraska Press, 1985).

26. Following Faragher, I use the term "interethnic" to describe French-Amerindian unions to avoid reifying a notion of race that was in this period not yet fixed in its modern connotation. The notion that the French state promoted "miscegenation" (a nineteenth-century word specifically attached to racialized thinking and thus anachronistic) as a strategy of colonial rule and assimilation in the seventeenth century has become common in Canadian and colonial historiography. For examples, see Jerah Johnson, "Colonial New Orleans: A Fragment of the Eighteenth-Century French Ethos," in Arnold R. Hirsch and Joseph Logsdon, eds., *Creole New Orleans: Race and Americanization* (Baton Rouge: Louisiana State University Press, 1992), 12–57. Questions about the precise moment when racial thinking emerged are beyond the scope of my argument, but for an excellent introduction to the problem see Guillaume Aubert, "'The Blood of France': Race and Purity of Blood in the French Atlantic World," *William and Mary Quarterly* 61:3, 439–78. See also Saliha Belmessous, "Assimilation and Racialism in Seventeenth and Eighteenth-Century French Colonial Policy," *American Historical Review* 110:2 (April 2005): 322–49.

27. JR 5:211. See also JR 8:49 and 10:27.

28. JR 8:49 and 10:27.

29. On the variety of ways that the French sought to integrate Amerindians and other colonial peoples, see Sara E. Melzer "The Magic of French Culture: Transforming 'Savages' into French Catholics in Seventeenth Century France," in Amy Wygant, ed. *The Meanings of Magic from the Bible to Buffalo Bill* (Oxford: Berghahn Books, 2006), 135–69. Cornelius Jaenen, *Friend and Foe: Aspects of French-Amerindian Cultural Contact in the Sixteenth and Seventeenth Centuries* (New York: Columbia University Press, 1976); Saliha Belmessous, "Etre français en Nouvelle-France: Identité française et identité coloniale aux dix-septième et dix-huitième siècles," *French Historical Studies* 27:3 (Summer 2004): 507–40.

30. JR 14:17–19.

31. Ibid., 21.

32. For examples of these principles in action, see JR 14:161–63; 15:101–9; 15:125; 17:31–33; 18:123–25.

33. For some of the complications regarding marriage, see Axtell, *Invasion Within*, 123–24.

34. JR 16:161–63. See also JR 14:235 and 15:125–27.

35. JR 20:211–13.

36. The *Jesuit Relations* is a poor souce for native-French liaisons; the Jesuits had obvious reasons not to dwell on the sexual behavior of French men when writing for a pious metropolitan audience. But, see the story about a native convert who took a non-Christian wife and was shunned by the convert community at St. Joseph. Although he was eventually reconciled with the community, the *Relations* note that he atoned publicly for the scandal he had caused, and that, despite living with the woman, "his fear of offending God and his respect for his baptism had prevented him from touching her although he was urgently solicited to do so—desiring that she should become a Christian before showing her the evidences of his affection." The story does not indicate what happened to his unbaptized wife. JR 18:173–77.

37. *Archivum Romanum Societatis Iesu (Rome), Gallia 109*, fol. 3, "Pierre de Sesmaisons: Raisons qui peuvent Induire Sa Sainteté à permettre aux Français ... d'épouser des

filles Sauvages..." cited in Jaenen, *Friend and Foe*, 164. Similar questions attracted the interest of the royal government. See BN Baluze 179 "Mémoire sur les mariages des Chrestiens catholiques avec les infideles, juifs, & heretiques," (n.d.) fol. 13–21.

38. JR 63:267.

39. On patterns of interaction between settlers and natives, see Greer, *Mohawk Saint*, 89–110.

40. Between 1698 and 1765, nearly 50 percent of the marriages registered at the French Great Lakes outpost of Michilimackinac united a native woman and French man. Gilles Havard and Cécile Vidal, *Histoire de l'Amérique Française* (Paris: Flammarion, 2003), 380.

41. Havard, *Empire et métissages*, 660–61. For an account of eighteenth-century debates between colonial officials and missionaries over interethnic marriages, see Charles Edwards O'Neill, *Church and State in French Colonial Louisiana* (New Haven, Conn.: Yale University Press, 1966), 246–55.

42. Greer, *Mohawk Saint*, 105.

43. For discussion of how gender ideology was "good to think with" in debates on conversion and confessional identity, see Keith Luria, *Sacred Boundaries: Religious Coexistence and Conflict in Early Modern France* (Washington, DC: Catholic University Press, 2005), esp. 193–245. For the missionaries' ideas about native women, see Greer, *Mohawk Saint*, 178–79.

44. Native Christian women's self-mortification was a hybrid practice that bore marked similarity to pre-conversion Iroquois spirituality. See Greer, *Mohawk Saint*, 115–24.

45. See, for example, the comments of Marie de l'Incarnation in Davis, *Women on the Margins*, pp. 284–85, n. 188.

46. Trudel, *Histoire de la Nouvelle France*, III:508.

47. JR 16:35.

48. JR 21:135–37.

49. JR 11:51.

50. JR 20:129. Trudel, *Histoire de la Nouvelle France*, III:508.

51. JR 11:53.

52. New France became the site of the first measure of this kind in France, predating the work of Vauban. See Robert Scafe, *The Measure of Greatness: Population and the Census under Louis XIV* (Unpublished PhD diss., Stanford University, 2005), 116–52.

53. On the Canadian census, see Robert Scafe, *The Measure of Greatness: Population and the Census under Louis XIV* (Unpublished PhD diss., Stanford University, 2005), 116–52. For more on the use of statistics, see James E. King, *Science and Rationalism in the Government of Louis XIV* (Baltimore: Johns Hopkins University Press, 1949), 116–46. For the significance of information to the developing administration, see Jay Smith, *The Culture of Merit: Nobility, Royal Service, and the Making of Absolute Monarchy in France, 1600–1789* (Ann Arbor: University of Michigan Press, 1996), 125–90.

54. "Memoire du roi pour servir d'instruction à Talon," (27 March 1665) and letter from Colbert to Talon (5 April 1667) in *Rapport de l'archiviste de la province de Québec* [hereafter RAPQ] 1930–31:5, 67.

55. Letter from the king to Frontenac (22 April 1675) in RAPQ 1926–27:80.

56. Edward Louis Montizambert, *Canada in the Seventeenth Century, from the French of Pierre Boucher* (Montreal: George E. Desbarats & Co., 1883), 64–69; W. J. Eccles, *Canada*

Under Louis XIV, 1663–1701 (London and New York: Oxford University Press, 1964), 1–5.

57. Carmen Bellerose, *La Fécondité des Canadiennes de moins de 20 ans au xviie siécle*. (MS Demography thesis, Université de Montréal, 1976); Allan Greer, *The People of New France* (Toronto: University of Toronto Press, 1997), 12–22; Trudel, *La Nouvelle France*, 515–16.

58. See Van Kirk, *Many Tender Ties*; Brown, *Strangers in Blood*; and Dickason, "From 'One Nation.'"

59. Yves Landry, *Les Filles du Roi au XVIIe siècle: Orphelines en France, pionnières en Canada* (Montreal: Leméac, 1992).

60. In order to discourage returns that drained manpower from the colony, Governor Frontenac was ordered not to sign passports for a French man "if he has no wife, children and establishment formed in the said country of New France that gives no room for doubt that he will return immediately." King to Frontenac (5 June 1672) RAPQ 1926–27:8.

61. "Il a esté distribués a quatre Capitaines, trois Lieutenans, cinq Enseignes et quelques bas officiers qui se sont establis et mariez en Canada le somme de 6,000 livres..." RAPQ 1930–31:108.

62. Landry, op cit.

63. Ann Laura Stoler, *Carnal Knowledge and Imperial Power*, 41–55.

64. Frontenac to Colbert (2 November 1672) RAPQ 1926–27:12. Trudel documents the relative importance of crimes related to sexuality and marriage in the "police blotter" he provides for the period 1636–63, II:453–63.

65. For attitudes toward polygamy, see above, chapter 1.

66. See *Edits, ordonnances royaux, declarations et arrêts du conseil d'état du roi concernant le Canada* (Quebec: E.R. Frechette, 1854), 67–68.

67. The letter advises the intendant to "entr[er] dans le destail de leurs petites affaires et de leur domestique." "Mémoire pour servir d'instruction à Talon" (27 March 1665) RAPQ 1930–31:17.

68. Marginal response of Talon to instructions dated 27 March 1665. RAPQ 1930–31:17.

69. RAPQ 1930–31:108. Landry, *Filles du roi*, 73–79.

70. In 1681, the departing intendant, Duchesneau, requested funds from Paris to subsidize the dowries of native girls who were graduating from the Ursuline school; nothing in his letter indicates that the preferred partners for these women were to be French. E.B. O'Callahan, ed., *Documents Relative to the Colonial History of the State of New York*. 15 vols. (Albany, NY: Weed, Parsons and Co, 1853–87) [hereafter DRCHSNY] 9:150. The following year, however, the budget allocation from Paris contained an allocation of 3,000 *livres* "pour dotter des filles de sauvages qui sortent de chez les Ursulines de Quebec, et ce qui se mariront aux François, à raison de cinquante livres chacunnes..." (AN Colonial Series C11a 6:fol 90–90verso). The new Intendant, De Meulles, responded by noting that at best one or two such marriages occurred per year, so a fund of 3,000 *livres* was excessive, "à moins que vouz nayez eu intention que lad somme de mil escus ayt estés distribüée a tous les pauvres gens qui se marient de ce païs icy, en leur donnant cinquante livres en se mariant, ce qui men a desja fait refuser quelques uns, ayant crû ester obligé de mattacher aux termes de l'Estat des gratifications..."

(ibid, fol. 90 verso). Governor de la Barre concurred that the terms of the allocation had been made in error. (DRCHSNY 9:207). From the responses of officials
on the scene, it is clear that the supposed subsidies for interethnic marriage
resulted from a bureaucratic error, not a considered policy decision, and that the
money was reallocated to other uses, including the habitual subsidies for settler
marriages.

71. See, in particular, Belmessous, "Assimilation and Racialism," and Jaenen, *Friend
and Foe.*

72. On the program to "Frenchify," see works cited in note 29, above. For a nuanced
discussion of missionaries' attitudes toward the assimilation of Christianized natives,
see Davis, *Women on the Margins,* esp. 107–22.

73. See Greer, *The People of New France.*

74. Gilles Havard and Cécile Vidal, *Histoire de l'Amérique Française* (Paris: Flammarion,
2003), 233–37.

75. De Meulles to Seignelay, 12 November 1682. AN (Colonial Series) C11a fol 90.

76. Greer, *People of New France,* 23.

77. Frontenac to Colbert (2 November 1672) RAPQ 1926–27:13.

78. "Mémoire de Talon sur l'état présent du Canada" (1667), RAPQ 1930–31:63.

79. Marie de l'Incarnation and Chrétien le Clerq quoted in Georges Sabagh, "The Fertility
of French-Canadian Women during the Seventeenth Century," *The American Journal of
Sociology* 47:5 (March 1942): 680.

80. Colbert to Frontenac (16 February 1674) RAPQ 1923–24:60.

81. Marie de l'Incarnation to Claude Martin, quoted in Davis, *Women on the Margins,*
113.

82. Duchesneau to Seignelay (13 November 1680) DRCHSNY 9:142.

83. Havard, *Empire et métissages,* 648–51. For the social, religious, and racial implications
of the ban on interethnic marriage in both New France and throughout the French
Atlantic, see also Belmessous, "Assimilation and Racialism"; Aubert, "The Blood of
France"; O'Neill, *Church and State*; Jennifer Spear, "'They Need Wives': Métissage
and the Regulation of Sexuality in French Louisiana, 1699–1730," in Martha Hodes,
ed., *Sex, Love, Race: Crossing Boundaries in American History* (New York: New York
University Press, 1999).

84. Denonville, "Memoire respecting Canada for M. Seignelay," January 1690.
DRCHSNY 9:442–43.

85. DRCHSNY 9:442.

86. Boucher, *Canada in the Seventeenth Century,* 71.

87. Denonville to Seignelay, 1685. DRCHSNY 9:276–77, 280.

88. Denonville to Seignelay, 25 August 1687. DRCHSNY 9:340.

89. DRCHSNY 9:278–79.

Chapter 5

1. This account of the case is drawn from the narrative in the *Cour des aides* decision of
1672 published in Gabriel Guéret and Claude Blondeau, eds., *Journal du Palais ou
recueil des principales décisions de tous les parlemens et cours souveraines de France* (Paris,
1680).

2. James Collins discusses the role of the *élus* in *Fiscal Limits of Absolutism: Direct Taxation in Early Seventeenth-Century France* (Berkeley: University of California Press, 1988), 167–72.

3. For the benefits offered in the edict of 1666, see appendix one.

4. On the significance of privilege for the state, see David Bien, "Offices, Corps and a System of State Credit: The Uses of Privilege under the Ancien Régime," in Keith Baker, ed., *The French Revolution and the Creation of Modern Political Culture Vol. I, The Political Culture of the Old Regime* (New York and Oxford: Pergamon, 1987), 89–114; on its significance for individuals, see William H. Sewell, Jr., *Work and Revolution in France: The Language of Labor from the Old Regime to 1848* (Cambridge: Cambridge University Press, 1980), 116–19.

5. Marcel Marion, *Dictionnaire des institutions de la France aux XVIIe et XVIIIe siècles* (Paris: Éditions A. & J. Picard & Cie, 1969), s.v. "privilèges," 458.

6. David Bien, "Offices, Corps, and a System of State Credit."

7. For the use of privilege to promote economic development, see C. W. Cole, *Colbert and a Century of French Mercantilism* 2 vols. (New York: Columbia University Press, 1939).

8. Michael Kwass discusses the social meanings of tax privileges in *Privilege and the Politics of Taxation in Eighteenth Century France: Liberté, Égalité, Fiscalité* (Cambridge: Cambridge University Press, 2000), 23–33; see also Sewell, *Work and Revolution in France*, 116–19.

9. Parents of workers in the stocking factories were also offered tax exemptions. BN MdC 148, fol. 248. Cole, *Colbert and a Century of French Mercantilism* 2:211, 253.

10. Roland Mousnier, *The Institutions of France under the Absolute Monarchy 1598–1789*, vol. 1 (Chicago: University of Chicago Press, 1979), 401.

11. Combles was offered a position as captain-chatellain. AN G7 1 (Colbert to d'Aguesseau, 27 November 1681).

12. BN Collection Clairambault 792:299–302. Le Cauchois was not alone in making this claim. A Monsieur Desmaux from Angoulême, whose noble status derived from city office and was revoked in March of 1667, later petitioned claiming that as the descendant of an echevin who had twelve children, his nobility should be confirmed. The provincial intendant d'Aguesseau was instructed to hold back on the decision pending discussions between Colbert and the king. AN H1 1688, 84.

13. Collins, *Fiscal Limits of Absolutism*, 200–13.

14. On the grand recherche de noblesse, see Jean Meyer, *La Noblesse Bretonne au XVIIIe siècle* (Paris: SEVPEN, 1966); James B. Wood, *The Nobility of the Election of Bayeux, 1463–1666: Continuity through Change* (Princeton, NJ: Princeton University Press, 1980).

15. Henri d'Aguesseau to Colbert, BN Clairambault 791:99–100 (26 November 1666). The work of modern historical demographers does not confirm d'Aguesseau's impressionistic analysis of elevated family sizes in Auvergne; insofar as regional differences characterized seventeenth-century France, the Northeast, Normandy, and the Île de France were the nation's fertile zones. See Alain Bideau and Jean-Pierre Bardet, "Une géographie très contrastée" in Jacques Dupâquier et al., *Histoire de la population française* 2:367–70.

16. François d'Herbigny warned that parents would donate their goods to their newly married minor sons to shield them from taxation. BN Clairambault 791:105–07

(8 December 1666); de Fortia in Auvergne warned of similar subterfuges. See BN Clairambault 791:109–14 (n.d.).

17. Applicants needed baptismal documents for all children, living or dead, which were to be copied into registers at the élection in the presence of local officials, as well as sworn testimony from two near relatives that the father indeed had the requisite number of living children. Fines for fraud were 1,000 *livres*, payable to the parish where the father lived, as well as the threat of criminal penalties.

18. Quoted in Marion, *Dictionnaire des institutions*, s.v. "taille personnelle," 527.

19. Pronatalist tax exemptions were offered to roturier fathers in the pays d'élection and in Burgundy, a pays d'état with a preexisting customary tradition of exempting fathers of twelve from taxes. I have found no evidence that non-noble fathers in the pays d'états successfully claimed the benefits offered in the royal edict of 1666. The uneven preservation of tax records and judicial records (from *Cours des aides*) makes it difficult to establish the precise boundaries within which pronatalist tax exemptions were offered. Edmond Esmonin suggested that pronatalist privileges were not offered to roturier fathers in Normandy, having never been registered by sovereign courts there. However, Esmonin's suggestion that such benefits were offered only in the jurisdiction of the *Cour des aides* of Paris is certainly untrue, as *élus* were registering the exemptions in Auvergne and Dauphiné, neither of which was in the jurisdiction of the Paris *Cour des aides*. For Esmonin's discussion, see *La Taille en Normandie au temps de Colbert, 1661–1683* (Geneva, Mégariotis Reprints, 1978; originally published 1913), 262.

20. Marion, *Dictionnaire des institutions*, s.v. "taille"; Kwass, *Privilege*, 48–51.

21. Vieuille, Nouveau traité des élections, quoted in Esmonin, *Taille en Normandie*, 174; Marion, *Dictionnaire des institutions*, s.v. "collecte, collecteurs."

22. For descriptions of how the system of repartition and collection worked, see Esmonin, *Taille en Normandie* and James Collins, *Fiscal Limits of Absolutism*, esp. 166–73.

23. *Épices* were noted irregularly. In 1671, Pierre Gaudo-Paquet and Claude Phelipot each paid twenty-four *livres* to register their claims to a pronatalist tax exemption, while Jean Freol paid twenty-one *livres*. AD Drôme C. 609. In 1687, Barthelemy Michel paid just twelve *livres*. AD Drôme C. 636. James Collins suggests that a median tax burden for the seventeenth century was probably in the vicinity of ten *livres*; the majority of households would have paid less than twenty *livres*. For these figures and explanation of the problems inherent in assessing average tax burdens, see Collins, *Fiscal Limits of Absolutism*, 171–77.

24. AD Nièvre, 1 C 411, declarations of Jacques Roy (1717) Claude Maucourant (1720).

25. BN Mélanges de Colbert 148 fol. 37 (2 April 1668).

26. BN Clairambault 792:299–302 (16 September 1670).

27. AD Yonne C. 85.

28. AD Yonne C. 85. A search of the archives did not turn up any actual tax rolls from Saint-Regnobert that could have confirmed these claims.

29. "... les notables riches et opulens sans contredit de toutte la parroisse," AD Yonne C. 85.

30. Pierre Goubert, "The Ancien Régime," quoted in Collins, *Fiscal Limits*, 173–74. Collins confirms the deep chasm between the large mass of the peasant population who paid little, and the upper quartile that paid significant sums.

31. AD Yonne C. 85.

32. Works by Collins and Goubert suggest that few individuals would have paid 300 *livres* of taxes in seventeenth-century France; on the other hand, Saint-Regnobert was not unique in the vast inequalities of assessment. See Collins, 173–77; Goubert, *Beauvais et les Beauvaisis*, 153.

33. Auxerre was incorporated into the province of Burgundy in mid-century. Therefore, Boucher, who claimed his exemption in 1665, was invoking the customary Burgundian exemption for fathers of twelve rather than the specific provisions of the royal prona-talist edict, which (according to local understanding) "confirmed" Burgundian tradi-tion in 1666.

34. The incident is described in AD Puy-de-Dôme, C. 1943 (1676–77).

35. AD Puy-de-Dôme, C. 1943. The town collected 2,000 *livres* in 1676 to pay expenses and "deniers royaux," in addition to 2,605 *livres* to pay debts. Most of the expense of trying to return fathers to the tax rolls came from the expenses of delegations to Clermont, the seat of the *généralité*, to confer with the intendant, legal experts, and the judges of the *Cour des aides*. Sieur Gaignac, deputized to make this journey, found himself caught in the mountains by winter weather for two weeks. The expenses for his trip and the valet who traveled with him came to 187 *livres*.

36. Collins shows that increases in taxation were not divided proportionally with respect to individual taxpayers. *Fiscal Limits of Absolutism*, 166–177.

37. See Bernard Vonglis, "L'établissement de la taille par commissaire et son contentieux dans l'élection de Paris (1760–1788)," in Marie-Hélène Bourquin et al., *Etudes d'histoire de droit parisien* (Paris, 1970), 317. See also Michael Kwass, *Privilege and the Politics of Taxation*, 130–33.

38. AN G7. 635 (14 March 1685).

39. "à cause . . . des grandes familles dont ils sont chargés, bien loin de pouvoir fere quelque proffict, ils sont réduicts à la pauvreté et misère." Quoted in Gabriel Esquer, Inventaire des archives communales de la ville d'Aurillac antérieures à 1790 (Aurillac, 1911), 1673.

40. To cite a few characteristic examples, one nobleman wrote to Colbert pleading for money to help him pay debts he had incurred in providing for his five sons. BN Mélanges de Colbert 153, fol. 73 (2 June 1669); a Sr. de la Violaye claimed that the loss of his office threatened his family with ruin and had forced him to neglect his children's education. Mélanges de Colbert 153, fol. 807 (26 June 1669); a group of officeholders warned that the loss of their tax privileges would "rob from them the means to give their children the education appropriate for their status, and that would make the children capable of serving the king." BN Clairambault 792: 465–66 (n.d.).

41. AD Yonne C 85. Emphasis mine.

42. AD Drôme C. 681 n. 13 (23 November 1710).

43. The experiences of Aurillac in 1676–77, discussed above, make this clear (AD Puy-de-Dôme C. 1943.) The repetition of this course of events in other places is strongly suggested by Colbert's correspondence with intendants in Lyon and Poitiers.

44. Gabriel Guéret and Claude Blondeau, *Journal du palais ou recueil des principales décisions de tous les parlemens et cours souveraines de France*. The journal appeared as a weekly from 1672–74, then at irregular intervals until 1695. Compilations were published in 1680, 1701, 1713, 1727, and 1755. See Jean Sgard et al., *Dictionnaire*

des Journaux 1600–1789 (Paris, 1991), n. 723. The court's decision also seems to have circulated between Colbert and the intendants: see the copy in AN G7 355.

45. "que du moment qu'on a jouy une fois, il se conserve toujours," *Journal du Palais* (Paris, 1680), 1: 42–51.

46. *Journal du Palais*, (Paris, 1680), 1: 42–51.

47. See the preamble to the Edict of 1666. Isambert 18:90.

48. *Journal du Palais*, (Paris, 1680), 1: 42–51.

49. The untranslated text reads as follows: Aussy est-il vray qu'il se passe dans l'acquisition du privilege une espèce de contrat sans nom entre l'état et les pères de douze enfants. Ils donnait leurs enfants à la république, et elle leur rend en échange l'affranchissement de tous les tributs, ou pour même dire, elle reçoit leurs enfans comme en quitte des charges dont ils estoient redevables, de sorte que le père n'en est que le depositaire, et ce n'est plus à luy mais à la république principalement qu'appartient le peril de leur vie." *Journal du Palais*, 1: 42–51.

50. Marcel Marion, *Dictionnaire des Institutions de la France au XVIIe et XVIIIe siècles* (Paris, 1969), s.v. "Cours des aides."

51. Marion, *Dictionnaire*, s.v. "Elections," 199.

52. On infant and child mortality, see Dupâquier et al., *Histoire de la population française*, 2:223–25.

53. Isambert, 19:413.

54. Colbert to de Marillac, intendant of Poitiers, in Lettres de Colbert 4:119 (14 December 1679).

55. Esmonin, p. 262, n. 4.

56. "The exemption should cease from the moment that one of the twelve children dies, unless there is written proof that the child died while serving in the king's troops. That is the policy you are obliged to have observed regarding this subject throughout your generality; and in the case that officers of the élections or Cours des aides make a ruling to the contrary, His Majesty will overturn their ruling." Quoted in Boislisle, Correspondence des Contrôleurs Géneraux des Finances 3 vols. (Paris, 1874–97), 1:119.

57. AD Puy-de-Dôme C. 1943. "Finally, regarding several cases involving the said Bavet, Delzons, Gourlat and also against the barrister Jacques Rocher on the same grounds, after having settled them [terminées à l'aimable], nevertheless fees were due for the case against Rocher, and for the preparation of documents, etc. . . . " A marginal note indicates these agreements were passed before a notary.

58. Pensions for noblemen with large families seem to have been paid regularly between 1667 and 1671, although the government limited its expenses by erecting additional criteria in addition to having ten or more living children. Most notably, it added investigations to prevent fraud and required that the nobleman place several of his sons in royal service. For additional information on the pensions paid to noblemen, see Leslie Tuttle, "Sacred and Politic Unions: Natalism, Families and the State in Old Regime France, 1666–1789." (Unpublished PhD diss., Princeton University, 2000), 157–78.

59. Bouchu to Contrôleur Général, 29 June 1699, in Boislisle 1:530.

60. Memorial Alphabetique des choses concernant la Justice, la Police & les Finances de France (Paris, 1742), s.v. "PERES." The entry, "Peres de famille taillables, ayant dix ou douze enfans, de quoi exempts" mentions the 1666 edict and its subsequent revocation in 1683.

61. AN G7 366, letters of Matthieu Chavagny, 28 February 1712 and 31 January 1714.
62. Shelby T. McCloy, "Government Aid to Large Families in Normandy, 1764–1786," *Social Forces* 18 (1940): 418.

Chapter 6

1. Thomas Le Blanc, *La Direction et la consolation des personnes mariées, ou les moiens infaillibles de faire un mariage heureux, d'un qui seroit malheureux* (Paris, 1664).
2. Claude Maillard, *Le Bon mariage, ou le moyen d'estre heureux et faire son salut en estat de mariage avec un traité des veuves* (Douai, 1643).
3. As anthropologist Caroline Bledsoe has observed, modern scholars "face an increasing struggle to understand both the experience of high fertility and the modes of social life that are constituted around it." *Contingent Lives: Fertility, Time, and Aging in West Africa* (Chicago: University of Chicago Press, 2002), 8–9.
4. Emmanuel Le Roy Ladurie, *Carnival in Romans* (New York: George Braziller, 1980).
5. René Favier, *Les Villes du Dauphiné aux XVIIe et XVIIIe siècles* (Grenoble: Presses Universitaires de Grenoble, 1993).
6. Jean-Pierre Rocher et al., *Histoire d'Auxerre des origines à nos jours* (Roanne le-Coteau: Horvath, 1984).
7. Archives Communales d'Auxerre GG 138 and 139 house the *procès-verbaux* recording these exemptions. GG 138, with information from 1664–1728, is currently missing but was summarized in an article published in a local history journal by Paul Richard. On the Burgundian precedent, see G. Robert, "Une politique familiale et démographie au XVIIe siècle," *Actes du Congrès des sociétés savantes* (1984): 142–50.
8. I am grateful to Michael Breen for the reference that first led me to Auxerre. In Auxerre, the city government kept records on inhabitants rewarded as *pères de familles nombreuses*. In Romans, the catalogue of *élection* records offered unusually detailed descriptions that facilitated my research. I have also found traces of the pre-1760 pronatalist program in the departmental archives of Aisne, Aube, Nièvre, Puy-de-Dôme, Savoie, and Seine Inférieure. The number of mentions in archival catalogues, however, surely underrepresents the extent of the archival evidence, most of it buried in the records of the *élections*, whose archives are spottily preserved and catalogued. In 1789, France contained 182 separate élection jurisdictions. See Marion, *Dictionnaire des institutions de la France au XVIIe et XVIIIe siècles* (Paris: Editions A. & J. Picard, 1969), s.v. "élection."
9. We would not expect to find many rural dwellers in the Auxerre municipal records, which deal with areas under the tax jurisdiction of city officials. Among the sixty-two fathers claiming rewards there just one claimed an agricultural occupation: Charles Gounot, a *laboureur* (farmer) who lived in the nearby hamlet of La Croix Pilate.
10. The following works have provided guidance on urban social categories: Marcel Couturier, *Recherches sur les structures sociales de Châteaudun, 1525–1789* (Paris: SEVPEN, 1969); James Farr, *Hands of Honor: Artisans and Their World in Dijon 1550–1650* (Ithaca, NY: Cornell University Press, 1988); Gregory Hanlon, *L'univers des gens de bien: Culture et comportements des élites urbaines en Agenais-Condomois au XVIIe siècle* (Talence: Presses Universitaires de Bordeaux, 1989); Julie Hardwick, *The Practice of Patriarchy: Gender and the Politics of Household Authority in Early Modern France* (University Park: Pennsylvania State University Press, 1998).

11. AD Drôme C. 656 (13 December 1693).

12. AD Drôme C. 632 (16 July 1675).

13. AD Drôme C. 636 (7 January 1687).

14. AC Auxerre GG. 138 and 139.

15. Lachiver, *La Population de Meulan du XVIIe au XIXe siècle* (Paris: SEVPEN, 1969), compiled from chart on 171. For couples married between 1670 and 1699, Bardet found all social groups except one termed "great notables" to have an average theoretical completed family size superior to six children. *Rouen*, 280.

16. Dupâquier, *Histoire de la population française*, 305.

17. These ages appear more in line with those common among urban elite groups in the sixteenth century. In her study of sixteenth-century Paris city councillors' families, Barbara Diefendorf found an average age at first marriage for women of twenty and one quarter (20.25) years. *Paris City Councillors*, 180–81.

18. Flandin, *Families in Former Times*, 184–187; Olwen Hufton, "Women, Work, and Family," in Natalie Z. Davis and Arlette Farge, eds., *A History of Women: Renaissance and Enlightenment Paradoxes* (Cambridge, Mass.: Belknap Press, 1993), 26–34.

19. AD Drôme C. 632, 263 verso–265.

20. See François Lebrun et Antoinette Fauve-Chamoux, "L'Amour et le mariage," in Dupâquier, ed., *Histoire de la population française*, 2:305.

21. Maurice Garden, *Lyon et les Lyonnais au XVIIIe siècle*, 104; *Histoire de la population française*, 2:316.

22. Officials' interpretation of the pronatalist law excluded children who had a different biological father from the children who could count toward the head-of-household's tally for the awards. If the mothers in these families had children from a previous marriage, or if the couples were raising the children of relatives alongside their own progeny, such children are never mentioned in the applications for pronatalist rewards of fathers in Auxerre or Romans. On blended families, see Micheline Baulant, "La famille en miettes" in Forster and Ranum, eds., *Family and Society: Selections from the Annales* (Baltimore: Johns Hopkins University Press, 1976), 116.

23. Only one couple showed evidence of a prenuptial conception; this does not appear to have affected their eligibility for a pronatalist reward, as the child was born while they were married.

24. On infant mortality, see Dupâquier, *Histoire de la population française*, 2:222–34.

25. Compiled from parish registers of Notre Dame-là-d'Hors, Auxerre, France.

26. *Histoire de la population française*, 2:238. The determining factor in the growing risk, demographers argue, is the mother's age rather than her repeated pregnancies, although the data for making such a conclusion is not clear. The mounting risk associated with births after the sixth is largely confirmed by John Knodel's result from six German villages in the eighteenth and nineteenth centuries. Knodel, *Demographic Behavior in the Past* (New York: Cambridge, 1988), 110–14.

27. Bardet, *Rouen*, 298.

28. For an example of this methodology used to delineate wet-nursing networks, see Alain Bideau, "L'Envoi des jeunes enfants en nourrice," in *Hommage a Marcel Reinhard* (Paris: Société de démographie historique, 1973), 49–58.

29. Sussman, 20–25.

30. Livre de raison of François Bastide, 1668–83, in Guibert, ed., *Livres de raison, registres de famille, et journaux individuels Limousin et Marchois* (Paris and Limoges, 1888), 204.

On wet-nursing, see Michael W. Flinn, *The European Demographic System 1500–1820* (New York: Harvester Wheatsheaf, 1981), 39–43. Children sent to wet nurses were subject to higher rates of infant mortality than those who were fed by their mothers, but the difference in infant mortality also varied by social class. Among artisans in eighteenth-century Rouen, for example, infant mortality was 22.9 percent for children fed by their mothers versus 34.5 percent for children fed by wet nurses. The children of *notables* when fed by their mothers suffered infant mortality of 19.8 percent, compared to 30.2 percent when fed by a wet nurse. See Dupâquier (whose results are drawn from Bardet's work), 228.

31. Sussman, 59.

32. See Lachiver, 123–33; Sussman, 50–58.

33. Linda Polllock, "Parent-Child Relations," in Kertzer and Barbagli, *Family Life in Early Modern Times, 1500–1789* (New Haven, Conn.: Yale University Press, 2001), 193–94; Daryl Hafter, "Women Who Wove in the Eighteenth-Century Silk Industry of Lyon," in Hafter, ed., *European Women and Preindustrial Craft* (Bloomington, Ind.: Indiana University Press, 1995), 52–54; Maurice Garden, *Lyon et les lyonnais au XVIIIe siècle* (Paris: Belles Lettres, 1970).

34. See Flandrin, *Families in Former Times*, 206–42.

35. Maillard, 344.

36. Moheau, quoted in Flandrin, 220.

37. Fromageau, *Dictionnaire des case de conscience*, quoted in Flandrin, 220.

38. Quoted in René Pillorget, *La Tige et le Rameau*, 123–24.

39. Jean Talon, quoted in Sigmund Diamond, "An Experiment in 'Feudalism': French Canada in the Seventeenth Century," *William and Mary Quarterly* 3:18 (1961): 9.

40. Agnès Walch, *La spiritualité conjugale dans le catholicisme français (XVIe–XXe siècle).* Paris: Editions du CERF, 2002. By the late seventeenth and eighteenth centuries, a more rigorist view, colored by Jansenism, came to dominate. Walch's survey of this literature allows scholars to contextualize the radically different conclusions of earlier scholars like Jean Delumeau and Jean-Louis Flandrin, who emphasized, respectively, the rigorist and laxist positions. See Delumeau, *La Peur en occident* (Paris: Fayard, 1978) and Flandrin, *Familles, parenté, maison, sexualité dans l'ancienne société* (Paris: Editions du Seuil, 1974).

41. John Bossy, *Christianity in the West, 1400–1700* (Oxford: Oxford University Press, 1985), 124.

42. AD Drôme C. 609, 1–2.

43. AD Drôme B 1720, 7 February 1686.

44. Abbé Cerné, *La Pedagogue des familles chretiennes contenant un recueil des plusieurs instructions sur diverses matières* (Paris, 1662). I have used the edition published in Paris in 1684, 148.

45. Cerné, *Pedagogue*, 152–55.

46. Ibid., 155–65.

47. Esprit Fléchier, *Mémoires sur les Grand Jours tenus à Clermont en 1665* (Paris: 1964), 22–23.

48. Pierre Lescuras, "Le Droit de Dîme, ou l'offrande à Dieu du dixième enfant d'une famille," *Bulletins et Mémoires de la Société Archaeologique et Historique de la Charente* (Angoulême) 1931, 201–4.

49. Maillard, 115.

50. Ibid., 112.

51. Ibid., 112–15.

52. For an intriguing analysis of a different way that motherhood fit into seventeenth-century notions of asceticism and sacrifice, see Larry Wolff, "Religious Devotion and Maternal Sentiment in Early Modern Lent: from the letters of Madame de Sévigné to the sermons of Père Bourdaloue," *French Historical Studies* 18:2 (1993): 359–95. My understanding of the potentially sanctifying value of suffering, particularly for women, is influenced by Caroline Bynum, *Holy Feast, Holy Fast: the Religious Significance of Food to Medieval Women* (Berkeley: University of California Press, 1988).

53. *Instructions Chrétienne pour les personnes qui aspirent au mariage ou qui y sont déja engagées* (Paris, 1730), 16–17.

54. McLaren, *A History of Contraception*, 149.

55. See, in particular, Flandrin, *Families in Former Times*, 212–42; Philippe Ariès, "Interpretation pour une histoire des mentalités," in Hélène Bergues et al., *La Prévention des naissances dans la famille* (Paris: PUF, 1960), 311–27; Burguière, "From Malthus to Weber"; Etienne Van de Walle, "Motivations and Technology in the Decline of French Fertility," in Wheaton and Hareven, eds., *Family and Sexuality in French History* (Philadelphia: University of Pennsylvania Press, 1980), 135–78.

56. Quoted in Charles de Ribbe, *Les familles et la société en France avant la Révolution, d'après des documents originaux* (Tours, 1879), 61, 268.

57. Mary Louise Roberts, *Civilization Without Sexes: Reconstructing Gender in Postwar France, 1917–1927* (Chicago: University of Chicago Press, 1994), 120–47; Miranda Pollard, *Reign of Virtue: Mobilizing Gender in Vichy France* (Chicago: University of Chicago Press, 1998); Cheryl Koos, "Gender, Anti-individualism and Nationalism: The Alliance Nationale and the Pronatalist Backlash against the Femme Moderne," *French Historical Studies* 19:3 (Spring 1996): 699–723.

58. For a review of these links, see McLaren, *A History of Contraception*, 175–80.

59. For an introduction to the patchwork of customary laws in early modern France, see Emmanuel Le Roy Ladurie, "A System of Customary Law: Family Structures and Inheritance Customs in Sixteenth-Century France," in Forster and Ranum, eds. *Family and Society: Selections from the Annales* (Baltimore: Johns Hopkins University Press, 1976), 75–103; for a theoretical exposition of how the practice of division worked, see, in the same volume, Pierre Bourdieu, "Marriage Strategies as Strategies of Social Reproduction," 117–44. For some clues about what parents of a range of statuses actually did when faced with such decisions, see Julie Hardwick, *The Practice of Patriarchy: Gender and the Politics of Household Authority in Early Modern France* (University Park: Pennsylvania State University Press, 1998), 143–58; Barbara Diefendorf, *Paris City Councillors in the Sixteenth Century: The Politics of Patrimony* (Princeton, NJ: Princeton University Press, 1983), 262–78; Gayle Brunelle, "Dangerous Liaisons: Mésalliance and Early Modern French Noblewomen," *French Historical Studies* 19:1 (Spring 1995): 75–103.

60. AD Drôme 2 E 15108 (15 January 1707).

61. Roman law required that all living children be mentioned in a will in order for it to be valid, even if the child was being "disinherited" and was to receive nothing.

62. "sy aucun desd. enfans veulent apprendre un mestier avant leurs majorité."

63. "la salle et cuisine du second etage de sa maison scituée en la grand place de cette ville . . ." from Marguerite Saligny's Will, AD Drôme 2 E 15108 (16 May 1729).

64. "pour son usage propre sans que le monnastaire s'en puissent prendre" ADD 2 E 15108.

65. Ibid.

66. Roman law required testators to mention all children, even if it was to specify their exheredation. Because Saligny mentions children in religious orders, but not Antoine and Laurence, it seems most likely that they had died.

67. AD Drôme 2 E 15108 (16 May 1729). On the use of *préciput*, see Le Roy Ladurie, "Customary Law," 61–65.

68. The total size of the estate is not specified in the will, so it is not possible to know precisely how much the heirs received. Consequently, the difference in scale between their portions and that of their brothers and sisters is approximate.

69. "et au deffaut dud Andre legataire lad Testatrice veut que led. Legs tourne au proffit de l'un de ses freres ou soeurs par ordre de primogeniture les males preferés."

70. AD Drôme 2 E 4144 (5 February 1714).

71. "Donne et legue par droit d'institution particuliere à Jean, François, Anne, Catherine, Estienne, Magdeleine, Joseph, Andre et Alexis Mantin ses enfans dud. Mantin au chacun la somme de quinze livres a laquelle elle porte la legitime paternelle et maternelle dun chacun desd enfans en lesgard aux engagements et debtes passees quelle a este obligé de contracter pour l'entretien, apprentissage et education de sesd. enfans..." AD Drôme 2 E 4151 (13 December 1721).

72. AD Drôme B. 1720 (28 January 1686).

73. "pour prevenir les difficultés qui pourroient naitre dans sa famille apres son deces," AD Drôme 2 E 15108 (16 May 1729).

74. For analyses of godparenting, see Hardwick, *Practice of Patriarchy* 167–81; see also John Bossy, "Blood and Baptism: Kinship, Community, and Christianity in Western Europe, from the Fourteenth to the Seventeenth Centuries" in Derek Baker, ed., *Sanctity and Secularity: The Church and the World* (Oxford: Blackwell, 1973).

75. Restif de la Bretonne, *My Father's Life*, trans. Richard Veasey (Gloucester: Alan Sutton, 1986), 112.

76. AD Yonne 3 E 7 252 (4 April 1742) partage des heritiers de Guillaume Pillard et Marie Ducrot.

77. Dominique Dinet, *Vocation et fidelité*, 38.

78. "au cas que lad. Helaine Bon sa fille veuille se faire Religieuse il luy legue la somme de trois mille livres et demies pour estre employées au payment de sa dot spirituelle et frais d'entrée en religion, et en ce cas les choses à elle leguées et specifiées aud. Estat appariendront a sond. heritier..." AD Drôme 2 E 15094 n. 48 (8 May 1710).

79. Antoine Sabliere and Marguerite Saligny both made provisions in their wills to provide their daughter, Marguerite, a nun, with a small pension. AD Drôme 2 E 15108 (15 Jan 1707 and 16 May 1729); Pierre Bon gave small pensions to his two daughters, one an Ursuline and one a Visitandine. AD Drôme 2 E 15094, n. 48.

80. Dominique Dinet, *Vocation et fidelité*, esp. 36–47, 168–95. Dinet attributes the collapse of the tradition in the eighteenth century to the financial instability of monastic institutions and to the influence of Jansenism. Jansenism, strong among the legal elite that had long supplied many postulants, made families hostile to the religious orders that accepted *Unigenitus*.

81. Dinet determined that in the dioceses he studied choir nuns originated in the following social groups between 1665 and 1734: officers and legal personnel (53.8 percent);

merchants (17.4 percent); bourgeois (13.6 percent); artisans (1 percent); peasants (0 percent); other (14.2 percent). Almost a quarter of the lay sisters in convents, however, came from the artisanal milieu. *Vocation et fidelité*, 174, 179. For a discussion of fertility and family strategy in the artisanal milieu, see Maurice Garden, "Bouchers et Boucheries de Lyon au XVIIIe siècle," *Actes du 92e Congrès Nationale des Sociétés Savantes, Section d'histoire* (Strasbourg, 1967): 47–80.

82. For essays that reflect on the interplay between economic and affective relationships in early modern families, see Hans Medick and David Sabean, eds., *Interest and Emotion: Essays on the Study of Family and Kinship* (Cambridge: Cambridge University Press, 1984).

83. On other ways that patterns of religious recruitment defy our expectations of family interest, see Barbara B. Diefendorf, "Give us Back our Children: Patriarchal Authority and Parental Consent to Religious Vocations in Early Counter-Reformation France," *Journal of Modern History* 68:2 (June 1996): 265–307.

Chapter 7

1. Restif de la Bretonne, *My Father's Life*, trans. Richard Veasey (Gloucester: Alan Sutton, 1986), 112.

2. See Dupâquier, *Histoire de la population française*, 4 vols. (Paris: PUF, 1988), 2: 52–70.

3. Ibid., 57.

4. For an overall introduction to this literature, see Jean-Claude Perrot, "Les économistes, les philosophes, et la population," in Dupâquier, ed., *Histoire de la population française*, 2: 499–551. Carol Blum, *Strength in Numbers: Population, Reproduction and Power in Eighteenth-Century France* (Baltimore: Johns Hopkins University Press, 2002), brilliantly reads this literature against the backdrop of gender and political crisis. J. J. Spengler, *French Predecessors of Malthus* (Durham, NC: Duke University Press, 1942) examined in depth the views of some of the most prominent authors. For bibliographic orientation to this rich literature, see Sauvy, Hecht and Lévy, *Economie et population: les doctrines françaises avant 1800* (Paris: INED, 1962) and the important recent work of Christine Théré, "Economic Publishing and Authors, 1566–1789," in Gilbert Faccarello, ed., *Studies in the History of French Political Economy: From Bodin to Walras* (London: Routledge, 1998), 1–56.

5. For a compelling analysis of these letters, see Blum, *Strength in Numbers*, 11–20. On their significance for later writers, see Sylvana Tomaselli, "Moral Philosophy and Population Questions in Eighteenth-Century Europe," *Population and Development Review* 14 (1988): 7–29.

6. Eric Brian, *La mesure de l'Etat: Administrateurs et géomètres au XVIIIe siècle* (Paris: Albin Michel, 1994), 169.

7. All English quotations are from *The Spirit of the Laws*, edited and translated by Anne M. Cohler, Basia Carolyn Miller, and Harold Samuel Stone (Cambridge: Cambridge University Press, 1989). This quotation is from Book 19, 310.

8. Book 23, 427–456. This quotation appears on 427.

9. I base this conclusion on my survey of eighteenth-century population writing. I found many more references to the 1666 pronatalist law dating from after the publication of *de l'Esprit des loix* in 1748 than before it.

10. *Spirit of the Laws*, 453.

11. Ibid, 23:28 "How one can remedy depopulation," 454.

12. Ibid., 23:11 "On the harshness of the government," 433–34.

13. On Montesquieu, see Claudie Bernard, *Penser la famille au XIXe siècle* (Saint-Étienne: Publications de l'Université Saint-Étienne, 2007), 199–205; on natural law, see Knud Haakonssen, *Natural Law and Moral Philosophy: from Grotius to the Scottish Enlightenment* (Cambridge: Cambridge University Press, 1996), 15–62.

14. *Spirit of the Laws* 23:2 "On marriages," 428.

15. Ibid., 23:4 "On families," 429.

16. Suzanne Desan, *The Family on Trial in Revolutionary France* (Berkeley: University of California Press, 2004), 36.

17. Tomaselli, "Moral Philosophy," 15–20; Blum, *Strength in Numbers*, 32–33.

18. For fascinating analysis of Jean-Jacques Rousseau's evolving position in these debates, see Blum, *Strength in Numbers*, 113–51.

19. [anon.] *L'Ami des hommes ou traité de la population* (Hamburg, 1758), 18–19.

20. Augustin Rouillé d'Orfeuil, *Alambic des Loix*, 227. Augustin Rouillé d'Orfeuil, author (according to Barbier and Cioranescu) of this work as well as *L'ami des françois* (1772) and *L'alambic moral* (1773), should not be confused with Gaspard Louis Rouillé d'Orfeuil, who served as royal intendant in the *généralité* of Champagne from 1764–1791.

21. *Alambic des Loix*, 227.

22. Ibid.

23. Louis Messance, *Recherches sur la population des généralités d'Auvergne, de Lyon, de Rouen, et de quelques provinces et villes de royaume* (Paris, 1766), 143.

24. Moheau did, however, approve of providing tax reductions to those who were married and had children, because "they already bear a considerable burden by virtue of the children they raise for the State." Moheau, *Recherches et considérations sur la population de la France*. Ed. by Eric Vilquin (Paris: INED, 1994), 264. His statement closely matches the logic of Old Regime administrators who granted such reductions.

25. Forbonnais, *Recherches et considérations sur les finances de France*, quoted in Charles E. Strangeland, *Pre-Malthusian Doctrines of Population* (New York: Columbia University Press, 1904); Jean-Louis Murat, *Mémoire sur l'état de la population dans le pays de Vaud* (Yverdon, 1766). For a different assessment of reactions to the 1666 pronatalist edict, see also James Riley, *Population Thought in the Age of the Demographic Revolution* (Durham, NC: Duke University Press, 1985), 67–68.

26. Necker, *Eloge de Jean-Baptiste Colbert, discours qui a remporté le prix de l'Académie française en 1773* (Paris, 1773). One of the contestants in competition for the prize that year, Jean Pechméja, did mention the Edict on Marriages, but only to criticize it. See Pechméja, *Eloge de Jean-Baptiste Colbert, discours qui a obtenu le second accessit, à jugement de l'Académie française, en 1773* (Paris, 1773), 26–27.

27. Serving as director general of finances from 1776 to 1781, Necker corresponded with provincial intendants about aid to fathers with many children.

28. Claude Lévy and Louis Henry, "Ducs et Pairs sous l'Ancien Régime: Caractéristiques démographiques d'une caste," *Population* 15:5 (October–December 1960): 807–30.

29. For declining family sizes among elites, see also Alain Bideau and Jean-Pierre Bardet, "Fluctuations chronologiques ou début de la révolution contraceptive," in Jacques

Dupâquier et al., *Histoire de la population française* 2:390–91. See also Jean-Pierre Bardet, *Rouen au XVIIe et XVIIIe siècles: les mutations d'un espace social* (Paris: Société d'édition d'enseignement supérieur, 1983), 263–346.

30. Puisieux, *Les Caractères*, quoted in Hélène Bergues, *La prévention des naissances dans la famille: ses origins dans le temps modernes* (Paris: INED, 1960), 258.

31. Le Guay de Prémontval, *La monogamie ou l'unité dans le mariage* (1751–52) quoted in Bergues, 259. The author's work is a response to the argument that polygamy was more fecund than monogamy. For more on this work, see Blum, 93–95.

32. Etienne Van de Walle, "Fertility Transition, Conscious Choice, and Numeracy," *Demography* 29:4 (November 1992): 487–502.

33. Louis Messance, *Recherches sur la population des généralités d'Auvergne, de Lyon, de Rouen, et de quelques provinces et villes de royaume* (Paris, 1766), 143–46. The author was interested in using what he first assumed would be a stable ratio between the annual number of births in a given population and its actual size to come up with a multiplier, the so-called "année commune des naissances." Having found this ratio, it could be used in the absence of a census to estimate total population by applying it to the number of births in a given group, data that was generally available in parish registers. Messance's chapter on large families, showing variations in marital fertility, served to highlight why estimations based on the number of households or marriages were inadequate for such estimation. On Messance, see Joshua Cole, *The Power of Large Numbers*, 30–31, and for the quest to measure population, see Eric Brian, *La Mésure de l'Etat*, 147–78. Note that Messance had his facts about the 1666 edict wrong, claiming that tax exemptions had been offered to men with ten children and pensions to those with twelve. See appendix 1 for the correct details.

34. Messance, 146.

35. He wrote, in relation to pronatalist laws, that marriage depended on human character and will, but "the fertility of marriages depends on causes absolutely independent of the will even of those who alone can contribute to it, and is for this reason above all human laws." Messance, 143.

36. Messance, 143–46.

37. For a survey of these views, see Bergues, 253–307.

38. L'abbé de Pezerols, quoted in Jacqueline Hecht, "Un problème de population active au XVIIIe siècle, en France: La querelle de la noblesse commerçante," *Population* 19:2 (1964), 280. What "fooling nature" actually meant in terms of contraceptive technique is uncertain, and has become a subject of some debate. See Etienne Van de Walle and Helmut V. Muhsan, "Fatal Secrets and the French Fertility Transition," *Population and Development Review* 21:2 (June 1995): 261–79.

39. Le Guay de Prémontval, quoted in Bergues, 259.

40. Jean-Henri Marchand, *Le noblesse commerçable ou ubiquiste* (1756), quoted in Bergues, 262.

41. There were exceptions, like Messance, who seemed to consider marital fertility outside human control. But the preponderance of evidence suggests that eighteenth-century observers assumed the cause of declining family size (as a phenomenon distinct from declining aggregate population) was deliberate family-limiting behavior of married men and women. For a survey of the evidence, see the excerpts from contemporary texts collected in Bergues, 253–307. See also the discussion by Van de Walle and Muhsam, "Fatal Secrets," esp. 273–76.

42. See Etienne Van de Walle, "Motivations and Technology in the Decline of French Fertility," in Robert Wheaton and Tamara Hareve, eds., *Family and Sexuality in French History* (Philadelphia: University of Pennsylvania Press, 1980): 135–78.

43. Denis Diderot, *Correspondance*, ed. Georges Roth (Paris: Editions de Minuit, 1955), 4:198–99.

44. Hans Kasper Hirzel, *Le Socrate rustique ou description de la conduite économique et moral d'un paysan philosophe* (Zurich, 1762). The quotations are from the 1768 Zurich edition, 214.

45. On Greuze, see Emma Barker, *Greuze and the Painting of Sentiment* (Cambridge: Cambridge University Press, 2005).

46. Diderot, *Salon de 1769*, quoted in Barker, 110. See also 103–4. Not all of Greuze's images of rural family life were as happy as *The Beloved Mother*. Lynn Hunt has focused on the painter's images of paternal curses and prodigal sons. See *The Family Romance of the French Revolution* (Berkeley: University of California Press, 1992), 36.

47. Claudie Bernard, *Penser la famille au XIXe siècle* (St. Étienne: Publications de l'Université de Saint-Étienne, 2007), 229–35.

48. P. J. Wagstaff, "Nicolas's Father: Restif and *La Vie de mon Père*," *Forum for Modern Language Studies* 16:4 (October 1980): 358–67; Pierre Testud, *Rétif de la Bretonne et la création littéraire* (Geneva: Droz, 1977); Charles Porter, "Life in Restif Country," *Yale French Studies* 40 (1968): 103–17.

49. Restif de la Bretonne, *My Father's Life*, trans. Richard Veasey (Gloucester: Alan Sutton, 1986), 108.

50. *My Father's Life*, 108–11.

51. Ibid., 109.

52. On the growing sentimentalization of paternal power, see Jeffrey Merrick, "Patriarchalism and Constitutionalism in Eighteenth-Century Parlementary Discourse," *Studies in Eighteenth-Century Culture* 20 (1990): 317–30 and "Fathers and Kings: Patriarchalism and Absolutism in Eighteenth-Century French Politics," *Studies on Voltaire and the Eighteenth Century* 308 (1993): 281–303; also, Lynn Hunt, *The Family Romance*, 17–52 and Allan Pasco, *Sick Heroes: French Society and Literature in the Romantic Age, 1750–1850* (Exeter: University of Exeter Press, 1997), 54–83.

53. *My Father's Life*, 112–14.

54. Ibid., 115–16.

55. Ibid., 116.

56. Barker, *Greuze*, 104.

57. Comments of Melchior Grimm, note in Diderot, *Salon de 1769*, 672, quoted in Barker, 104. Barker offers some evidence that this comment by Geoffrin is apocryphal. See note 74, 268–69. For additional insight into women's responses to population issues, see Christine Théré, "Women and Birth Control in Eighteenth-Century France," *Eighteenth-Century Studies* 32:4 (1999): 552–64.

58. AD Gironde C. 2476, Fargès to subdelegates, 11 June 1768.

59. Ibid.

60. See for example, AD Marne C. 938, Rouillé D'Orfeuil to ? (n.d.).

61. AD Gironde C. 2476, D'Ormesson to Fargès, 1768.

62. Michael Kwass, *Privilege and the Politics of Taxation in Eighteenth-Century France: Liberté, Egalité, Fiscalité* (Cambridge and New York: Cambridge University Press, 2000), 23–61.

63. Kwass, *Privilege and the Politics of Taxation*, 119–54.

64. AD Gironde C. 2476, Fargès to subdelegates, 11 June 1768.

65. AD Marne C. 938, "Etat des Peres de famille aiant [dix enfans] vivans et plus auxquels M. L'Intendant de Champagne a accordé différens privilèges" (n.d.). The document does not indicate whether some families received benefits for multiple years.

66. AD Calvados C. 233.

67. I have found evidence of the eighteenth-century benefits to fathers of large families in the following provincial archives (corresponding intendancy in parentheses): Bouches-du Rhône (Aix); Orne (Alençon); Gers (Auch); Gironde (Bordeaux); Calvados (Caen); Marne (Chalons); Haute-Vienne (Limoges); Aisne (Soissons); Seine Inférieure (Rouen), and Savoie (Savoie).

68. On the free funds of the capitation, see Kwass, *Privilege and the Politics of Taxation*, 55–56.

69. The appearance of archival files that record aid to *pères de familles nombreuses* may be a reflection of new scrutiny of provincial intendants. After 1765, the royal council exercised more control over how the free funds of the *capitation* were spent. See Françoise Mosser, *Les Intendants de Finances au XVIIIe siècles: Les Lefèvre d'Ormesson et le "département des impositions" (1715–1777)* (Geneva and Paris: Droz, 1978), 141.

70. Provincial administrators sometimes mentioned other ways that they addressed aid to fathers of large families, including the *moins imposé*, or reduction on the *taille*, reductions in the *vingtièmes*, and exemption from the *corvée*. Grants from the *fonds libres de la capitation*, however, was the most common practice.

71. AD Calvados C. 233.

72. AD Haute-Vienne C. 256.

73. Quoted in Shelby T. McCloy, "Government Aid to Large Families in Normandy, 1764–1786," *Social Forces* 18 (1940): 418–24.

74. AD Marne C. 938, 26 February 1785. Rouillé's claim about the costs of the program is no doubt exaggerated. Accounts prepared in the early 1770s, some fifteen years earlier, suggest that he had spent much less—2,989 *livres*—providing tax reductions to 323 families. See AD Marne C. 938, "État des pères de famille aiant [torn] vivans et plus auxquels M. L'intendant de Champagne à accordé différens privilèges," [n.d.—1772?].

75. AD Calvados C. 991, Feydeau de Brou to subdelegates, 12 May 1784.

76. For an analysis of taxpayers' petitions, see Kwass, 119–54. For more detail on prolific fathers' petitions, see Leslie Tuttle, "Celebrating the *Père de Famille*: Pronatalism and Fatherhood in Eighteenth-Century France," *Journal of Family History* 29:4 (2004): 366–381.

77. AD Calvados C. 1017.

78. AD Marne C. 938, 6 November 1783.

79. AD Calvados C. 993.

80. AD Gironde C. 2476.

81. Kwass, *Privilege and the Politics of Taxation*, 83.

82. Figure compiled from data in AD Calvados, C. 1017. Michael Kwass estimates that the average weight of *capitation* and *tailles* on non-noble households in the généralité at twenty-nine *livres* per year.

83. Compiled from AD Gironde C. 2476. The records do not always make clear who has noble status and who does not.

84. AD Calvados C. 1017, Duroset d'Entrement case file.

85. AD Gironde C. 2475.

86. AD Calvados C. 1017, Laverdy to intendant, 18 November 1765.

87. AD Bordeaux C. 2475, Demothes to intendant, 22 July 1764.

88. AD Bordeaux C. 2475 request of Gérard Dupleix Cadignan, n.d. For a discussion of issues surrounding the position of military nobles in the eighteenth century, see Smith, *The Culture of Merit*, esp. 213–61. See also Jay Smith, *Nobility Reimagined: The Patriotic Nation in Eighteenth-Century France* (Ithaca, NY: Cornell University Press, 2005).

89. AD Bordeaux C. 2475, 27 December 1765.

90. For the administrative correspondence about Dupleix, see AD Bordeaux C. 2475, letters of 30 May and 9 June 1767.

91. AD Calvados C. 233, 26 February 1776.

92. See, for example, the notes and comments offered by curés and local officials in AD Caen, C. 993 and 1017.

93. AD Caen C. 1017, form dated 1784.

94. AD Aisne C. 990.

95. See on this subject, André Burguière, "Le déstabilisation de la société française," in Dupâquier et al., *Histoire de la population française*, 2: 475–92; Olwen Hufton, *The Poor of Eighteenth-Century France, 1750–1789* (Oxford: Oxford University Press, 1975); Robert M. Schwartz, *Policing the Poor in Eighteenth-Century France* (Chapel Hill, NC: University of North Carolina Press, 1988).

96. Burguière, 481.

97. Kathryn Norberg, *Rich and Poor in Grenoble, 1600–1814* (Berkeley: University of California Press, 1985), 178.

98. AD Gironde C. 2475, Fargès to ?, 1768.

99. Jean-Pierre Bardet, "La chute de la fécondité," in Jacques Dupâquier, ed., *Histoire de la population française* 3: 365.

100. Restif de la Bretonne, quoted in Bernard, *Penser la famille*, 229.

Conclusion

1. AD Puy de Dôme 1 C., 7359 (15–28 October 1788).

2. J. P. Bardet, *Rouen aux XVIIe et XVIIIe siècles*, 272 and 318.

3. Montesquieu, *Spirit of the Laws* 23:1, 427.

4. See Lynn Hunt, *The Family Romance of the French Revolution* (Berkeley: University of California Press, 1992), esp. 17–25; Jean Delumeau and Daniel Roche, eds. *Histoire des pères et de la paternité* (Paris: Larousse, 2000; original edition 1990), 251–61; Allan Pasco, *Sick Heroes: French Society and Literature in the Romantic Age, 1750–1850* (Exeter: University of Exeter Press, 1997).

5. AD Aisne, D. 10 "Projet d'un nouveau dispositif de la loi du Novembre 1666" (1787). Among the improvements the society proposed were provisions that exempted the eldest sons of large families from the militia, and provisions that specifically included widows' children from first marriages in the count of children necessary to qualify for an award.

6. Phillips, "Attack on Celibacy," 169.

7. Ibid.

8. Louis Dupuy, quoted in Blum, 158.

9. Deputy Azéma, quoted in Jacques Mulliez, "Révolutionnaires, nouveaux pères? Forcément nouveaux pères! Le droit révolutionnaire de la paternité," in Michel Vovelle, ed. *La Révolution et l'ordre juridique privé* (Orléans, 1988), I:397, n. 119.

10. Roland Le Vayer de Boutigny, *De l'autorité du roy touchant l'âge nécessaire a la profession solemnelle de religion* (Paris, 1669), 195.

11. Roland Le Vayer de Boutigny, *Reflexions sur l'édit touchant à la reformation des monastères* (Paris, 1667), 216.

12. A royal edict of March 1768 raised the age for taking religious vows from sixteen for both men and women to eighteen for women and twenty-one for men (as compared to twenty for women and twenty-five for men, as was proposed in 1666). The new regulations came on the heels of the Commission des Reguliers, a kingdom-wide investigation of monasteries for men, and a generation after the work of the Commission des Secours, which investigated female religious houses. On these measures, see John McManners, *Church and Society in Eighteenth-Century France: The Clerical Establishment* (Oxford: Oxford University Press, 1999), 505–614 and Elizabeth Rapley, *A Social History of the Cloister* (Montréal and Kingston: McGill-Queen's University Press, 2001).

13. Desan, *The Family on Trial in Revolutionary France* (Berkeley: University of California Press, 2004), esp. 15–92; quotation from 55.

14. See Blum, 159.

15. Poncet de la Grave, *Considérations sur le celibat rélativement à la politique, à la population, et aux bonnes moeurs* (Paris, 1801), described in J. J. Spengler, *French Predecessors of Malthus* (Durham, NC: Duke University Press, 1942), 106–8.

16. See Blum, 155–63; Phillips, "Attack on Celibacy."

17. See Desan, 283–310.

18. Blum, 178.

19. Angus McLaren, *A History of Contraception* (Oxford: Blackwell, 1990), 181.

BIBLIOGRAPHY

Abbreviations

AD Archives Départmentales
AN Archives Nationales, Paris
BN Bibliothèque Nationale, Paris

Archival and Manuscript Sources

Archives Nationales, Paris

Series G7: Contrôle générale de Finance
Series H1: Pays d'états, Pay d'élections, intendances
H1 1688–91 Correspondence of Henri d'Aguesseau, intendant in Limoges, 1666–72

Bibliothèque Nationale, Paris

Collection Clairambault 446, 613, 791
Mélanges de Colbert 33, 153, 154
Cinq Cents de Colbert 160, 195
Manuscrits Français 17407, 21265
Collection Morel de Thoisy 415–18
Collection Baluze, 179
Reports, memoranda, correspondence of royal officials, especially Jean-Baptiste Colbert, related to legal reform, marriage, monastic celibacy, and to the formulation and implementation of the 1666 Edict on Marriage

Bibliothèque de l'Arsenal, Paris

Recueil Le Camus, IV (MS 674) memorandum of Nicolas Le Camus on proposed pronatalist legislation

Archives Départmentales de l'Aisne

Series C. Provincial Administration
C. 832 Élection de Guise: Sentences, 1666–80
C. 946 Intendance de Soissons: Instructions regarding the *fonds libres de la capitation* (1787–89)
C. 990 Intendance de Soissons: *Fonds libres de la capitation* (1788–89)
C. 1010 Assemblée de l'élection de Guise: aid to large families
Series D. Science, Arts and Instruction
D. 10 Bureau d'Agriculture de Laon et de Soissons, mémoires et rapports (1787)

Archives Départmentales de Calvados

Series C. Provincial Administration

C. 233 Intendance de Caen: Report by Cordier Delaunay, 1787

C. 991–1018 Intendance de Caen: aid to large families, 1771–89

Archives Départmentales de la Drôme

Series B. Courts and jurisdictions

B. 1720, 1721 Judicature de Romans: Probate inventories

Series C. Provincial Administration

C. 599, 609, 610, 656, 663–65: Élection de Romans: registers and decisions, 1668–1701

Series 2E Fonds Notariaux

Wills, marriages, contracts, etc. of families who received pronatalist tax exemptions

Archives Départmentales de la Gironde

Series C. Provincial Administration

C. 84, 85 Intendance de Bordeaux: Correspondence, 1776–77

C. 2475–79 Intendance de Bordeaux: Accounting and correspondence regarding aid to large families, 1719–89

C. 2481 Intendance de Bordeaux: charitable aid and pensions. 1773–78

C. 2482 Intendance de Bordeaux: payment orders, 1776–77

C. 2493 Intendance de Bordeaux: charitable aid, gratifications, 1779–86

Archives Départmentales de la HauteVienne

Series C. Provincial Administration

C. 142 Intendance de Limoges: taxation, 1783–90

C. 234 Intendance de Limoges: *Vingtièmes*, 1763–74

C. 245, 256 Intendance de Limoges: *Capitation*, 1778–90

C. 267–69 Intendance de Limoges: *Fonds libres de la capitation*, 1776–97

Archives Départmentales de la Marne

Series C. Provincial Administration

C. 938. Intendance de Champagne: aid for large families, 1666–1788

Archives Départmentales de la Nièvre

Sub-Series 1 C. Administration

1 C 411 Élection de Clamecy: requests for reductions in the *taille* 1708–85

Archives Départmentales du Puy de Dôme

Series C. Provincial Administration

C. 1943 Intendance d'Auvergne: Communal Affairs of Aurillac, 1676–83

C. 7359 Assemblée d'élection d'Aurillac: *Procès verbaux*, 1788

Sub-series 4C. Provincial Administration, 1787–90

4 C 21, 24, 111 Assemblée Provinciales et commission intermédiaire d'Auvergne: *procès verbaux*

Archives Départmentales de l'Yonne
Series C. Provincial Administration
C. 85 Élection d'Auxerre: tax matters, 1634–1741
Geneaological Resources
Parish registers of Notre Dame là d'Hors, Auxerre; St. Eusebe, Auxerre; St. Pierre-en-Vallée, Auxerre, 1660–1800

Archives Municipales d'Auxerre
GG. 139: *procès-verbaux* recording fathers of ten or more living children seeking exemption

Bibliothèque Municipale de Sens
MS 208: Traités sur les mariages, Bergeret, Abraham, de Gomont

Bibliothèque Municipale de Toulouse
MS 433–36: Judicial Reform: memoranda by jurists and administrators for the preparation of reform ordinances (1664–72)

Printed Primary Sources

Bodin, Jean. *Les Six livres de la République*. Paris: Fayard, 1986. Originally published in 1576.

Boislisle, Correspondence des Contrôleurs Généraux des Finances. 3 vols. Paris, 1874–97.

Bossuet, Jacques-Bénigne. *Politique tirée des propres paroles de l'écriture sainte*. Paris, 1709.

Boucher, Pierre. *Canada in the Seventeenth Century from the French of Pierre Boucher*. Edited by Edward Louis Montizambert. Montreal: George E. Desbarats and Co., 1883.

Cernay, l'Abbé. *La Pedagogue des Familles chrestiennes, contenant un recueil de plusieurs Instructions sur diverses matières*. Paris, 1684.

Clément, Pierre, ed. *Lettres, instructions et mémoires de Colbert*. 7 vols. Paris, 1861–73.

Diderot, Denis. *Correspondence*. Collected and annotated by Georges Roth. Paris: Éditions de Minuit, 1955.

Fortin, Philippe Sieur de le Hoguette. *Testament ou conseil d'un père à ses enfans*. Amsterdam, 1696.

———. *Les elemens de la politique selon les principes de la nature*. Paris, 1663.

Guibert, ed. *Livres de raison, registres de famille, et journaux individuels Limousin et marchois*. Paris and Limoges, 1888.

Isambert, François et al., eds. *Recueil général des anciennes lois françaises depuis l'an 420 jusqu'à la révolution de 1789*. 29 vol. Paris, 1821–33.

Journal du Palais ou Recueil des principales décisions de tous les Parlemens et Cours Souveraines de France. Gabriel Guéret and Claude Blondeau, eds. 2 vols. Paris, 1701.

Lahontan, Louis-Armand, Baron de. *New Voyages to North America*. Reuben Gold Thwaites, ed. Chicago: A. C. McClure, 1905.

Le Blanc, Thomas. *La Direction et consolation des personnes mariées, ou les moyens infaillibles de faire un mariage heureux, d'un qui seroit malheureux*. Paris, 1664.

Léry, Jean de. *Histoire d'un voyage fait en la terre du Brésil* (1580). Geneva: Droz, 1975.

Le Vayer de Boutigny, Rolland. *Reflexions sur l'édit touchant à la reformation des monastères* n.p., 1667.

Anon. *Le Nombre des Ecclesiastiques de France, celuy des Religieux et des religieuses, le temps de leur Etablissement, ce dont ils subsistent & à quoy ils servent.* n.p., n.d.

Marie de l'Incarnation. *L'Ecole Sainte, ou explication familiere des mystères de la foy.* Paris, 1684.

Messance, Louis. *Recherches sur la population des généralités d'Auvergne, de Lyon, de Rouen, et de quelques provinces et villes de royaume.* Paris, 1766.

Mirabeau, Victor Riqueti, Marquis de. *L'Ami des hommes ou traité de la population.* Hamburg, 1758.

Moheau, Jean-Baptisk. *Recherche et considérations sur la population de la France.* Edited by Eric Vilquin. Paris: INED, 1994.

Montaigne, Michel de. *Complete Essays of Montaigne.* Donald Frame, translator. Stanford: Stanford University Press, 1965.

Montesquieu, Charles-Louis de Secondat, Baron de. *The Spirit of the Laws.* Edited and translated by Anne M. Cohler, Basia Carolyn Miller, and Harold Samuel Stone. Cambridge: Cambridge University Press, 1989.

Montpensier, Anne-Marie Louise D'Orléans, duchesse de. *Against Marriage.* Edited and translated by Joan deJean. Chicago: University of Chicago Press, 2002.

O'Callahan, E. B. and Berthold Farnow, eds. *Documents Relative to the Colonial History of the State of New York,* 15 vols. Albany, NY, 1853–87.

Perrier, François. *Arrests Notables du Parlement de Dijon, recueillis par M. François Perrier...avec les observation sur chaque Question, par Gauillaume Raviot Ecuyer.* 2 vols. Dijon, 1735.

Poulain de la Barre, François. *Three Cartesian Feminist Treatises.* Vivien Bosley, translator. Chicago: University of Chicago Press, 2002.

Pure, Michel de. *La Prétieuse, ou le mystère des ruelles.* Edited by Emile Magne. Paris: E. Droz, 1938.

Rapport de l'archiviste de la province de Québec. 1926–27, 1930–31.

Ribou, Jean. *Les Delices de la poésie galante.* Paris, 1667.

Rothschild, James Baron de. *Les Continuateurs de Loret: Lettres en Verse de la Gravette de Mayolas, Robinet, Boursault, Perdou de Subligny, Laurent et autres (1665–1689).* 3 vols. Paris: 1882–83.

[Rouillé d'Orfeuil] *L'alambic des loix.* Paris, 1773.

Tamizey de Larroque, ed. *Livre de Raison de la Famille de Fontainemarie.* Agen, 1889.

Thwaites, Reuben Gold, ed. *The Jesuit Relations and Allied Documents: Travels and Exploration of the Jesuit Missionaries in New France, 1610–1791,* 73 vols. Cleveland, Ohio, 1896–1901.

Thiers, Jean-Baptiste. *Traité des superstitions qui regardent les sacraments selon l'écriture sainte, les décrets des conciles et les sentiments des saints pères et des théologiens.* Paris, 1703–04.

Secondary Sources

Accampo, Elinor. *Blessed Motherhood, Bitter Fruit: Nelly Roussel and the Politics of Female Pain in Third Republic France.* Baltimore, MD: Johns Hopkins University Press, 2006.

Adams, Julia. *The Familial State: Ruling Families and Merchant Capitalism in Early Modern Europe.* Ithaca, NY: Cornell University Press, 2005.

Antoine, Michel. *Le Gouvernement et l'administration sous Louis XIV: Dictionnaire Biographique.* Paris: CNRS, 1978.

Ariès, Philippe. *Centuries of Childhood: A Social History of Family Life.* New York: Alfred A. Knopf, 1962.

————. *Histoire des populations françaises et de leurs attitudes devant la vie depuis le XVIIIe siècle.* Paris: Editions du Seuil, 1971.

Aubert, Guillaume. "'The Blood of France': Race and Purity of Blood in the French Atlantic World." *William and Mary Quarterly* 61:3 (2004): 439–78.

Axtell, James. *The European and the Indian: Essays in the Ethnohistory of Colonial North America.* Oxford and New York: Oxford University Press, 1981.

Bardet, J. P. *Rouen aux XVIIe et XVIIIe siècles mutations d'un espace sociale.* Paris: Société d'édition d'enseignement supérieur, 1983.

Beasley, Faith E. *Salons, History and the Creation of Seventeenth-Century France.* Burlington, Vt.: Ashgate, 2006.

Bell, David A. *Lawyers and Citizens: The Making of a Political Elite in Old Regime France.* New York: Oxford, 1994.

Belmessous, Saliha. "Assimilation and Racialism in Seventeenth and Eighteenth-Century French Colonial Policy." *American Historical Review* 110:2 (April 2005): 322–49.

————. "Etre français en Nouvelle France: Identité française et identité coloniale aux dix-septième et dix-huitième siècles." *French Historical Studies* 27:3 (Summer 2004): 507–40.

Bergues, Hélène. "La Population vue par les utopistes." *Population* 6:2 (April–June 1951): 261–86.

————. *La Prévention des naissances dans la famille.* Paris: PUF, 1960.

Bernard, Claudie. *Penser la famille au XIXe siècle.* Saint Étienne: Publications de l'Université de Saint-Étienne, 2007.

Bledsoe, Caroline H. *Contingent Lives: Fertility, Time, and Aging in West Africa.* Chicago: University of Chicago Press, 2002.

Blum, Carol. *Strength in Numbers: Population, Reproduction and Power in Eighteenth-Century France.* Baltimore, MD: Johns Hopkins University Press, 2002.

————. "Of Women and the land: Legitimizing husbandry," in John Brewer and Susan Staves, eds. *Early Modern Conceptions of Property.* London: Routledge, 1995.

Bosher, J. F. *French Finances 1770–1795: From Business to Bureaucracy.* Cambridge: Cambridge University Press, 1970.

Bourdieu, Pierre. "Marriage Strategies as Strategies of Social Reproduction," in Forster and Ranum, eds., *Family and Society: Selections from the Annales.* Baltimore: Johns Hopkins University Press, 1976.

Bourgeon, Jean-Louis. *Les Colbert avant Colbert: Destin d'une famille marchande.* Paris: PUF, 1986.

Bossy, John. *Christianity in the West, 1400–1700.* Oxford: Oxford University Press, 1985.

————. "Godparenthood: The Fortunes of a Social Institution in Early Modern Christianity," in *Religion and Society in Early Modern Europe, 1500–1800.* Edited by Kaspar von Greyerz. London, 1984.

Breen, Michael. *Law, City and King: Legal Culture, Municipal Politics, and State Formation in Early Modern Dijon.* Rochester, NY: University of Rochester Press, 2007.

Brian, Eric. *La Mesure de L'État: Administrateurs et géomètres au XVIIIe siècle.* Paris: Albin Michel, 1994.

Brooke, Michael Z. *Le Play: Engineer and Social Scientist.* London: Longman, 1970.

Brouard-Arends, Isabelle. *Vies et images maternelles dans la littérature française du dix-huitième siècle.* Oxford: The Voltaire Foundation, 1991.

Brown, Jennifer S. H. *Strangers in Blood: Fur Trade Companies in Indian Country.* Vancouver and London: University of British Columbia Press, 1980.

Brunelle, Gayle. "Dangerous Liaisons: Mésalliance and Early Modern French Noblewomen." *French Historical Studies* 19:1 (Spring 1995).

Burguière, André. "From Malthus to Weber: Belated Marriage and the Spirit of Enterprise," translated by Patricia Ranum in Robert Forster and Orest Ranum, eds., *Family and Society: Selections from the Annales*. Baltimore, MD: Johns Hopkins University Press, 1976, 237–50.

Burke, Peter. *The Fabrication of Louis XIV*. New Haven, Conn.: Yale University Press, 1992.

Charbonneau, Hubert. *Tourouvre-au-Perche aux XVIIe et XVIIe siècles: Etude de démographie historique*. Paris: PUF, 1970.

Chianea, Gérard. "La Mère et l'Enfant dans le Droit Dauphinois." *Cahiers d'Histoire* 25 (1980).

Childers, Kristin Stromberg. *Fathers, Families and the State in France, 1914–45*. Ithaca, NY: Cornell University Press, 2003.

Church, William F. *Constitutional Thought in Sixteenth-Century France*. Cambridge, Mass.: Harvard University Press, 1941.

———. "The Decline of the French Jurists as Political Theorists, 1660–1789." *French Historical Studies* 5:1 (Spring 1967): 1–40.

Clancy Smith, Julia and Frances Gouda, eds. *Domesticating the Empire: Race, Gender and Family Life in French and Dutch Colonialism*. Charlottesville: University of Virginia Press, 1998.

Cole, Charles Woolsey. *Colbert and a Century of French Mercantilism*. 2 vols. Hamden, Conn.: Archon, 1964.

Cole, Joshua. *The Power of Large Numbers: Population, Politics and Gender in Nineteenth-Century France*. Ithaca, NY: Cornell University Press, 2000.

Collins, James. "The Economic Role of Women in Seventeenth-Century France." *French Historical Studies* 16:2 (Fall 1989): 436–70.

———. *Fiscal Limits of Absolutism: Direct Taxation in Early Seventeenth-Century France*. Berkeley: University of California Press, 1988.

———. *The State in Early Modern France*. Cambridge, Mass.: Cambridge University Press, 1995.

Cott, Nancy. *Public Vows: A History of Marriage and the Nation*. Cambridge, Mass.: Harvard University Press, 2000.

Crawford, Katherine. *Perilous Performances: Gender and Regency in Early Modern France*. Cambridge, Mass.: Harvard University Press, 2004.

Crowston, Claire Haru. *Fabricating Women: The Seamstresses of Old Regime France*. Durham, NC: Duke University Press, 2001.

Darmon, Pierre. *Le Mythe de la procréation à l'âge baroque*. Paris: J. J. Pauvert, 1977.

Davis, Natalie Zemon. "Ghosts, Kin and Progeny: Some Features of Family Life in Early Modern France." *Daedalus* 106:2 (Spring 1977): 87–114.

———. *Women on the Margins: Three Seventeenth-Century Lives*. Cambridge, Mass.: Harvard University Press, 1995.

Davis, Natalie Zemon and Arlette Farge, eds. *A History of Women in the West III: Renaissance and Enlightenment Paradoxes*. Cambridge, Mass.: Belknap Press, 1993.

De Baecque, Antoine. *The Body Politic: Corporeal Metaphor in Revolutionary France, 1770–1800*. Stanford: Stanford University Press, 1997.

DeJean, Joan. *Tender Geographies: Women and the Origins of the Novel in France*. New York: Columbia University Press, 1991.

Delaney, Carol. "The Meaning of Paternity and the Virgin Birth Debate." *Man* (new series) 21:3 (September 1986).

Delumeau, Jean. *Sin and Fear: The Emergence of the Western Guilt Culture 13th–18th Centuries.* New York: St. Martin's Press, 1990.

Delumeau, Jean and Daniel Roche, eds. *Histoire des Pères et de la Paternité.* 2nd edition. Paris: Larousse, 2000.

Dent, Julian. *Crisis in Finance: Crown, Financiers and Society in Seventeenth-Century France.* London: David and Charles Newton Abbot, 1973.

Desan, Suzanne. *The Family on Trial in Revolutionary France.* Berkeley: University of California Press, 2004.

Diefendorf, Barbara B. *From Penitence to Charity: Pious Women and the Catholic Reformation in Paris.* New York: Oxford University Press, 2004.

—————. "Give Us Back Our Children: Patriarchal Authority and Parental Consent to Religious Vocations in Early Counter-Reformation France." *Journal of Modern History* 68 (June 1996): 265–308.

—————. *Paris City Councillors in the Sixteenth Century: The Politics of Patrimony.* Princeton, NJ: Princeton University Press, 1983.

—————. "Widowhood and Remarriage in Sixteenth-Century Paris." *Journal of Family History* 7 (Winter 1982).

—————. "Women and Property in ancien régime France. Theory and practice in Dauphiné and Paris," in John Brewer and Susan Staves, eds., *Early Modern Conceptions of Property.* London: Routledge, 1996, 170–93.

Donzelot, Jacques. *The Policing of Families.* New York: Pantheon, 1979.

Dupâquier, Jacques et al. *Histoire de la population française.* 4 vols. Paris: Presses Universitaires de France, 1988.

Dupâquier, Jacques and Michel Dupâquier, eds. *Histoire de la Démographie: La statistique de la population des origines à 1914.* Paris: Librairie Academique Perrin, 1985.

Eccles, W. J. *Canada Under Louis XIV, 1663–1701.* London and New York: Oxford University Press, 1997.

Esmein, Adhémar. *Le Mariage en droit canonique.* New York: B. Franklin, 1968.

Esmonin, Edmond. *Etudes sur la France des XVIIe et XVIIIe siècles.* Paris: PUF, 1964.

—————. *La Taille en Normandie au temps de Colbert 1661–1683.* Geneva: Mégariotis Reprints, 1978.

Farr, James R. *Authority and Sexuality in Early Modern Burgundy 1550–1730.* New York: Oxford University Press, 1995.

—————. *Hands of Honor: Artisans and Their World in Dijon, 1550–1650.* Ithaca, NY: Cornell University Press, 1988.

Farragher, John Mack. *A Great and Noble Scheme. The Tragic Story of the Expulsion of the French Acadians from their American Homeland.* New York: W. W. Norton, 2005.

Favier, René. *Le Villes du Dauphiné aux XVIIe et XVIIe siècles.* Grenoble: Presses Universitaires de Grenoble, 1993.

Fildes, Valerie. *Wet-Nursing: A History from Antiquity to the Present.* Oxford: Blackwell, 1988.

Flandrin, Jean-Louis. *Families in Former Times: Kinship, Household and Sexuality.* Cambridge: Cambridge University Press, 1979.

—————. *Sex in the Western World: The Development of Attitudes and Behaviour.* Translated by Sue Collins. Chur, Switzerland: Harwood Academic Publishers, 1991.

Flinn, Michael W. *The European Demographic System, 1500–1820*. New York: Harvester, 1981.

Forster, Robert. *The Nobility of Toulouse in the Eighteenth Century: A Social and Economic Study*. Baltimore: Johns Hopkins University Press, 1960.

Foucault, Michel. *Discipline and Punish: the Birth of the Prison*. New York: Vintage Books, 1979.

———. *The History of Sexuality Volume I: an Introduction*. New York: Vintage Books, 1990.

Fuchs, Rachel G. *Contested Paternity: Constructing Families in Modern France*. Baltimore: Johns Hopkins University Press, 2008.

———. *Poor and Pregnant in Paris: Strategies for Survival in the Nineteenth Century*. New Brunswick, NJ: Rutgers University Press, 1992.

Gager, Kristen. *Blood Ties and Fictive Ties: Adoption and Family Life in Early Modern France*. Princeton, NJ: Princeton University Press, 1996.

Ganiage, Jean. *Trois Villages de L'Ile-de-France: Etude démographique*. Paris: PUF, 1963.

Garden, Maurice. "Bouchers et boucheries de Lyon au XVIIIe siècle." *Actes du 92e Congrès national des Sociétés savantes*. Strasbourg, 1967.

———. *Lyon et les Lyonnais au XVIIIe siècle*. Paris: Flammarion, 1975.

Gautier, Etienne and Louis Henry. *La Population de Crulai, paroisse Normande: Etude historique*. Paris: PUF, 1958.

Gelbart, Nina Rattner. "Delivering the Goods: Patriotism, property and the midwife mission of Mme du Coudray," in John Brewer and Susan Staves, eds., *Early Modern Conceptions of Property*. London: Routledge, 1995.

———. *The King's Midwife: A History and Mystery of Madame du Coudray*. Berkeley: University of California Press, 1998.

Gélis, Jacques. *History of Childbirth: Fertility, Pregnancy and Birth in Early Modern Europe*. Translated by Rosemary Morris. Cambridge, UK: Polity Press, 1991.

Gerber, Matthew Dean. *The End of Bastardy: Illegitimacy in France from the Reformation Through the Revolution*. PhD dissertation. University of California, Berkeley, 2004.

Giesey, Ralph E. "Rules of Inheritance and Strategies of Mobility in Prerevolutionary France." *American Historical Review* 82 (1977): 271–89.

Gillispie, Charles Coulson. *Science and Polity in France at the End of the Old Regime*. Princeton, NJ: Princeton University Press, 1980.

Goodman, Dena. *The Republic of Letters: A Cultural History of the French Enlightenment*. Ithaca, NY: Cornell University Press, 1994.

Gordon, Daniel. *Citizens Without Sovereignty: Equality and Sociability in French Thought, 1670–1789*. Princeton, NJ: Princeton University Press, 1994.

Goubert, Pierre. *Beauvais et les Beauvaisis de 1600 à 1730: Contribution à l'histoire sociale de la France au XVIIe siècle*. Paris: SEVPEN, 1960.

Grafton, Anthony et al. *New Worlds, Ancient Texts: The Power of Tradition and the Shock of Discovery*. Cambridge, Mass.: Belknap Press, 1992.

Greer, Allan. *The Jesuit Relations: Natives and Missionaries in Seventeenth-Century North America*. Boston and New York: Bedford St. Martins, 2000.

———. *Mohawk Saint: Catherine Tekakwitha and the Jesuits*. New York: Oxford University Press, 2005.

———. *The People of New France*. Toronto: University of Toronto Press, 1997.

Hafter, Daryl, ed. *European Women and Preindustrial Craft*. Bloomington: Indiana University Press, 1995.

———. *Women at Work in Preindustrial France*. University Park: The Pennsylvania State University Press, 2007.

Hanley, Sarah. "Engendering the State: Family Formation and State Building in Early Modern France." *French Historical Studies* 16:1 (Spring 1989): 4–27.

―――."Family and State in Early Modern France:The Marriage Pact," in Marilyn J. Boxer and Jean H. Quataert, eds., *Connecting Spheres:Women in the Western World, 1500 to the Present*. Oxford: Oxford University Press, 1987.

―――."'The Jurisprudence of the Arrêts': Marital Union, Civil Society and State Formation in France, 1550–1650." *Law and History Review* 21:1 (Spring 2003): 1–20.

―――."The Monarchic State in Early Modern France: Marital Regime Government and Male Right," in Adrianna Bakos, ed., *Politics, Ideology and the Law in Early Modern Europe: Essays in Honor of J.H.M. Salmon*. Rochester, NY: University of Rochester Press, 1994.

―――. "Social Sites of Political Practice in France: Lawsuits, Civil Rights, and the Separation of Powers in Domestic and State Government, 1500–1800." *American Historical Review* 102:1 (February 1997).

Hanlon, Gregory. *L'univers des Gens de bien: Culture et comportements des élites urbaines en Agenais-Condomois au XVIIe siècle*. Talence: Presses Universitaires de Bordeaux, 1989.

Hardwick, Julie. *The Practice of Patriarchy: Gender and the Politics of Household Authority in Early Modern France*. University Park: Pennsylvania State University Press, 1998.

―――. "Women Working the Law: Gender, Authority and the Legal Process in Early Modern France." *Journal of Women's History* 9:3 (Autumn 1997): 28–49.

Harrington, Joel F. *Reordering Marriage and Society in Reformation Germany*. Cambridge: Cambridge University Press, 1995.

Harth, Erica. *Cartesian Women:Versions and Subversions of Rational Discourse in the Old Regime*. Ithaca, NY: Cornell University Press, 1992.

―――. *Ideology and Culture in Early Modern France*. Ithaca, NY: Cornell University Press, 1983.

Hastrup, Kirsten. "The Semantics of Biology: Virginity," in Shirley Ardener, ed., *Defining Females:The Nature of Women in Society*. London: Croom Helm, 1978.

Hatin, Eugène. *Bibliographie historique et critique de la presse periodique française*. Paris: Librairie de Firmin Didot Frères, 1866.

Havard, Gilles. *Empire et métissages: Indiens et Français dans le Pays d'en Haut, 1660–1715*. Paris: Presses de l'Université de Paris-Sorbonne, 2003.

Havard, Gilles and Cécile Vidal. *Histoire de l'Amérique Française*. Paris: Flammarion, 2003.

Hecht, Jacqueline. *"l'Idée de denombrement jusqu'à la Révolution,"* in *Pour une histoire de la statistique*. Paris: INED, 1976.

Heckscher, Eli. *Mercantilism.* Translated by Mendel Shapiro. London: G. Allen & Unwin ltd., 1935.

Henry, Louis. *Anciennes familles genèvoises: etude démographique, XVIe–XXe siècles*. Paris: PUF, 1956.

Henry, Louis and Claude Lévy. "Ducs et pairs sous l'ancien régime: Caractéristiques démographiques d'une caste." *Population* 15:5 (1960): 807–30.

Hoffman, Philip T. and Kathryn Norberg, eds. *Fiscal Crises, Liberty, and Representative Government, 1450–1789*. Stanford: Stanford University Press, 1994.

Horowitz, Maryanne Cline. "The 'Science' of Embryology Before the Discovery of the Ovum," in Marilyn J. Boxer and Jean H. Quataert, eds., *Connecting Spheres: European Women in a Globalizing World, 1500 to the Present*. 2nd ed. New York: Oxford University Press, 2000.

Hufton, Olwen. *The Poor of Eighteenth-Century France*. Oxford: Clarendon Press, 1974.

Hunt, Lynn. *The Family Romance of the French Revolution*. Berkeley: University of California Press, 1992.

Hurt, John J. *Louis XIV and the parlements: The assertion of royal authority*. Manchester: Manchester University Press, 2002.

Jaenen, Cornelius. *Friend and Foe: Aspects of French-Amerindian Cultural Contact in the Sixteenth and Seventeenth Centuries*. New York: Columbia University Press, 1976.

Jouanna, Arlette. *Ordre social: mythes et hiérarchies dans la France du XVIe siècle*. Paris: Hachette, 1977.

Kaplan, Steven L. *Bread, Politics and Political Economy in the Reign of Louis XV*. 2 vols. The Hague: Martinus Nijhoff, 1976.

Keohane, Nannerl. *Philosophy and the State in France*. Princeton, NJ: Princeton University Press, 1980.

King, James E. *Science and Rationalism in the Government of Louis XIV 1661–1683*. Baltimore: Johns Hopkins University Press, 1949 (The Johns Hopkins University Studies in Historical and Political Sciences Vol. LXVI).

Knibiehler, Yvonne and Catherine Fouquet. *L'Histoire des mères du Moyen-Age à nos jours*. Paris: Montalba, 1980.

Knodel, John E. *Demographic Behavior in the Past: A study of fourteen German village populations in the eighteenth and nineteenth centuries*. Cambridge: Cambridge University Press, 1988.

Kuczynski, R. R. "British Demographers' Opinions on Fertility," in *Political Arithmetic: a Symposium of population studies*. Edited by Lancelot Hogben. New York: Macmillan Company, 1938.

Kwass, Michael. *Privilege and the Politics of Taxation in Eighteenth-Century France: Liberté, Égalité, Fiscalité*. Cambridge: Cambridge University Press, 2000.

Lachiver, Marcel. *La Population de Meulan du XVIIe au XIXe siècle*. Paris, SEVPEN: 1969.

Landes, Joan. *Women and the Public Sphere in the Age of the French Revolution*. Ithaca, NY: Cornell University Press, 1988.

Landry, Yves. *Les Filles du roi au XVIIe siècle: Orphelines en France, pionnières en Canada*. Montreal: Leméac, 1992.

Lansing, Carol. "Gender and Civic Authority: Sexual Control in a Medieval Italian Town." *Journal of Social History* (Fall 1997): 33–59.

Laqueur, Thomas. *Making Sex: Body and Gender from the Greeks to Freud*. Cambridge, Mass.: Harvard University Press, 1990.

Laslett, Peter, Karla Osterveen and Richard M. Smith. *Bastardy and its Comparative History*. Cambridge, Mass.: Harvard University Press, 1980.

Lefebvre, Charles. *Cours de doctorat sur l'histoire du droit matrimonial français*. Paris, 1908.

Le Roy Ladurie, Emmanuel. "A System of Customary Law: Family Structures and Inheritance Customs in Sixteenth-Century France," in Robert Forster and Orest Ranum, eds., *Family and Society: Selections from the Annales*. Translated by Elborg Fortster and Patricia Ranum. Baltimore: Johns Hopkins University Press, 1976.

Lesthaeghe, Ron. "Motivation et légitimation: conditions de vie et régimes de la fécondité en Belgique et en France du XVIe siècle au XVIIIe siècle," in Alain Blum, Noël Bonneuil and Didier Blanchet, eds., *Modèles de la démographie historique*. INED Congrès et colloques n. 11. Paris: PUF, 1992.

Levin, Lawrence Meyer, *The political doctrine of Montesquieu's Esprit des lois: its classical background*. New York: Publication of the Institute of French Studies, Inc., Columbia University, 1936.

Lougee, Carolyn C. *Le Paradis des Femmes:Women, Salons and Social Stratification in Seventeenth-Century France*. Princeton, NJ: Princeton University Press, 1976.

Luria, Keith. *Sacred Boundaries: Religious Coexistence and Conflict in Early Modern France*. Washington, DC: Catholic University of America Press, 2005.

Lynch, Kathleen. *Family, Class, and Ideology in Early Industrial France: Social Policy and the Working-Class Family*. Madison: University of Wisconsin Press, 1988.

McLaren, Angus. *A History of Contraception: From Antiquity to the Present Day*. Oxford: Blackwell, 1990.

————. *Reproductive Rituals:The Perception of Fertility in England, 16th–19th Centuries*. London and New York: Methuen, 1984.

————. *Sexuality and the Social Order:The Debate over the Fertility of Women and Workers in France, 1770–1920*. New York: Holmes & Meier, 1983.

McClintock, Ann. *Imperial Leather: Race, Gender and Sexuality in Colonial Conquest*. New York: Routledge, 1995.

McCloy, Shelby T. "Government Aid to Large Families in Normandy, 1764–1786." *Social Forces* 18:3 (1940): 418–24.

McHugh, Tim. *Hospital Politics in Seventeenth-Century France: The Crown, Urban Elites, and the Poor*. Aldershot and Burlington, Vt.: Ashgate, 2007.

Marion, Marcel. *Dictionnaire des institutions de la France aux XVIIe et XVIIIe siècles*. Paris: Editions A. & J. Picard & Cie, 1969.

————. *Les Impôts Directs sous l'Ancien Régime principalement au XVIIIe siècle*. Paris, 1910.

Melzer, Sara. *"France's Colonial History*....

Merrick, Jeffrey. "The Cardinal and The Queen: Sexual and Political Disorders in the Mazarinades." *French Historical Studies* 18 (1994): 667–99.

————. "Fathers and Kings: Patriarchalism and Absolutism in Eighteenth-Century French Politics." *Studies on Voltaire and the Eighteenth Century* 308 (1993).

————. "Sexual Politics and Public Order in Late Eighteenth-Century France:The *Mémoires secrets* and the *Correspondence secrète." Journal of the History of Sexuality* 1:1 (July 1990): 68–84.

Meuvret, Jean. "Comment les Français voyaient l'impôt," in *Comment Les Français voyaient La France au XVIIe siècle*. Bulletin de la Société d'étude du XVIIe siècle, 1955.

Meyer, Jean. *La Noblesse Bretonne au XVIIIe siècle*. Paris: SEVPEN, 1966.

————. "Un problème mal posé: La Noblesse pauvre." *Revue d'histoire moderne et contemporaine* 18 (April–May 1971).

Mollenauer, Lynn Wood. *Strange Revelations: Magic, Poison, and Sacrilege in Louis XIV's France*. University Park: Pennsylvania State University Press, 2007.

Monteil, A. Alexis. *Histoire financière de la France*. Paris: Bibliothèque Nouvelle, 1872.

Moogk, Peter. *La Nouvelle France: The Making of French Canada—A Cultural History*. East Lansing: Michigan State University Press, 2000.

Morgan, Jennifer. "'Some Could Suckle Over their Shoulder': Male Travelers, Female Bodies, and the Gendering of Racial Ideology, 1500–1770." *The William and Mary Quarterly*, 3rd series, 54:2 (January 1997): 167–92.

Mosser, Françoise. *Les Intendants des Finances au XVIIIe Siècle: Les Lefèvre d'Ormesson et le "Département des Impositions"(1715–1777)*. Geneva: Librairie Droz, 1978.

Motley, Mark. *Becoming a French Aristocrat: the Education of the Court Nobility, 1580–1715*. Princeton, NJ: Princeton University Press, 1990.

Mousnier, Roland E. *The Institutions of France under the Absolute Monarchy 1598–1789.* 2 vols. Chicago: University of Chicago Press, 1979.

———, ed. *Un Nouveau Colbert: Actes du Colloque pour le tricentennaire de la mort de Colbert.* Paris: SEDES, 1983.

Murat, Inès. *Colbert.* Charlottesville: University Press of Virginia, 1984.

Norberg, Kathryn. *Rich and Poor in Grenoble, 1600–1814.* Berkeley: University of California Press, 1985.

Nye, Robert. *Masculinity and Male Codes of Honor in Modern France.* New York: Oxford, 1993.

Olivier-Martin, François. *Histoire du droit français des origines à la Révolution.* Paris: D. Montchrestien, 1948.

———. *La Coutume de Paris: Trait d'union entre le droit romain et les législations modernes.* Paris, 1925.

O'Neill, Charles Edwards. *Church and State in French Colonial Louisiana.* New Haven, Conn.: Yale University Press, 1966.

Ozment, Steven. *When Fathers Ruled: Family Life in Reformation Europe.* Cambridge, Mass.: Harvard University Press, 1983.

Pagden, Anthony. *European Encounter with the New World: From Renaissance to Romanticism.* New Haven, Conn.: Yale University Press, 1993.

Paris, Charles B. *Marriage in XVIIth Century Catholicism: The origins of a religious mentality: The teaching of "L'école française" (1600–1660).* Tournai: Desclée, 1975.

Pasco, Allan H. *Sick Heroes: French Society and Literature in the Romantic Age, 1750–1850.* Exeter: University of Exeter Press, 1997.

Pateman, Carole. *The Sexual Contract.* Stanford: Stanford University Press, 1988.

Perrot, Jean-Claude. *Une histoire intellectuelle de l'économie politique, XVIIe–XVIIIe siècle.* Paris: Editions de l'Ecole des hautes etudes en sciences sociales, 1992.

Peterson, Jacqueline and Jennifer S. H. Brown. *The New Peoples: Being and Becoming Métis in North America.* Lincoln: University of Nebraska Press, 1985.

Pillorget, René. *La Tige et le Rameau: familles anglaise et française, XVIe–XVIIIe siècle.* Paris: Calmann-Lévy, 1979.

Pollock, Linda A. *Forgotten Children: Parent-Child Relations from 1500 to 1900.* Cambridge: Cambridge University Press, 1983.

Prévost de Lavaud, Etienne. *Les Théories de l'Intendant Rouillé d'Orfeuil.* Thèse pour le doctorat sciences politiques et économiques. Rochechouart, 1909.

Ranum, Orest. *Artisans of Glory: Writers and Historical Thought in Seventeenth-Century France.* Chapel Hill, NC: University of North Carolina Press, 1980.

Rapley, Elizabeth. *A Social History of the Cloister: Daily Life in the Teaching Monasteries of the Old Regime.* Montréal & Kingston: McGill-Queen's University Press, 2001.

Ribbe, Charles de. *Les familles et la société en France avant la Révolution d'après des documents originaux.* Tours, 1879.

Richter, Daniel K. *The Ordeal of the Longhouse: The Peoples of the Iroquois League in the Era of European Colonization.* Chapel Hill and London: University of North Carolina Press, 1992.

Riley, James C. *Population Thought in the Age of the Demographic Revolution.* Durham, NC: Duke University Press, 1985.

———. *The Seven Years War and the Old Regime in France: the Economic and Financial Toll.* Princeton, NJ: Princeton University Press, 1986.

Roberts, Mary Louise. *Civilization Without Sexes: Reconstructing Gender in Postwar France, 1917–27*. Chicago: University of Chicago Press, 1994.

Roche, Daniel. *France in the Enlightenment*. Cambridge, Mass: Harvard University Press, 1998.

Rocher, Jean-Pierre et al. *Histoire d'Auxerre des origines à nos jours*. Roanne: Horvath, 1984.

Sabagh, Georges. "The Fertility of French-Canadian Women during the Seventeenth Century." *The American Journal of Sociology* 47:5 (March 1942): 680–89.

Scafe, Robert. *The Measure of Greatness: Population and the Census under Louis XIV*. PhD diss. Stanford University, 2005.

Schalk, Ellery. *From Valor to Pedigree: Ideas of Nobility in France in the Sixteenth and Seventeenth Centuries*. Princeton, NJ: Princeton University Press, 1986.

Schneider, Zoë. "Women Before the Bench: Female Litigants in Early Modern Normandy." *French Historical Studies* 23:1 (Winter 2000): 1–32.

Schochet, Gordon. *Patriarchalism in Political Thought*. New York: Basic Books, 1975.

Schwartz, Robert M. *Policing the Poor in Eighteenth-Century France*. Chapel Hill, NC: University of North Carolina Press, 1988.

Scott, Joan. *Only Paradoxes to Offer: French Feminists and the Rights of Man*. Cambridge, Mass.: Harvard University Press, 1996.

Secombe, Wally. "Starting to Stop: Working-Class Fertility Decline in Britain." *Past and Present* 126 (February 1990): 151–88.

Seifert, Lewis, "Eroticizing the Fronde: Sexual Deviance and Political Disorder in the Mazarinades." *L'Ésprit créateur* 35 (1995): 22–36.

Solomon, Howard M. *Public Welfare, Science, and Propaganda in Seventeenth Century France: The Innovations of Théophraste Renaudot*. Princeton, NJ: Princeton University Press, 1972.

Smedley-Weill, Anette. *Les Intendants de Louis XIV*. Paris: Fayard, 1995.

Smith, Jay. *The Culture of Merit: Nobility, Royal Service, and the Making of Absolute Monarchy in France, 1600–1789*. Ann Arbor: University of Michigan Press, 1996.

Spear, Jennifer. "'They Need Wives': Métissage and the Regulation of Sexuality in French Louisiana, 1699–1730," in Martha Hodes, ed., *Sex, Love, Race: Crossing Boundaries in American History*. New York: New York University Press, 1999.

Spengler, Joseph J. *French Predecessors of Malthus*. Durham, NC: Duke University Press, 1942.

Stone, Lawrence. *The Family, Sex and Marriage in England 1500–1800*. Abridged edition. London, 1979.

Strangeland, Charles Emil. *Pre-Malthusian Doctrines of Population: A Study in the History of Economic Theory*. New York: Columbia University Press, 1904.

Strasser, Ulrike. *State of Virginity: Gender, Religion and Politics in an Early Modern Catholic State*. Ann Arbor: University of Michigan Press, 2004.

Stuurman, Siep. *François Poulain de la Barre and the Invention of Modern Equality*. Cambridge, Mass.: Harvard University Press, 2004.

Thomas, Keith. "Numeracy in Early Modern England." *Transactions of the Royal Historical Society* (5th series) 37. London, 1987.

Traer, James. *Marriage and the Family in Eighteenth-Century France*. Ithaca, NY: Cornell University Press, 1980.

Treasure, Geoffrey. *Louis XIV*. Harlow, England: Longman, 2001.

Trigger, Bruce G. *The Children of Aataentsic: A History of the Huron People to 1660*. Montreal and London: McGill-Queen's University Press, 1976.

Trudel, Marcel. *The Beginnings of New France, 1524–1663.* Translated by Patricia Claxton. Toronto: McClelland and Stewart, 1973.

——. *Histoire de la Nouvelle France,* 3 vols. Montreal: FIDES, 1963.

Tucker, Holly. *Pregnant Fictions: Childbirth and the Fairy Tale in Early-Modern France.* Detroit, Mich.: Wayne State University Press, 2003.

Van de Walle, Etienne. "Fertility Transition, Conscious Choice, and Numeracy." *Demography* 29:4 (November 1992).

——. "Motivations and Technology in the Decline of French Fertility," in Wheaton and Hareven, eds. *Family and Sexuality in French History.* Philadelphia: University of Pennsylvania Press, 1980.

Van Kirk, Sylvia. *Many Tender Ties: Women in Fur Trade Society, 1670–1870.* Norman: University of Oklahoma Press, 1980.

Vilquin, Eric. "Le Pouvoir royal et la statistique demographique," in *Pour une histoire de la statistique.* Paris: INED, 1976.

Walch, Agnès. *La spiritualité conjugale dans le catholicisme français.* Paris: Editions du Cerf, 2002.

Weil, Rachel. *Political Passions: Gender, the Family and Political Argument in England, 1680–1714.* Manchester: Manchester University Press, 1999.

Wellman, Kathleen. *Making Science Social: The Conférences of Théophraste Renaudot, 1633–1642.* Norman: University of Oklahoma Press, 2003.

Wolf, John B. *Louis XIV.* New York: W. W. Norton, 1968.

Wood, James B. *The Nobility of the Election of Bayeux, 1463–1666: Continuity through Change.* Princeton, NJ: Princeton University Press, 1980.

Wrigley, E. A. "Family Limitation in Pre-Industrial England." *Economic History Review* 19 (1966): 82–109.

Zanger, Abby E. *Scenes from the Marriage of Louis XIV: Nuptial Fictions and the Making of Absolutist Power.* Stanford: Stanford University Press, 1997.

INDEX